To my brother, Ron
on his 18th birthday.
November 28, 1956

-Al

THE GOLFERS OWN BOOK

THE Golfers OWN BOOK

EDITED BY

Dave Stanley and George G. Ross

LANTERN PRESS · PUBLISHERS · NEW YORK

The editors and publishers wish to thank all of the authors, their representatives, publishers, publications and organizations for their kind permission to use material in this book. Full copyright notices of previously copyrighted work are given on the pages on which the material appears.

The comic cartoons in this volume appear by courtesy of and are copyright 1956 by Art Paul, Laughs Unlimited, 106 West 45th Street, New York, 36, N. Y.

Library of Congress Catalog Number: 56-13027

CONTENTS

GOLF FICTION AND HUMOR

ANECDOTES, ODD FACTS, OFF BEAT DATA

INDEX OF GOLF INFORMATION

THE GOLFERS OWN BOOK

THE 19TH HOLE

"Golf is an exercise which is much used by the Gentlemen of Scotland. A large common in which there are several little holes are chosen for the purpose. It is played with little leather balls stuffed with feathers; and sticks made somewhat in the form of a bandy-wicket. He who puts a ball into a given number of holes, with the fewest strokes, gets the game. The late Dr. M'Kenzie, author of the essay on Health and Long Life, used to say that a man would live longer for using this exercise once or twice a week."

Dr. Benjamin Rush in *Sermons to Gentlemen,* 1772.

"In forecasting a big and solid future for golf business, look at family play at those golf nurseries, miniature courses. Parents are bringing so many little tots out to putt that putters for small youngsters are becoming standard equipment at miniature courses."

Picture caption in *Golfdom,* "The Business Journal of Golf."

"The indoor golf practice range has gone scientific. A Connecticut manufacturer of electronic instruments got a patent this week for a system that computes where a captive ball would go and projects a picture of the ball and its flight on a screen."

N.Y. Times dispatch, August 19, 1955

TEEING OFF

by Dave Stanley

In the past half-century, golf has risen from an aristocratic sport to a democratic fever. Where only a few decades ago a handful of golf courses nestled sleepily in the suburbs, now there are hundreds of modern, turbo-jet golf operations. And increasingly, the advancing population is pushing golf courses further and further out, and inland. If it keeps up we will have concentric strips of golf courses all over the nation, back-to-back.

Saturday and Sunday mornings are post-time for millions. They bounce out of bed, rip toward the family car carefully demolishing junior's play pen, and race off for tee-off time. And with the crowds so thick, they sign up at the unworldly hour of 7 A.M., and go back to bed, to return a few hours later.

Whatever the obstacles a) high cost of clubs as compared to a tennis racket b) green fees c) waiting d) the pre-dawn waking, golf is more popular than rock 'n' roll.

Which brings us to a story. There is a young bald-headed TV and resort funnyman we know, who is in a sorry dilemma. Everybody in his crowd is going to the psychiatrist but him. And wherever he goes he is assailed with suggestions that he join the horizontal men on the foam rubber slats.

Finally, a member of his "crowd," went up to him and said, "Bernie, I'm surprised at your attitude. I'm just shocked that you're not going. Don't you think that you ought to see a psychiatrist and find out why?"

Well, those who don't want to play golf are in a similar psychological squeeze. Everywhere you go, you hear about golf.

Men, women, boys, girls, society bells, dental assistants, and chefs in eat 'n run luncheonettes, are dancing the fairway fandango. The "voice of the turtle" is not heard in the land, it's the plop of ball against club.

And in every country that Rand McNally has a color for, the sport is enjoyed. Egypt has courses right smack in the desert. Southeast Asia countries have fairways right alongside rice paddies; golfers are playing in their best Brooks Brothers blazers against the grim backdrop of nationalistic movements.

Recently, for example, the chronicler of upper and middle-class folkways, the *New Yorker* magazine (Dec. 3, 1955) had a fascinating "Letter From Bangkok." The major emphasis in this report was on the fabulous popularity of golf in Siam. Incidentally, Oriental ingenuity there has worked out a scheme where pre-conditioned crows are used to flush out lost balls!

A multi-million dollar affair, golf is now big business. It has a trade-paper "Golfdom," which covers the business end of the sport. Golf also has its scientific side. Soil chemists and feed experts are constantly at work in the lab, the hot-house and the greens trying to develop a grass that does as well in the wet and cold Maine climate as in the dry, hot Texas heat.

Daily, golf seems to be winning more and more partisans than any other field except possibly hi-fidelity. And there seem to be factors that are speeding its growth. Mostly, there is a steady decline in the work week and a gain in leisure-time. John Diebald, the automation expert, further predicts that advanced technology will enable us to produce so many products and services with less human effort that more free time for people is in sight. "It is entirely reasonable," he says, "to expect a three-day weekend within the next decade."

Adding to the golf boom is the 1955 U.S. Supreme Court decision barring segregation from municipally supported links, thus opening up golf to more Negro players; which is a move that should be applauded by all good sportsmen. Also, prejudice against women is disappearing; for they are becoming very skillful at the game, despite those Billie Burke-type cartoons that still flourish.

In every way golf seems to be spiralling upward in audience response. Besides sociology there is the simple attraction of the sport itself. Golf is played in the open air (healthy), on serene, rolling hills (scenic), with people (sociability), and requires control and judgment (skill). Once the high cost of clubs and playing (Green fees, tipping, etc.) and crowded conditions are vanquished, golf may one day be the major participant sport in America.

Popular as the game is, I'd like to suggest that you don't have to play golf. Even if you don't want to play, you can lead a perfectly normal, well-adjusted life, and reach the statistical age that insurance experts say you can live to. Even though everybody's swinging and slicing, you can rest on your haunches —and individualism.

But if you enjoy the game, or are thinking of sampling the sport, buying clubs, waiting in line at the tee, going out with crochety unstable members of a foursome, paying tips to the caddies, let me not dissuade you. If you want to join the millions, from chief executives to small shop-keepers, who have given in to the fevers of the game, there are many nice things to look forward to.

For one thing, it will definitely help you in business. *Time Magazine*, as you will see later on in the book, recently added a postscript to Dale Carnegie-ism. It proclaimed that many a contract, impossible to nail down in an oak-panelled office has been pinned down on the grassy-green fields of a golf course. There is even the story of the Madison Avenue gray-flannel suiter who called up the office one day, and said he was ill, and couldn't report to the golf course that morning!

THE GOLFER'S OWN BOOK is designed to sharpen your pleasure of the game. It's a golf sampler, a fairway swatch of the best professional advice you can get from the nation's top golfers.

Adding a human touch to this "How-To" material are fine well-written short stories by such famous story tellers as Paul Gallico, P. G. Wodehouse and others.

THE GOLFER'S OWN BOOK also has some unique features, special material on country clubs, municipal courses, resort links, which is hard to come by. To use the TV language of understatement, this book, combining fact, fiction, humor, is breezy, entertaining and helpful, and is a "must."

Buy extra copies for your foursome friends to mark special events: Christmas (Dec. 25), New Years (Jan. 1), St. Valentine's Day (Feb. 14), The Earthquake at San Francisco (Apr. 18-19), Queen Victoria's birthday (May 24), The Destruction of the Bastille (July 14), The Capitulation of Sedan (Sept. 1), Columbus discovered America (Oct. 12), The Boston Tea Party (Dec. 16), New Jersey Ratified the U.S. Constitution (Dec. 18) and all other festive occasions.

Fore!

CLUBS, GOLF TERMS, RULES

☿☿☿☿☿☿☿☿☿☿☿☿☿☿☿☿☿☿☿☿☿☿☿☿☿☿☿☿☿☿☿☿

HOW TO BUY CLUBS THAT FIT
From GOLF DIGEST

Ask your Pro for help in selecting new clubs, which should be correct in weight, length, flexibility, grips and faces.

Buying a set of golf clubs can be as personal as buying a suit, and corresponding care should be taken.

The best suggestion of course is to ask your professional to help you in your selection of new clubs. It's like getting a prescription from your doctor.

However, no matter how you buy your clubs, there are certain general hints which can be of value. The two things most important to consider in club-buying are length and weight. Get clubs of the wrong length or incorrect weight and you will never be able to play up to your potentialities.

The proper length is controlled by two factors—how tall you are, and how far you ordinarily stand from the ball. This can vary according to the length of your arms and whether you have a flat or upright swing.

A short player might take longer clubs than most players of his height because he stands fairly far away from the ball and takes a flat swing. On the other hand, a tall player might employ an upright swing, and therefore take shorter clubs.

Weight controls the tempo of your golf swing, which as you know should be smooth. If your clubs are too light for your strength, you will not be able to "feel" the clubhead as you swing. If the clubs are too heavy, you won't be able to swing as quickly as desirable, and you will lose valuable clubhead speed.

The grips, club face angles and flexibility of the shafts are also points to be given consideration. The grips, of course, should be of the proper size for your hands, and for the way you hold a club. Club face angles are usually slightly hooked, but if you are a chronic hooker it would be wise to buy a set of clubs with perfectly straight faces. A rule of thumb on shaft flexibility is that the stronger you are, the stiffer shaft you will use. The gradations are extra stiff, stiff, medium-stiff, medium and soft. Medium is the most popular shaft among the average male golfers, but some women and older men may prefer the more flexible soft shafts. Only above average golfers can use the stiffer shafts to good advantage.

Whatever you do, pick out some clubs in which you can place your full confidence. It stands to reason that you can't play your best unless you have complete faith in your clubs.

ALL ABOUT THE CLUBS

In your golf bag you carry the tools of the sport. The main section of the bag is devoted to carrying space for your clubs. Here you will have two kinds of golf clubs—the "woods" and the "irons." You will generally carry from nine to fourteen clubs, depending on your experience, preferences and ability. Your golf bag also has pockets for balls, tees, gloves, and the addenda which contribute to the necessity and the comfort of the player.

There is a direct relationship of one club to another—just as there is a relationship between any fine tool and another when found in a master mechanic's kit. Each golf club has a specific job it can perform best and learning this best function will help you enjoy the game of golf even more. There is a definite job for each club just as there is an overall job for all the clubs together. This relationship concerns the problems of play—i.e., the matter of distance you want to hit the ball; the situation, as teeing off, or blasting from sand, or putting; and the conditions of play, as in grass, sand, or on the putting surface.

In the old days, circa 1928-1929, all the golf clubs had names. But just around that time the trend grew to drop the names and refer to the various clubs by number—thus, the Brassie became the number 2 Wood and the Spoon, the number 3 Wood. A complete listing of all the clubs in your bag by name and by number follows; with a special detachable "permanent reminder" for refresher purposes, which is affixed on a perforated page. Simply rip the page out along the perforations, place the page in your golf bag, and you'll have a constant handy-dandy reminder of the names, functions and distances of each club.

With the exception of the Driver, the Pitching Wedge and the Putter, practically every club is today referred to by number. The simplicity of calling for a club by number, a specific number designating a specific club to do a specific job, caught on like wildfire when it was first introduced—and is very nearly exclusively used now.

NAMES OF CLUBS	NUMBERS OF CLUBS	DISTANCES (Average Player)
Driver	#1 Wood	210-250 yds
Brassie	#2 Wood	190-230 yds
Spoon	#3 Wood	180-220 yds
Short Spoon	#4 Wood	175-205 yds
Cleek	*(has become #5 Wood)*	160-175 yds
Driving Iron	#1 Iron	*(Rarely found today)*
Midiron	#2 Iron	180-185 yds
Midmashie	#3 Iron	170-175 yds
Jigger	*(has no corresponding # today)*	
Mashie Iron	#4 Iron	160-165 yds
Mashie	#5 Iron	150-155 yds
Mashie Niblick	#6 Iron	140-145 yds
Pitcher	#7 Iron	130-135 yds
Spade Mashie	*(has no corresponding # today)*	
Pitching Niblick	#8 Iron	120-125 yds
Niblick	#9 Iron	115 yds-2 in. from green
	#10 Iron	" " " " " "
	#11 Iron	" " " " " "
Pitching Wedge	—	70 " " " " "
Wedge	—	For sand blasting.
Dynamiter (Sand Club)	—	For sand blasting.
Putter	—	On putting green.

THE PRO GETS MORE MILEAGE

As a matter of reference, the Professional golfer, understandably, gets more distance. To compare the Pro's blast with your own, add roughly 35-50 yards more on the drive—then about 20-40 yards more with the other woods. This gives the Pro golfer a drive ranging from about 265 to 300 yards; a shot of 245 to 270 yards with the #2 Wood; 220 to 250 yards with the #3 Wood; and about 215 to 230 yards with the #4 Wood.

THE WOODS

When you step up to the tee, you reach for the Driver. Naturally—for you know that, other things being equal, this is the club which will give you the longest distance. But why is this so? Considering that you might have some interest in the "why" of the thing, herewith is a brief description, explanation and resume of usage of the Woods.

The Woods—Description and Use

Driver: This is the largest of the clubs. The Driver is used for teeing purposes only, within the teeing area. It is a block of wood with lead inserted either on the back or bottom of the clubhead. The head, itself, is 1½" deep; and 1¼" to 1⅞" in height. The Driver has 2 degrees of loft. The average golfer gets about 210-250 yards with this club.

#2 Wood (Brassie) : This is the second largest wood. It is used for hitting the ball equal, or slightly shorter, distances than the Driver, but without using a tee and not within a teeing area. The #2 Wood has 2 degrees MORE LOFT than the Driver, hence 4 degrees of loft. The average golfer gets 190-230 yards.

#3 Wood (Spoon) : This is the third largest club and its use is to hit the ball shorter distances than the #2 Wood would be called on to do. The average golfer gets about 180-220 yards with #3 Wood. This club has 6 degrees of loft.

#4 Wood: This is the fourth Wood in the bag, and the same reasoning applies here. The #4 Wood has 8 degrees of loft to it. The average golfer should get, roughly, 175-205 yards with the #4.

The Driver and the #2 Wood are the same height—42½ to 43 inches overall. The clubheads are nearly identical, with the exceptions noted above. The #3 Wood and the #4 Wood vary one inch shorter. However, the clubhead of the #3 Wood is appreciably smaller than the Driver and the #2. The clubhead of the #4 Wood is still smaller in size.

THE IRONS

The various Irons in your bag, with the exception of the Wedge, the Pitching Wedge and the Putter, are all identified by number. All Irons are grouped according to a "long iron"-"medium iron"-"short iron" classification. This means pretty well what it says, and refers to distance.

Irons range from the #1 Iron, called a "Driving Iron" and not generally found in the average bag, up numerically to the #9 Iron. To these you add the Wedge, the "Pitching Wedge" and the #10 Iron and #11 Iron, plus the Putter.

The "short irons" which run up from #7 Iron through #11 Iron are also called "Pitching Irons" and are used for pitching purposes, from an inch or two off the green on out to about 135 yards from the green. #2 Iron thru #4 Iron are "long irons"—#5 & #6 are "medium."

The Irons—Description and Use

#2 Iron: The #2 Iron is used in play mainly to hit to a green from a distance of about 180-185 yards. It is generally made of stainless steel with a chrome finish, weighing about 15 ounces. It stands 38½" in length to 39" and has 3 degrees of loft in the clubhead.

#3 Iron: The face of the #3 Iron is exactly the same as that of the #2 Iron, except that it has 2 degrees more of loft. The overall length of this club is a bit shorter than #2 Iron. This is true in all Irons as the numbers get larger. This Iron is used to hit to the green from distances ranging about 170-175 yards.

#4 Iron: The face of this club is also exactly the same as that of the #2 Iron, but this has additional degrees of loft; in this case, 7 degrees of loft. It is used to hit to the green for distances of 160-165 yards.

#5 Iron: This is the first of the "Medium irons" and here the face of the club shows the first difference from numbers 2, 3 and 4 in the Irons. Here the face becomes slightly "wider" or

"deeper" offering more surface while the additional 2 degrees of loft take us to 9 degrees. This club is noticeably heavier than the preceding ones and the shaft is a bit shorter. The #5 Iron is used to hit to the green from distances of 150-155 yards.

#6 Iron: Another "medium iron" with slightly shorter shaft than #5 Iron; with 11 degrees of loft in the clubhead; and used to hit to the green from about 140-145 yards out.

#7 Iron: This is the first of the "short irons" or the "pitching irons." These clubs are heavier still than the preceding ones with progressively shorter shafts and increasing degrees of loft. This club is used for pitching; higher arc in the air, clear an obstacle, shorter distance, greater accuracy. The face of this club is even "wider" than that found on the medium irons. It is used to hit to the green from distances of 130-135 yards away.

#8 Iron: The face of this Iron is wider still; the shaft is shorter; it has 2 degrees more loft; and is heavier. It is used to hit for distances of approximately 120-125 yards out on to the green.

#9 Iron: The face of this club is still wider than the others; the loft is greater, here being 17 degrees of loft; the shaft is shorter; and the club is heavier. #9 Iron is used to get to the green from distances of about two inches out, all the way to 115 yards away. (The same applies to the following Irons; the Wedge, the Pitching Wedge, the #10 and the #11 Irons. All are pitching clubs.)

#10 Iron and #11 Iron are identical Irons. Can be used to blast from sand and can also be used for pitching to the green. The main difference is that #10 has 19 degrees of loft—while #11 Iron has 21 degrees of loft. Otherwise, either can be used from distances covering an inch or two off the green on out to about 115 yards away. Here the shafts are shorter than the others and the clubs are still heavier.

Pitching Wedge is very similar to the above two clubs, the #10 Iron and the #11 Iron, being used to pitch to the green from an inch or two on out to about 70 yards away. It can be best used from sand or for just pitching-in purposes.

Wedge: Now here is a beauty. This is called the golfer's "trouble shooter" and is especially designed to blast out of sand. The wedge has a wide flange for added weight to carry thru sand or heavy grass. The flange also acts as a plane-ing surface in the sand which prevents the club from digging in the sand and actually stopping the club in the sand.

The wedge can be used either to blast or pitch, and in some cases, to chip.

Distances can be from about a foot (usually if in heavy fringe grass around green) to 80 yards. The trend has been to use the "pitching wedge" (or wedge as a pitching club from further out. The pros almost invariably use the wedge to 100 yards with excellent results. The wedge will give more loft to a shot than a #9 iron, and therefore may be more desirable.

This club has become the pro's magic wand in cutting down scores, and therefore, the average golfer should devote more practice than usual to this club. The dividends obtained will be compensating.

Putter: The Putter is used mainly for putting the ball into the hole—on the putting surface or green. It has about 1 degree of loft in the clubhead, altho the Putter comes in various shapes, assorted stylings, and different lengths. On occasion the Putter will be used when the ball is resting on the apron of the green, or the fringe area adjacent to the carefully clipped short lawn of the putting green itself.

GETTING THE MOST OUT OF YOUR CLUBS

The heart of any golf club is the shaft. The flexibility of the shaft is what determines whether or not you get maximum compression on your ball when you hit it. As the years pile up, your swing will change, insidiously, implacably. Clubs which suited you once just dandy are no longer good—now they rob you of distance, of accuracy, of some of the fun in golf. Why?

A Tip: To compensate for the loss of clubhead speed and sheer power in your swing as you gracefully grow older, see your Pro about a more flexible shaft. You may begin anew to add yards of distance.

Question—See my Pro?

Answer—YES! SEE YOUR PRO! He's the man who will nip bad habits in the bud. His experienced eye will catch insipient faults before they ruin your swing or your stance or your grip.

His professional experience will select the proper length of shaft, the correct flexibility necessary in your swing, the just-right club for you.

Your Pro can tell by watching you whether or not a too-stiff shaft has spent its kick before impact, thereby causing you an anguished loss of distance and direction.

Proper fitting is very, very important when it comes to selecting golf clubs. You should be as careful about this matter as you are in fitting your shoes, or your suit. This is not said lightly.

Call on your Pro—because your club can change your swing, unless periodically checked. You may start with the sweetest, smoothest swing on the course—but an improperly fitting club can change that swing—change it just enough to spoil the fun for you.

A Tip: When outfitting yourself, it is most advisable to call on your Pro for help in selecting the clubs best for you. Do not rely on a salesman's spiel alone—he may be right, but not for you! Clubs vary enough today to call for expert knowledge in initial selection. Play the percentages in your favor. Call on your Pro. He's an expert!

When losing distance or direction, it is most advisable to call on your Pro. Perhaps the clubs themselves are the culprits. He can spot your faults immediately and prescribe for you.

HOW LONG SHOULD GOLF CLUBS LAST

Most Pros agree, a good set of clubs should and will last you a lifetime—but you won't want them to! The club of today is so greatly superior and so vastly improved—that it is often to your advantage to make a change. But once again, it takes a Pro to know this. For example: the manufacturers are constantly experimenting with newer, more flexible materials in order to achieve greater play in the shaft.

A Tip: Consult your Pro regularly, and keep abreast of the equipment situation. It won't cost you a cent; and he'll be happy to keep you informed. Don't worry; when something comes along which will improve your game, he'll be the first to let you know. In any case, ask him about whatever bothers you. There's no charge for conversation, and it's the Pro who is on top of the improving equipment situation. That's his business.

TIPS ON BUYING GOLF EQUIPMENT

Contrary to general opinion, golf need not be an expensive sport. Considering the growth of the public course and the improvements in the modern, well-built golf clubs and other equipment, the cost of the game should not be excessive for any budget over a period of years.

Golf clubs, and the bags you carry them in, vary in price of course. They vary to suit your taste, your pocketbook or your needs. But there are certain tips which will guide you when buying clubs and a bag and which will save you money.

A Tip: Buying the cheapest set of clubs can sometimes be the most expensive means of learning the game.

First of all, cheap equipment, in any line, will not stand up under hard usage as well as a more costly line of goods. This applies to golf clubs as well as automobiles. For a clincher, replacing broken and wornout clubs will cost you as much in the long run as buying a good set of clubs originally. Then, consider the matter of learning bad habits (which will only have to be un-learned) due to poorly balanced clubs, improperly fitted clubs, stiff shafts, too-long or too-short clubs, etc. In brief, when you shop around, don't automatically look for price "bargains." They may cost you more.

PRICES OF GOLF CLUBS

1. Woods: From about $20.00 on up to $84.00, for four. (In the most expensive category, you buy top-grade, "registered" sets. In a "registered" set, before the club is put together, every single part of it is weighed—precisely—to achieve perfect, hairline balance. What makes the big difference is the workmanship that goes into each club in a "registered" set and the care. Materials are about the same, with minor differences; but generally you'll find persimmon wood used for the clubhead, and an aluminum sole plate on the bottom, plus a fiber insert on the face.

2. Irons: From about $35.00 to $129.00 a set, this for top-grade clubs.

A Tip for the Beginner: When buying clubs, the beginner would be at a disadvantage if he incurs the full expense of the very best right from the start. This is unnecessary, and even harmful to his learning of the game. Paradoxical as it may seem, today's Professional prefers a beginner to buy a set of clubs somewhere in the middle-to-lower price bracket. The reason for this is that the Pro can then, after he watches the neophyte for a while, recommend and fit him to a set of clubs with enough flexibility in the shafts to help his swing improve sooner.

THE GOLF BAG

The golf bag can be dismissed shortly. The bag exists only to carry your golf clubs. If you carry a full set of clubs, you'll need a bag big enough and strong enough to stand the gaff. The more clubs you want to carry, the more reinforced stitching you'll need in your bag—therefore, the more expensive it will be. 'Nuff said.

KEEPING YOUR CLUBS IN SHAPE

by Robert Scharff

Condensed from

SCIENCE AND MECHANICS Magazine

Check over your woods first. If the finish is in good shape, rubbing with a soft cloth and raw linseed oil will brighten the surface. For stubborn dirt, grass stains or white ball marks, wash the entire head with a detergent (*Tide, Surf*) and warm water. Dirt in face corrugations can be routed out with a toothpick or a sharpened tee. After the club head has dried thoroughly, apply a coat of furniture polish, hard wax or silicone. A cloth made particularly for golf clubs (available from sporting goods stores and pro shops) applies a silicone coating as you rub the club.

If the wood finish is cracked, badly scarred or bleached and flaky, your best bet is to remove it completely and start over. Try soaking the whole head in a can of acetone or other lacquer thinner. As the wrinkled-up finish accumulates on the head, wipe it off and continue soaking until all the old finish is removed. If the surface doesn't react to the acetone treatment, it may be a varnish base. Try any good paint and varnish remover to get down to the bare wood. If neither of these methods works, scrape the finish off with a hand scraper or piece of glass. Smooth the surface with 3/0 or 4/0 sandpaper or medium steel wool.

Clean the face and sole of the club with steel wool before

applying the new finish. If the face has no ivory, plastic or fiber insert, the old finish, after softening with remover, may be cleaned from the corrugations with a golf tee. Insert should be cleaned only with soap and water and no finishing need be applied to them. If inserts are loose, remove the screws that hold them, fill the holes with *Smooth-On* and coat the surface with a quick-drying adhesive like *Duco Household Cement* or *Miracle Adhesive* before rescrewing the insert in place. Replace inserts after refinishing head.

To clean the sole plate, wrap a piece of fine emery cloth

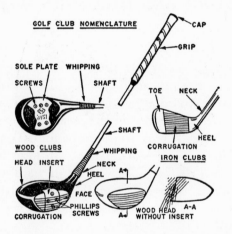

around a small file and go over the whole face lightly to smooth sharp edges or nicks. Tighten the screw holding sole plate or fill holes the same as for inserts if screws are loose.

Most of the pro shops refinish wood heads by first applying mahogany or walnut stain with a flat brush. If the stain is too dark, wipe some of it off with a lint-free cloth after 5-15 minutes. If you should wipe off too much and the stain is too light, apply a second coat after at least 24 hours. Be careful not to stain the sole plate.

When the stain is dry, apply a coat of paste filler (available at hardware and paint stores) with an old, short-bristle brush. Thin the filler with turpentine if necessary to make it brushable. Allow the filler to set for 15-20 minutes, until the gloss disappears, then wipe off the excess with burlap—first across the grain, then lightly with the grain. Filler should not be gouged out of the wood pores. Let filler dry for about 48 hours before sanding the surface.

Top coats may be spar varnish, clear brushing lacquer or one of the new plastic finishes such as *Liquid Plastic* (available at hardware stores). Lay on two full coats, but not thick enough to sag or ripple. Sand lightly with 6/0 garnet paper between

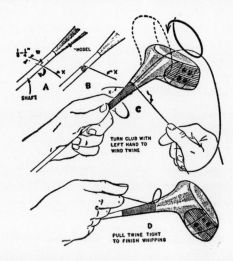

coats. Allow the final coat to dry for three days. You can leave the full gloss finish, but dirt and mud will clean off more readily if the final coat is rubbed with pumice and linseed oil on a felt pad. Rub with the grain and don't press hard enough to burn the top coat. When the gloss is gone, wipe clean with a dry cloth. An occasional wiping with a silicone cloth or furniture polish will keep the club new-looking all season.

Replacing loose or missing whipping is a common repair needed for wood clubs. Whipping finishes off ends of the grip and covers the point between the neck of the head and the shaft. Special golf twine, made for this purpose, is available at sports stores or you can use shoemaker's 3- or 4-ply linen thread. Wrap on the whipping.

Your irons will require little care except periodic cleaning and care of the grips. Use ordinary scouring powder on stainless steel, chromium or nickel plated heads. Then wash with a detergent, cleaning corrugations with a sharpened golf tee. When dry, wipe heads with a silicone cloth. For iron heads likely to rust, such as polished steel, clean with a medium fine emery cloth or a fine buffing wheel. Wipe them with a lightly oiled cloth.

Check all edges of your irons to make sure they are not sharp enough to cut a ball. File down sharp edges and deep nicks with a fine mill file. If the head on any of your clubs is loose, the head should be removed and reset at the factory. Loose heads can be dangerous, so don't take any chances. The same goes for cracked, bent or warped shafts. They should be repaired at the factory, or replaced.

Grips are among the most important parts of your golf clubs, as they control the club's "feel and action." Saddle soap or a leather conditioner, like *Lexol,* lubricates and preserves leather grips. Composition and rubber grips require only an occasional washing with a mild soap.

To preserve metal shafts, wash occasionally with detergent and warm water. After drying thoroughly, rub with a silicone cloth and then with a lightly oiled cloth. Remove any rust spots with 00 steel wool before rubbing with mineral oil.

During the season you can keep your clubs in good condition by always wiping them dry with an oily cloth after using them.

GLOSSARY OF GOLF TERMINOLOGY

In any line of endeavor, it takes but a moment to separate the sheep from the goats. Those "in the know" about anything generally speak the lingo. Golf, too, has a lingo—sharp, precise, crystal-clear terminology that helps you communicate your ideas with exactness leaving no margin for possible misinterpretation. For the uninitiated to sit in on a conversation between engineers or lawyers or dentists—or for that matter, golfers—can lead to the hideous conclusion that either you are on another planet, or the language you are listening to has been made up by the auditors and consists of an idioglossia understood only by themselves, leaving you in the dank, isolated cold.

Since you wish to browse through a golf book, here are some of the more common golf terms—plus some of the definitions.

COMMONLY USED GOLF TERMS

1. *Match play*—golf in which each hole is a separate contest. The winner is the player or team winning the most holes. *Stroke play* ("medal" play)—golf in which total strokes for the round or rounds determine the winner.
2. *Par*—the number of strokes a good player ordinarily would need to play a hole without a mistake under ordinary conditions. Always allows two putts on the green. *Birdie*—one stroke under par. *Bogey*—an arbitrary standard; usually one stroke over par. *Eagle*—two strokes under par.
3. *Up*—number of strokes a player is ahead of opponent. *Down*—number of strokes (or holes) a player is behind opponent.

4. **Tee**—First; little peg on which ball is placed in elevation before striking from teeing ground. Second; the teeing ground itself.

  Fairway—the specially tended, closely cropped area between tee and green, intended for regular play.

  Green—the putting green surface.

  Approach—a stroke along the way to the green.

5. **Divot**—a chunk of sod gouged out by a player's club. (Always replace your divots and then press them down with your palm or shoe.)

6. **Away**—The ball farthest from the hole, and therefore the one to be played first.

  Honor—the right to drive or play first. This is determined by lowest score on previous hole; with lowest score playing first or "having the honor." (On first hole, toss a coin.)

7. **Slice**—a right-handed player "slices to the right"—result of stroke which gives ball clockwise spin that makes it arc to the right in flight. (Left-handed player just the opposite.)

  Hook—a right-handed player "hooks to the left"—the stroke caused the ball to rotate counterclockwise in flight and spins it off to the left. (Again, opposite for left-handed golfer.)

8. **Press**—hitting beyond one's normal power. Usually results in poor swing.

  Top—to hit the ball above its center.

9. **Lie**—situation of a ball, good or bad. (The "lie" of a club is the angle which the shaft makes with the ground when the club is sitting naturally.)

10. **Fore**—the warning cry to golfers in your line of play.

11. **Handicap**—strokes given to equalize player's abilities.

12. **Halved**—when each side has played a hole in the same number or strokes, the hole is said to be "halved."

  Dormie—when one side is as many holes ahead as there remain holes to play, they are said to be "dormie."

DEFINITIONS

Amateur—one who plays the game of golf solely as a non-remunerative sport; non-profit-making pastime.

Professional—derives profit or income or remuneration from golf. This includes prize money; prizes in excess of $100 in retail value; prizes of a nature making them easily convertible to cash.

Exceptions: prizes of only symbolic value, such as metal trophies; scholarships won as prizes in recognized competitions before the 18th birthday.

After 18th Birthday: a golfer loses amateur status if he receives compensation for serving as an assistant to a pro; works in a golf shop making, repairing or cleaning clubs at a golf course; takes any other action which clearly indicates his intention of becoming a professional golfer.

Also: a golfer loses amateur status if he gives instruction in golf for compensation; lends his name or likeness for the advertisement or sale of anything except in the normal course of business as a dealer, manufacturer or inventor.

Also: if, because of your golf skill or reputation, you receive compensation directly or indirectly from anyone dealing in golf merchandise; this includes money, balls, clubs or other golf equipment without appropriate payment.

Also: "ghost writing" articles or books on golf of which he is not the author can lose an individual's amateur status.

Also: because of golfing skill, accepting the benefits of a scholarship or any other inducement to become a student in an institution of higher learning.

All of these can cause the loss of amateur standing. In addition—*AFTER THE 21st BIRTHDAY*—receiving compensation as a caddie; a caddie-master; or assistant caddie-master will likewise cause you to lose amateur status.

DO YOU REALLY PLAY GOLF?

by Joseph C. Dey, Jr.

Executive Director, United States Golf Association

*You don't unless you observe the official rules—and
some of them may surprise you. Here are 25 questions
and answers that will test your knowledge*

The rules of golf are as important to the game as its shots, because they make the sport standard for every player—in 56
printed pages which still leave a fair number of ifs and buts.
The rules are based on three fundamental principles: that the
golfer must play the ball as it lies, play the course as he finds it,
and finally, where neither of the first two principles can apply,
settle all questions by fair play. Only the golfer who strictly
follows these principles and the regulations developed from
them can say he really plays golf.

Here's a round with the rules, which should serve as a good
test. The questions and answers are based on match play—one
player against another on a hole-by-hole basis. In stroke play,
where the total score for the full round determines the winner,
the same penalties usually apply, except that an infraction
which costs the hole in match play normally calls for a loss of
two strokes in stroke play. The rules are in the official code of
the U.S. Golf Association. The answers are the same in friendly
play or tournament competition, whether your opponent is
Ben Hogan or your next-door neighbor.

"His firm won't do a thing without his consent."

1. If I accidentally break a club, may I borrow another from my partner to finish the round we're playing?

No. You may not borrow from anybody playing on the course. The idea is to prevent embarrassing an opponent by asking him to lend you a club to help you defeat him. You may replace a broken club, however, by sending back to the club-house for another. But if you should break the club in anger and not in the "normal course of play," it may not be replaced. Penalty is less of each hole in which a violation occurred. (Rule 3)

2. Suppose I try to play a fairly long carry over some trees, but just fail to make it. I still believe I can make the carry, however; may I drop another ball and play it over the trees for practice?

No. You are not allowed a practice stroke with a ball during the play of a hole. The penalty is loss of the hole. (Rule 8)

3. My opponent asks me which club I used as he prepares to play his shot. Am I supposed to tell him?

No. Asking for advice is forbidden, and your opponent loses the hole. (Rule 9-1)

4. We're all even as we play the 18th hole. As we get in front of the green my opponent asks me how many strokes I've had. "Five," I tell him. Just after he plays, I remember a shot I didn't count. I've really played six, and I tell him so. Is that all right?

You lose the hole. Since you did not correct your mistake before your opponent played, he may have based his tactics on your misinformation. (Rule 10-2)

5. I discover after the match is over that I was entitled to a handicap stroke on the 15th hole which I didn't know about. If I'd

counted the handicap stroke, I'd have won the match. May I take the stroke now?

No, it's too late to claim the 15th hole. Any claim in match play must be made before the players tee off on the next hole, or, if the claim involves the last hole of the round, before they leave the putting green. (Rule 11-1)

6. If my opponent drives off first when I am entitled to the honor, may I claim the hole?

No, there is no penalty. In match play—but not in stroke play—you may require him to replay any shot in proper order. Whether or not you do so is up to you. The same ruling applies if he drives off ahead of the markers on the teeing ground. In stroke play the competitor *must* tee off again, counting any strokes he may have taken on the hole before his legal drive. (Rules 12-3a, 20-2, 35-2b, 13-1 and 13-2)

7. I hit a long drive right down the middle of the fairway, but my ball comes to rest in a divot mark left by some preceding player. Can't I nudge my ball onto a level spot? If I can't, why should my good drive be penalized by someone else's carelessness?

You have to play the ball as it lies or be penalized by loss of the hole. That is the keystone of the rules of golf. Sometimes you get a good break, as when a ball headed out of bounds strikes a tree and rebounds onto the fairway; other times you get a bad break. We can't equalize all the breaks, and must accept them as they come. (Rule 16)

8. May I have relief without penalty if my ball comes to rest in the fairway just behind
(a) an anthill?
(b) a mound made by a gopher?
(c) a little knoll of sand?
(d) a rock imbedded in the ground?

(a) The anthill is a loose impediment and may be removed. (Definition 17, Rule 18-1)

(b) Since the gopher mound was made by a burrowing animal, the rules permit the ball to be lifted without penalty and dropped over the shoulder as near as possible to the spot where it lay, but not nearer the hole. (Rule 32-1)

(c) You get no relief from the knoll of sand. (Rule 17-1)

(d) You get no relief from the imbedded rock. (Rule 17-3)

9. My ball lands in very long grass. In order to see it, I part the grass and press it down slightly. My opponent says that is not permissible. Who is right?

Your opponent, and you lose the hole. You are not allowed to improve your lie, and you're not necessarily entitled to see the ball when you play it. (Rule 17-2)

10. I tee my ball and on my backswing discover that a branch of a large shrub interferes. I stop my backswing and break off the branch, contending my action is proper because the ball is not in play until I actually have struck it. Am I right?

No. You are not permitted to improve your line of play by moving, bending or breaking anything fixed or growing, with certain exceptions which do not apply here. Your penalty is loss of the hole. (Rule 17-3)

11. I use a club to pull my ball out from under a bush where it came to rest, counting the operation as one stroke. Did I score this correctly?

No. Your penalty is loss of the hole for not hitting at the ball "fairly" with the clubhead. (Rule 19-1)

12. I play my opponent's ball by mistake in the fairway, and he plays mine. Should we swap balls and go back to where they first lay?

No. You automatically lost the hole for playing the wrong ball, even though your opponent did the same later. There is no penalty, however, if you play a wrong ball in a hazard, provided you then play your own, since the rules do not permit you to pick up a ball in a hazard in order to identify it. (Rules 21-2 and 23-1)

13. My ball starts to roll down a hill toward out-of-bounds. I hit it while it is moving. My opponent says I violated the rules. Is he right?

Yes. You lose the hole. (Rule 25-1)

14. My shot lands in shallow water off a beach. There is a stiff wind and it looks as if the waves and wind will move the ball close enough to let me play it. How long may I wait?

You may not wait at all. The penalty for delay is loss of the hole. (Rule 25-2)

15. What is the ruling in a match when my ball strikes
(a) someone not connected with the match?
(b) my opponent or his caddie?
(c) me or my caddie?

(a) You play the ball where it comes to rest, without penalty. (Rule 26-1)
(b) Your opponent loses the hole. (Rule 26-2b)
(c) You lose the hole. (Rule 26-2a)

16. In looking for my ball, my caddie accidentally kicks it. Am I penalized?

Yes, one stroke. You play the ball as it now lies. However, if your opponent's caddie kicks your ball in searching for it, there is no penalty against anybody, since he was doing you a courtesy in looking for your ball. You must now drop it as near as possible to the spot from which it was moved. (Rules 27-1c and 27-1b)

17. My opponent's ball knocks mine into the hole. What then?

In match play, you are credited with holing out on your last stroke. In stroke play, you would be obliged to replace your ball. (Rules 35-2c and 27-3)

18. My opponent says that when my ball is lost, I must drop another ball near the spot where the first was lost and add a penalty stroke. Is that right?

No. You play another ball as nearly as possible from the spot where the first ball was *played,* and add a penalty stroke. Failure to do so loses the hole. (Rule 29-1)

19. Thinking my drive is lost, I go back to the tee and signify my intention of driving again and accepting the attendant penalty. Before I drive, however, my caddie yells he has found my ball. May I still play it?

Yes, provided it was found within five minutes after the search began. (Definition 6)

20. My ball comes to rest in the branches of a tree, ten feet above the ground. What happens if I
(a) try to climb the tree and the ball falls to the ground?
(b) stand on the ground and shake the tree so that the ball comes down?
(c) throw a club at the bough and knock the ball down?
(d) stand on a ladder to play the ball?
(e) climb the tree and, standing on a limb, hit the ball?

(a) You are penalized one stroke for moving the ball accidentally. (Rule 27-1c)
(b) You lose the hole for not playing the ball as it lies and for

improving its position by moving something growing. (Rules 16, 17-3)

(c) You lose the hole for not playing the ball as it lies and for not striking at it fairly. (Rules 16, 19-1)

(d) You lose the hole for building a stance. (Rule 17-4)

(e) No penalty, provided you don't violate the rule which states: "Players shall at all times play without undue delay." (Rule 37-7)

21. My ball stops behind a young tree which is supported in part by a guy wire. The tree and the wire together interfere with my stroke. May I drop the ball away, without penalty?

Yes. As the guy wire is artificial and qualifies as an obstruction under the rules, you may drop the ball without penalty within two club-lengths of the guy wire—but not nearer the hole than its original position. Since the tree is a natural obstacle, theoretically you are not entitled to relief from it. But if dropping the ball away from the guy wire also happens to provide relief from the tree, that's your good luck. (Definition 20 and Rule 31-2)

22. May I lift and drop my ball from soft, mushy ground in the rough?

Only if it lies in "casual water," which means a temporary, visible accumulation of water. Snow and ice are "casual water"; mud is not. (Definition 8, Rule 32-1a)

23. If my opponent is off on his putt, his ball might carom off mine, which lies just to the side of the hole, and still drop in. May I lift my ball before he plays?

No. You may not lift the ball of your own volition. However, your opponent has the right to require you to lift it. (Rule 35-2a)

24. My opponent's ball stops on the very lip of the cup. He claims he may wait 60 seconds to see whether it will fall into the hole. Is he right?

No. If there is any doubt whether his ball has come to rest, he is entitled to only a momentary delay—a few seconds—to settle the doubt. Otherwise, play must proceed immediately. (Rule 35-1f)

25. Is it all right to play "winter rules" in the summer?

It's not all right to play them at any time. There is no recognized code of "winter rules." The ball must be played as it lies unless there are abnormal conditions, in which case the local committee may adopt specific but temporary local rules and rescind them when conditions improve. Scores made at any time of year under local rules (generally permitting the lie of the ball to be improved) are not acceptable for handicaps under the USGA Handicap System.

GOLF CLOTHES

What is the best outfit when playing golf?

Wear loose-fitting, non-restricting, light clothing. It frees your movements, improves your sense of enjoyment, and helps your game. Recommended are loose sport shirts, a light windbreaker or sweater, and lightweight slacks. A cap is suggested, since it shields the golfer from glare and distraction.

Highly recommended, although not arbitrarily insisted upon by the authorities, are golf shoes. The different types are:

1. "Spike" shoes—these give the best purchase on any type of turf. Prevent skidding and give excellent footing.
2. "Cleats"—best in sand and soft turf.
3. "Others"—includes all types of carved-sole shoes designed to improve traction and footing; styled in rubber, leather and canvas.

You may wear any type shoe you prefer, of course, but the spikes are most highly recommended by experienced golfers, for best all-round utility wear and endurance. The cost of a pair of good golf shoes runs from about $12.00 to $30.00.

SUNGLASSES

Investigation seems to indicate that, surprisingly perhaps, sunglasses seem to hinder a golfer's game rather than help. Whether it be that you lose the sharpness and clarity of contrast in vision; or whether the reason lies elsewhere, the fact is that so few good golfers wear them the consensus agrees—sunglasses are no great aid on a golf course. Better to wear a cap with a good dark visor.

WHERE TO PLAY

ALL ABOUT THE PUBLIC COURSES

As Jimmy Durante would say, "Everybody's trying to get into the act." The act, being public or municipal golf. Everybody and his second cousin is out there these days, hooking, driving, hollering "Fore." About a quarter of a century ago, there were just a handful of publicly run links; they were as rare as motels. Today, the public courses are jammed with a golf-hungry populace; they're as crowded as a suburban supermarket on Saturday, at high noon.

If you're statistical, here's the jump expressed in figures. In 1930, there were fewer than 300 public courses. In 1956, some sports C.P.A. reported more than 2,000 courses—with more being logged monthly. Aided by the National Golf Foundation of Chicago, more and more communities are building an 18-hole answer to hypertension.

By and large, the public courses are superior installations, supplying golf to every kind of player under the sunniest and most attractive conditions. They offer you carefully tended golf courses, hospitable clubhouses and tenderness toward your budget. This awareness of economy and shunning of frivolous garnishings while still making available the "ne plus-ultra" in facilities is the impetus toward even wider acceptance of the public and Municipal Course.

For example, the Bethpage Golf Course in New York, operated under the supervision of the Long Island State Park Commission, offers four different 18 hole golf courses; with a fifth now nearing completion; plus a truly magnificent clubhouse. Each course, designated red, blue, green and black, is harder than the last one, giving any golfer a good game, from the beginner to the Pro. The truth of the matter is that the "championship" course at Bethpage is as tough as any in the nation.

WHAT IS A PUBLIC COURSE

Are "public" and "Municipal" courses the same?

1. The Public Course—is open to everybody.
2. The Municipal Course—is open only to residents of a certain area. (A permit is issued. *Tip:* Apply to the Commissioner of Public Works.)

This business of restricting Municipal facilities for the primary enjoyment of the local residents is not as heartless and discriminatory as it may at first appear. Place yourself in a lovely suburban residential neighborhood, then pay your tax for public works, then battle all the strangers who drive up from the city eventually to push you right out of the golf picture. In sheer self defense, many communities are leaning toward some sort of "Municipal" exclusivity for the protection of the local gutta percha enthusiasts. But the other face of the coin is the rapid rate at which "public" courses, open to all, are being built.

For the sake of clarity and simplicity, from here on in, unless specifically noted otherwise, both Municipal and public links will be referred to as public courses.

WHERE ARE THE PUBLIC COURSES

If you want to locate public golf courses in your locality, what's the quickest, easiest way?

1. Use the classified section of your local telephone book; look under: "Golf Courses—Public."
2. Contact the local Chamber of Commerce.
3. Contact the Office of the Commissioner of Public Works (under whose department public golf courses fall, in most communities.

WHAT DOES IT COST

How much will it cost each time I go out to play a round? Roughly, about $2.25 on weekdays; $3.25 weekends. The beauty of the public golf course is its minimum cost for maximum enjoyment. The above figures, varying slightly from community to community, break down as follows:

1. Greens fee   = $1.50 (weekdays)
   Caddy cart, rental =   .35 (per round)
   Locker, w/1 towel =   .40
                     $2.25 *TOTAL*

2. Greens fee   = $2.50 (weekends)
   Caddy cart, rental =   .35 (per round)
   Locker, w/1 towel =   .40
                     $3.25 *TOTAL*

Note: You generally have to leave a $1 deposit for rental of a caddy cart which, of course, is returned.

Notice—a caddy is not a necessary expense; the caddy cart serves nicely, at a fraction of the cost. *TIP:* Never haul your cart onto the green but always leave it at the tee side. The wheel tracks can deface the putting surface. (This is the reason most private clubs prohibit the use of the inexpensive caddy cart on the links.)

Notice that you pay only for what you use. Naturally there are as many "extras" as you may wish to indulge. Should you want to hire a caddy, the cost generally runs to $1.00 for nine holes; $2.00 for eighteen. (Double this for two players.) You may also rent a yearly locker for a very nominal $5.00 to $7.00, rarely more. Extra towels are available to everybody for, usually, ten to twenty cents apiece.

Tips: Take advantage of all the facilities, to the fullest extent. They are carefully figured out to keep individual costs down. This means; rent the locker by the year—you'll save money. Use a caddy cart—you'll save money. If you prefer a caddy, arrange for him before you leave the caddymaster. If you prefer an experienced caddy, ask for him before you start to play. This means at the "starting point"—"first tee"—"clubhouse." But do it in advance—you'll save time and wear and tear on your temper. Plan to register for tee-off first, then have a snack at the clubhouse. Food is tasty and inexpensive—you'll save time and money.

HOW DO YOU PAY

Do you receive a bill, as at a private club, or do you "pay as you go"?

At practically all public courses, the method is cash on the line, "pay as you go." This applies to the "Pro Shop" as well, found at all public courses.

TIPS ON TIPPING

Who gets tipped at a public course, and how much?

The rules followed here are identical with the ones you practice anywhere in public places. If your practice is to tip a bartender a set sum, then follow your conscience. So far as waiters are concerned, generally speaking the clubhouse set-up at a public course follows cafeteria-style service—hence, no tipping is necessary.

1. If you hire a caddy, from 50¢ to $1.00 is common per round. Double this for two players. Those bags are heavy.
2. In the parking lot—there are rarely attendants. When there are, tipping is not the rule.

Tipping on the public course, as you can see, is a rather minor item, unlike its counterpart at a private club or country club, where an automatic 15% gratuity is added to dining room and bar checks.

FAMILY AND GUESTS

May a golfer bring non-playing guests to a public course?

Yes, of course. Everybody's welcome. However, only players may actually go out on the links. Non-players may make full use of the other facilities. The clubhouse, the bars and lounges, the restaurant, the gardens, the walks and the area around the various practice tees and putting greens are theirs for the asking. Many public courses offer more than this. The aforementioned Bethpage Golf Course on Long Island includes a polo field, riding stables, picnic grounds, game rooms, facilities for organized group games and scheduled baseball games. They also feature the area as a winter sports center when weather conditions permit, with skiing and sleighing on the numerous slopes, often lighted at night.

ETIQUETTE AT THE PUBLIC COURSE

Are there any "house rules" at a public course?

Yes. The common courtesies of good manners and consideration for your fellow man apply here as well as everywhere else. Check the bulletin board at the main desk for any special local customs which may prevail.

1. ETIQUETTE IN THE CLUBHOUSE: House rules are posted for your guidance.
2. ETIQUETTE ON THE LINKS: For the most part public courses honor the rules as laid down by the *UNITED STATES GOLF ASSOCIATION*. (Reprinted toward end of book.)

You'll find that public courses, as a general rule, are more lenient than private clubs about many things. However, there are certain "musts" no matter where you play golf—and one of these is: "Learn the rules of etiquette" as listed on your score card! Read your score card! Your score card will be your guide to fuller enjoyment on the course. On it will be listed all local rules pertaining to the particular course you are playing, plus the exceptions noted for local preference. You will speed up play and make your own game more enjoyable by observing the reminders listed on the score card; a sample card to familiarize you with one typical example, follows:

MEMO TO GOLFERS

You can speed up play and make your game more enjoyable by observing the following reminders:

1. *Be ready to hit the ball when it is your turn. Have ball, tee and club ready, don't fumble for them at the last minute.*

2. *Watch your ball; mark it by a tree, bush or a dark clump of grass and go directly to it. Assist other members of your party in locating a lost ball and wave following party thru if there is a delay in finding it.*

3. *Leave your bag or caddy cart on tee side of green. Do not take bags or carts on green.*

4. *Line up your putt ahead of time, hole out and step aside at once so next man may putt.*

5. *When all players are on the green on Par Three holes let the next party tee off, then putt out.*

6. *If you wish to take your time, let the following party thru.*

7. *REMEMBER: Golf is a game, and also a Golf Course is a place of beauty.*

8. **Replace all divots; they will grow.**

THE PRO

Does every public course have a professional?

Yes. And here, as at a private course, the Pro is in business. The practice of remuneration varies from course to course. But it suffices to know that whether the public course, city administration, public works commission or whoever controls the golfing facilities pays the Pro a full salary, a partial salary and commission, or operates thru his hands a concession, nevertheless the Pro is there to operate the Pro Shop and to give lessons.

Individual golf instruction runs around the $3.00-$4.00 per half-hour level. This is less expensive than the amount charged at country clubs; yet the instruction is pretty much of the same high caliber. The Pro Shop at a public course is pretty much the same sort of store you find at a country club; and they handle the same golf necessities.

ANYBODY CAN PLAY GOLF

Is there an age limit at a public course?

No . . . you are neither too young nor too old when you come to play golf at a public course. Of course, non-playing children are discouraged but the usual facilities of the park are there to take care of their needs. Bethpage Golf Course reports that children age eight and nine have come out to play golf, carrying a full set of nine clubs . . . and have enjoyed the game and have brought pleasure to all who participated or watched. But of arbitrary restrictions on age—there are none.

THE GOLFING SEASON

What is the usual golfing season? Can you play all year round?

Weather permitting—golf can easily be played all year 'round. However, the climate of the locality generally determines what is designated as the local "season"—the South's running months longer than colder climes. Speaking practically, so long as there is no snow on the ground, the courses are kept open and available; altho the Pro Shop may be closed down for the three or four winter months. But even at that, play is possible from Washington's Birthday on through the Christmas season in some localities.

A WORD TO THE WISE—SPECIAL HINTS

Are there any tips which will help a person going out to a public course to make playing more pleasant?

Avoid the morning jamup!

Public courses, since they invite one and all to come out and play golf, are obviously crowded places, some more than others; some only so at certain times. However; there are times when you can anticipate crowded conditions. One of these is the early morning registering time. If you can manage to arrange your time so as to play in the afternoon, or even the late morning, you'll find little or no wasted time. The times to avoid are the hours between 6 a.m. to 11 a.m.

Anticipate Sunday and holiday crowds!

If possible, avoid weekend play, when things do get sticky. Try to play during the week. With daylight saving time, you can count on good golfing conditions until very nearly nine o'clock at night.

Arrive early. The earlier the better!

If you can only play weekends, or on holidays; then by all means the earlier you arrive the better. Plan to skip breakfast that morning; get out to the course; register around 5 a.m. to 6 a.m.; then relax for a while. You'll have time for a leisurely breakfast at the clubhouse restaurant. What you are after this way is the earliest possible tee-off time assignment; and it's first-come-first-served at public courses.

Dress properly!

Check the early-morning weather reports. A glance out the dawn-obscured window is rarely too accurate an indicator of the day you can expect. This way, raincoats, or sweater, or very light clothing may be packed into the car or carried, with at least a modicum of accuracy on the day's weather ahead.

Learn the rules of etiquette! (On all score cards)

Remember this—public courses invite golfers with all degrees of skill. Know this in advance. Also constantly bear in mind that some are rank neophytes, who just don't know any better. So—don't become impatient with a beginner. It will save you many an anguished moment and keep your blood pressure normal.

For safety's sake, keep your wits about you!

Check the people ahead; check the players behind you; and anticipate what MIGHT happen, so *think*. Generally speaking, courtesy and consideration on the course is the greatest safety-control factor in golf today.

Use the "ball washer"

To help you follow your ball; and to aid in more accurate drives; make use of the ball washers at each tee. In fact, caring for your equipment will help your game and the fuller enjoyment of the day on the golf course in many ways.

Enjoy yourself—while waiting!

Take advantage of the driving tees and the putting greens for practice while you wait for tee-off time. Most public courses will rent you a large bucket of balls for 50¢ or a dollar and you can loosen up while you wait.

Be considerate!

This means in everything. You are out for a game of golf, so play your game at your own leisurely pace. But, if you want to take your time, how about permitting a following party to play thru? How about replacing divots? They'll grow again, and the course will retain its beauty and utility. How about keeping caddy carts and heavy bags off the greens? How about smoothing out tracks, foot prints and heel gouges? How about putting empty cigarette packages and other trash into your pocket until you reach a trash can instead of just cluttering up the course with paper and refuse? How about parking your car within the white lines which denote a one-car space instead of straddling two spaces?

These are, briefly and concisely, some of the hints it would be well to bear in mind. They all work both ways, since observing them will not only help others but will also help you.

As you can see, there is really little reason for the average golfer to join a private club when a modern public course is available. True, private clubs and country clubs generally are less crowded and encourage a fuller social life. But the public courses more than make up for this with lower cost to the golfer and more than adequate facilities for socializing.

Considering the financial status of today's average golfer, plus the happy progress made in the construction of public courses during the last thirty years and particularly in the last ten, the growth of the game of golf in public parks comes as no great surprise. And all indications point to a continuing healthy development in this direction.

ALL ABOUT THE COUNTRY CLUBS

So you want to join a country club. You're a bit fat of purse and you want the seclusion and prestige of a club. Well, here is a capsule portrait of how country clubs work; how much it costs to join; club etiquette; and other tidbits of intelligence that you may find informative. The material is based upon a painstaking survey of many clubs throughout the nation, and interviews with those walking encyclopedias—Club membership chairmen.

At the start, remember that country clubs are as indigenously American as pheasant under glass. However, in the past decade, they have lost some of that snobbish aristocratic lustre; democracy has breached the dikes, not entirely, but enough to make a difference.

Today, because of the young married set with the two and three kids, the country club has become an enormously flexible institution; it is part "Y", part dance-hall, part teen-age center; part swimming pool, and an oasis for much married men of the type James Thurber described so well in cartoon and text.

And now the facts about country clubs and what they have to offer.

WHERE ARE THE COUNTRY CLUBS

If you want to locate country clubs in your locality, what's the quickest, easiest way?

1. Use the classified section of your local telephone book; look under: "Country Clubs."
2. For a more complete listing of country clubs in and around

your community, it is suggested you write to: United States Golf Association, 40 East 38th Street, New York 16, N.Y.

MEMBERSHIP FEES

How much does a country club membership cost?

You may anticipate only one fee for yourself as a member of a country club. This is the membership fee—with an additional initiation fee added the first year only. The actual cost to you will range from:

1. For membership—as high as $3,500 a year to as low as $250 a year.
2. For initiation—as high as $5,000 to as low as $100.

When you visit the membership chairmen of the various country clubs during your "search" period, be on the lookout for the following tip-offs to good, bad or indifferent club management. Is the driveway and parking area well kept, clean and neat? Does the attendant come quickly and with a smile? Is the lobby freshly painted and is the furniture well-selected? Check the bulletin board immediately—this can be the key! Is it up-to-date, neatly hung; and does it give the story of activities "right now" or are last week's events interfering with this week's announcements. Sloppy management generally means a sloppy country club, with all the extra costs and extra delays such management means in any business. Talk to some of the members and get their reactions to their own club. Is the atmosphere relaxed and friendly? Are the members happy in their membership—ask the folks you meet during your visit whether there are delays when they want to get out and play nine or eighteen holes? Stroll out of the clubhouse and look at the grass yourself. Are the lawns and greens of the course well-manicured? These are the questions only you can get the answer to—on the spot.

FAMILY AND GUESTS

For the most part, country clubs follow this pattern. Only the individual who actually signs up for membership is free to use the facilities of the club. However, most every club permits an arrangement whereby your wife or your children or your guests may come with you to enjoy the activities presented. However, a nominal charge is made for their use of these facilities. Where you may play golf, then take a dip in the pool and attend the dance at night—all without additional charge beyond your own club membership—even your wife, in most cases, will have to pay the small charge for accompanying you, if she does not have her own membership in the club.

Depending on the club itself, all guests, which includes members of your family, are usually charged whenever they take advantage of your club's activities. Most clubs offer a two-week "guest membership" card which you are encouraged to arrange for. This permits "guests" freedom of action without hampering your own movements. If they wish to play golf in your absence they simply pay the greens fee, from $3.00 to $10.00 themselves.

HOW DO YOU PAY

Do you "pay as you go" at a country club, or do they send you a bill?

For the most part, true all over the country, no cash is ever used at a country club—with two exceptions. As a matter of convenience to both yourself and your guests, this has proven to be the simplest and most gracious way to handle payment of bills. Guests, where they run up their own bar and restaurant bills, are billed personally. Whenever you would normally pay a bill, at the country club you sign a "Chit." Chits are tabulated monthly and itemized bills are mailed out. Both members and guests who have incurred charges receive separate bills.

Your purchases from the Pro Shop—where such articles as golf shoes, sox, sports shirts, slacks and caps are offered, as well as the standard golf equipment including clubs, golf bags, tees, golf balls and gloves—are all signed for via the "Chit" method. No cash is involved. When you get your monthly bill, you will find that one amount is for the total of your purchases at the club Pro Shop—the other will be for the total of every other service, such as restaurant, bar and special assessments.

TIPS ON TIPPING

As a general rule common to most country clubs—no cash tipping is permitted, with two exceptions. Your dining room check is signed as a "Chit" with a 15% "gratuity" added as the waiter's tip. No cash is necessary or permitted. The same holds true at the bar, in the lounge and for other special services. Cash tipping is frowned upon as an inconvenience since the proper tips are well taken care of thru regular channels.

The two exceptions—here is where you do pay in cash!

1. The parking lot attendant. From a quarter to a dollar is common practice.
2. The caddy. From 50¢ to $5.00 is common—with the well-accepted practice averaging about $1.00.

Tipping, a necessary evil, is often honored more widely in the breach than in the observance—therefore, be on the lookout, during your preliminary visits as to whether or not the club follows this rule. Winking at the "no cash tipping" rule, and this is easily observed if you keep an eye cocked toward the lounge and the dining room while you stroll the clubhouse and grounds area, can add appreciably to the cost of membership, considering that you are going to be charged the 15% gratuity anyway, on service "Chits." If the particular country club you are visiting has established cash tipping in addition to the regular 15%, note this fact carefully and be advised that the practice can be expected to extend in all directions, such as with the club Pro, waiters, bartender, musicians, life guard at the pool, etc. Note that all of these people are paid salaries and their tips are well cared for thru "Chit" gratuities. Additional outlay of cash is unnecessary.

ETIQUETTE IN THE CLUBHOUSE

What are the "House Rules" at a country club?

The country club is yours to use—its golf course, its restaurant, its swimming pool, its gymnasium, its parking lot, its bar and its dance floor. The common courtesies of good manners, and consideration for the welfare of your fellow-members prevail.

House rules generally are posted for the guidance of all members. Altho these vary in subtle and minute fashion, most are surprisingly similar.

ETIQUETTE ON THE LINKS

What are the rules when you are out on the golf course?

For the most part country clubs honor the rules as laid down by the *United States Golf Association,* which are as follows:

1. No one should move, talk or stand close to or directly behind the ball or the hole when a player is addressing the ball or making a stroke.

2. The player who has the honor should be allowed to play before his opponent or fellow-competitor tees his ball.

3. No player should play until the players in front are out of range.

4. In the interest of all, players should play without delay.

5. Players searching for a ball should allow other players coming up to pass them; they should signal to the players following them to pass, and should not continue their play until those players have passed and are out of range.

6. Before leaving a bunker, a player should carefully fill up all holes made by him therein.

7. Through the green, a player should ensure that any turf cut or displaced by him is replaced at once and pressed down, and that, after the players have holed out, any damage to the putting green made by the ball or the player is carefully repaired.

8. Players should ensure that, when dropping bags or the flagstick, no damage is done to the putting green, and that neither they nor their caddies damage the hole by standing close to the hole or in handling the flagstick. The flagstick

should be properly replaced in the hole before the players leave the putting green.

9. When the result of a hole has been determined, players should immediately leave the putting green.

Priority on the Course

In the absence of special rules, singles, threesomes or four-somes should have precedence of and be entitled to pass any other kind of match. A single player has no standing, and should give way to a match of any kind.

Any match playing a whole round is entitled to pass a match playing a shorter round.

If a match fail to keep its place on the course and lose more than one clear hole on the players in front, it should allow the match following to pass.

THE PRO

The Professional is at the country club as a businessman. General practice is to pay him a rather small salary, but then to encourage him to augment his income in several ways. This he does happily via the Pro Shop, which he usually owns, plus the lessons he gives to members. For these he charges fees ranging from $5 a half-hour to as much as $50 or even more per half-hour, as in the case of the "big name" boys whose pictures grace the sports pages of the newspapers regularly. Unless your particular club has such a "top" name, you can count on lessons within the $5 to $10 per half-hour bracket. Lessons, by custom, run a half hour, altho more and longer tutelage can easily be arranged for by phoning in advance. Need it be pointed out that this is an excellent investment—for improving your game, especially by means of a tip-top golfer's advice, can add immeasurably to your enjoyment of golf.

And so we come full circle—as the golf Pro, an important cog in the country club wheel, takes his place with all the other factors, to lay bare the inner workings of "the Club." But remember this—the main purpose of the country club is two-fold

—good golf and good fellowship. Therefore, whatever part of the story you review; be it financial, guest policy, tipping, etiquette or special advantages; the purpose and the function remain the same. That's why country clubs came into existence and that's why they are flourishing today.

ALL ABOUT THE RESORT COURSES

If you turn to the resort section of your favorite newspaper or that telephone book of tempting escapism, *Holiday* magazine, you will find ads of resorts featuring that magic four-letter word: "GOLF!" Sometimes, the word is accompanied by a spot drawing of a golfer in a tremendous downswing, as the sun beams on joyously.

Yes, throughout the nation, Joe Hotel Owner is spreading out the grass-green carpet for buffs in windbreakers. And it would be foolish not to take advantage of this invitation to links pleasure. If you're going away for a week's vacation or a weekend, you might as well go to a resort which has a 9 or 18 hole course. It's better to spend your money on this than to pay for head-shrinkers, n'est ce pas?

These slumbering, peaceful courses are the product of a sharp post-war battle for the vacationer's holiday dollar. During World War II, you were lucky enough to get in anywhere; the customer was a lowly ant. After the war the customer was king, and the dollar, his scepter. So hotel owners got busy—with the result a fabulous mushroom growth of golf courses built alongside resort hotels.

Ideal for beginners—excellent instruction was available right from the start, since "name" pros were hired to run the Pro shops and give lessons. This proved to be an inspiration to hotel owners looking for another attraction to inveigle the weary vacationist to his hostelry. Joining forces with swimming pools, indoor and outdoor; topnotch shows; bigtime dance bands; and boating, fishing and what-have-you, the resort golf course quickly made a place for itself in the vacation atmosphere scheme of things.

It quickly developed that crowds are no problem at the resort links, except for the hours of 9 to 11 a.m.; which makes it perfect for leisurely enjoyment and a welcome change from the rat race of big city golfing. And they discovered, and the word spread, that golfing in a vacation atmosphere added to the fun.

Resort golf is located wherever you find a concentration of hotels thus bringing in the element of competition for the customers. Naturally, there are many hotels which also offer golf due to the demand for it . . . but examining the resort picture, does show a pattern as having been established. In the East, and perhaps leading the rest of the country as to number of courses, quality of challenge, and excellence of instruction because of the "Pro" is the Catskill Resort area of New York State. Hard on its heels, altho trailing in number of courses if not quality of personnel, is Florida and its pitch for the vacation crowd, particularly the winter trade. Each year more hotels are adding golf to the holiday menu. There is a growing network of vacation spas which offer everything from putting greens thru pitch and putt courses up to nine and even eighteen hole layouts. New York, Florida, California, North Carolina, Pennsylvania, are just a few places where golfers are making that happy discovery. The Caribbean resort industry is also out trying to win the Yankee dollar that way; also Bermuda.

Which works out real fine for the golfers who don't mind mixing pleasure with pleasure as they rid themselves of the 20th century blues at hotels which feature their game.

WHERE ARE THE RESORTS WITH GOLF COURSES

What's the easiest, quickest way to locate a hotel which has a golf course?

1. Look in your local newspaper's "vacation section."
2. Write to the local Chamber of Commerce in the area where you wish to vacation.

3. Write to: The United States Golf Association, "Golf House," 40 East 38th Street, New York 16, N.Y.
4. Write to: The National Golf Foundation, Mr. Herb Graffis, 407 South Dearborn Street, Chicago 5, Illinois.

HOW LONG IS RESORT GOLFING SEASON

The golf season corresponds exactly with the hotel season—which means, generally, from about April 15th to November 1st. Exceptions are common, as in winter resorts when the weather permits, guests are invited to use the golf course even if the Pro shop is closed. Golf, therefore, can be played all year 'round, weather permitting.

ARE THE GOLF COURSES GOOD

How much of a challenge to a good golfer is the typical resort course?

Frank Scelzo the P.G.A. Pro at the bouncing Laurels Hotel and Country Club in the Catskills of New York State, states that resort courses are not toy or midget jim-crack affairs.

1. His course at the Laurels, altho temporarily a nine hole course, is soon to be enlarged to a full eighteen hole course. But even now, using double tees, he insists: ". . . this particular course is a good test of golf. It's one of the toughest courses in the country, from the long tee. The hazards, distances, and grooming are all big-time."

2. Twice around this nine hole course totals 6,705 yards from the short tees; 7,004 yards from the long tees, in a double match.

ARE THE COURSES CROWDED

Are resort golf courses crowded, or at least busy enough to cause long waits before tee-off time?

Peculiarly enough, crowds are no problem at most of the resort hotels. Despite the most lushly inviting facilities, apparently swimming, handball, boating and the infinite variety of activity offered by the modern resorts manages to spread the guest list thin over all. Frank Scelzo mentions that at the

Laurels he averages between 60 to 100 people a day; and on weekends, there is little change. This is, to interpret, a very small traffic; and it means no waiting. A possible exception seems to be the one common to most resorts and hotels—and this is the after-breakfast rush to the links. Even at that, the wait is generally ten minutes in duration, hardly longer than twenty at the outside. Just avoid this 9 to 11 a.m. concentration and you will be master of the course.

WHAT TIME DOES COURSE OPEN

Are you limited by "hours" when you want to play?

No—you can even play by moonlight, if you think you can follow the flight of your golf ball. The resort courses are generally yours for the using, no matter the time of day or night. But the Pro Shop keeps hours, altho they follow the pattern of vacationing guests.

1. Using Mr. Scelzo's Laurel's Hotel as the typical example: he opens his shop at 8:00 a.m., sometimes as early as 6:00 a.m.; and he closes, supposedly, at 6:00 p.m. but usually much closer to 8:00 p.m. Weekdays and weekends are the same as to hours.

IS EQUIPMENT AVAILABLE

Must I bring my own golf bag, clubs, balls, etc., or can I rent them at the hotel?

The typical resort golfing setup is very similar to the typical CC or public course in that you will almost always find a completely equipped Pro Shop there for your convenience, including full rental as well as sale merchandise. Naturally, most golfers prefer their own clubs at all times; but if you need to fill in an item or two, you'll undoubtedly find it at the Shop. This section is particularly interesting and valuable to beginners—for most resorts provide complete golf equipment for rental, so if you want to give it a try on vacation, go to it.

WHAT OTHER FACILITIES ARE OFFERED

Do these resorts and hotels have locker rooms, shower rooms; can you get lessons; use practice greens, etc.?

Most all of the resort golf courses have practice putting reens, and practically all of them make some sore of provision or storage of your bag and clubs, as well as cleaning facilities or your spikes and equipment. But this latter varies with the lub and the type of vacationer who makes a practice of using he facilities. Some resorts even go so far as to have steam ooms, massage and rubdown facilities, complete locker-room ervice in a luxurious clubhouse, but this is the exception ather than the rule. When you consider that you are at a vacaion spot to begin with, it is rather a simple matter to cross the oad to your own room and there, shower at your own conenience.

. Facilities, such as massage tables, etc., are usually found at those resorts where the golf course is distant from the main house of the hotel. For example, at the Laurels, there is no real clubhouse since the golf course is directly across the street from the hotel. The Concord, with the golf course far from the hotel, has a big clubhouse.

. Lockers are unnecessary at those courses where the links are close to the hotel; but club storage is provided, for a fee of about 50¢ a day, $1.50 on weekends, and perhaps $2.00 for a full week's storage.

FEES AND OTHER COSTS

Some resort golf courses permit registered guests to play at o additional cost; at these there is no green fee; altho most otel golf courses do charge a small fee.

. Greens fee—for registered guests—$1.50
Greens fee—for outsiders; friends of registered guests; strangers—$3.00-$4.00

The above prices are those charged at the Laurels in the atskills. These fees vary from place to place. Their range encompasses:
From nothing at all to as much as $3.00 for registered guests.

Most resorts maintain a policy of sorts—usually that onl
registered guests may play the hotel golf course. But in practic
this is most elastic. What usually happens is, if the course is no
congested, the Pro will permit the non-registered individual t
play the course for the higher greens fee.

2. Caddy fee—Range from: $1.50-$2.50 (single nine), $3.0(
   $4.50 (double nine), $2.00-$6.00 (from single to doubl
   eighteen)
3. Carts—where permissible, price generally runs from 25¢ t
   no more than 75¢ a day. Some of the real palaces may charg
   $1.00 a day.

Summary: When you play a resort course, as you can see th
fees and other costs are relatively low, yet most places do charg
something. At the average resort; barring the ultra-ultra an
the fleabag; you can play (at a cost to yourself) of:

Greens fee: $1.50
Caddy: 2.50
              ―――――
              $4.00—total.

LESSONS

Can I get lessons at a resort golf course, and how much d
they cost?

All resorts worthy of the name, at least ambitious enough t
provide a golf course, be it a nine-hole or eighteen-hole cours
will have a Pro; and in the prominent vacation areas, chance
are you will discover to your delight that he is one of the bigge
"name" pros. But he is there to operate his golf shop (yes, al
golf shops "belong" to the Pro running them by P.G.A. ruling
and to give lessons. Good teachers come high in any line, ye
you will find the cost of lessons not exorbitant, especially cor
sidering that you may be a pupil of say, Frank Scelzo at th
Laurels, Jimmy Demaret at the Concord, Joe Turnesa at Gro
singers; etc.

1. Lessons range from: $5.00-7.50 per half-hour; $25.00-35.00 per six half-hour lessons.

2. It is advisable to arrange for an appointment when you want a lesson. You'll be sure the Pro is there so no time is wasted. The Pro will be prepared for you; you derive full benefit of the lesson. Being sure of your time adds to the anticipatory enjoyment.

3. It is most advisable to take a lesson or two while at a resort —because, your teacher is apt to be one of the very best in the business—you are in a more relaxed and receptive mood —the lack of pressure gives you more for your money and extra time on each lesson, plus the handiness of the course being available to practice on right now. Add to this the convenience of being able to get to the Pro and the course so easily; and these are potent "yeas" for the resort or hotel lesson.

ARE RESERVATIONS NECESSARY

For playing the resort golf course—generally not, except for heavy week-end or holiday play. For taking a golf lesson—Yes!

ALL ABOUT COLLEGE GOLF

by Bernie Wohl, Golf Instructor Brooklyn College, Adult Education Division

All over the nation, lights are burning brightly in college gyms as businessmen, lawyers, accountants, bakery truck drivers, home-makers are taking their stance and learning the fundamentals of golf. The courses aren't expensive and they've proven very useful. So if you really want to learn from qualified teachers, investigate a nearby college.

In the past decade, there has been a tremendous increase in college golf, reflecting the growing interest of the general public. Golf is the fastest-growing participant-sport in America today. The Adult Education classes in various educational institutions, including Community Centers and "Y's," have caught on phenomenally. Our groups at Brooklyn College, started in 1950, have run as high as nine classes per session. Each class is limited to 20 students and registration is usually closed almost as soon as the rolls are opened. More and more institutions are adding such instruction.

COST OF COURSES

In New York City, the fees run from a nominal $1.00 at the City Community Centers to $15.00 per course at Brooklyn College. In some Community Centers, in order to get competent instructors, the P.T.A. which often sponsors the group, adds the amount necessary from its treasury or charges an additional 4 or 5 dollars per person.

"They say this is the longest course in Texas."

KNAPP
MENGES

EQUIPMENT PROVIDED

The equipment used varies considerably depending upon the funds available and the competency of the instructor. When I inaugurated the course at Brooklyn College, I shopped the market for suitable equipment. It soon became evident that for a course combining group and individual instruction, a driving cage was not suitable; each student would get only about five minutes practice in a two hour class.

For use with the woods, I finally selected the Par Golf Company's "Masterpiece Golf Device." This is a rubber mat with a captive rubber ball at which the student swings. This device has certain psychological advantages for teaching the basic fundamentals of the full golf swing, superior to anything else I have been able to find. Students soon learn to keep the head steady during the swing.

For use with the irons, the students are supplied with good quality "cocoa" mats and the new plastic golf balls. These simulate the flight of a real ball and cannot cause injury.

A beginning student should not have to buy clubs since it takes some knowledge of the game to be able to select the kind he or she prefers. On the other hand, a student who has his or her own sticks is encouraged to bring them to class, since it is preferable to learn with the tools you are later going to use. For my students, I have at least ten of each of the major types of clubs necessary for the different types of lessons—woods; long, medium, and short irons; and putters—in all about fifty to sixty clubs. In addition, there is at least one set of left-handed clubs.

For putting we provide the Ben Hogan "Golf Green" and real golf balls. Since putting comprises half the game of golf and requires constant practice, provision is made for instruction and practice at every session.

CONTENT OF THE COURSE

The organization of these courses varies from place to place. The National Golf Foundation publishes an "Instructors Handbook" outlining 16 lessons. Some Community Centers give a series of ten lessons; some keep open four nights a week and students may drop in any time or all the time for practice and informal instruction.

At Brooklyn College we give a series of 8 lessons to a course, and hold three sessions during the year—Fall, Winter, and Spring. Each of the 8 lessons consists of group lectures and demonstrations, discussion, and individual practice, with supervision and analysis. My program for the 8 lessons at Brooklyn College is as follows:

First through fourth lessons:
> the full swing using the woods and the rubber "Masterpiece" device, putting theory and practice; description of the game, differences among clubs and uses for each, golf etiquette; need for practice.

Fifth lesson—the long iron and general iron play

Sixth lesson—the medium iron, review of general iron play, emphasis on chipping.

Seventh lesson—the short irons, approaching, pitching, explosions from sand traps and review of full iron plays.

Eighth lesson—general review, any and/or all clubs; difficult lies; mental attitude towards the "game"

GETTING THE MOST FROM A COURSE

As in learning any manual skill, PRACTICE is the keynote. Therefore, students should be encouraged to practice frequently and for short periods of time between weekly lessons.

Certain books and pamphlets are available and valuable for specific purposes, but they can also be confusing, if not used correctly. In general, "book-larnin'" is best used to remind the student of various phases of instruction which he has already received, not as an outright text. For example, after the instructor has taught how the club should be held, the pupil, during practice, may refer to the pictures in a book as a check.

COURSE CREDIT FOR GOLF

Aside from Adult Education, many colleges have added golf to their regular curriculum, especially for Physical Education majors. In some institutions, credit is allowed to those taking the course as a leisure-time, non-competitive activity, as well as to those who play on the college golf team.

THE FULL PICTURE

The golf course is the worst place to learn to play golf. Well, then can one learn to play golf, really learn, in such atmosphere as is provided by a school course? By all means, as is being proven all the time and with thousands of students. No one should go out on a golf course without a fair knowledge of the fundamentals and some slight ability to apply them. With this knowledge, practice and practice alone will turn the duffer into a golfer, regardless of the type of instruction—individual, group, or a combination of the two. At any rate, I repeat, the golf course is the worst place to learn to play golf.

THE FUNDAMENTALS
OF GOLF

GRIP AND STANCE
AS THEY RELATE TO THE ENTIRE SWING
by Cary Middlecoff

Allow me to revert to fundamentals again and attempt to impress you with the fact that *the proper grip and stance for each individual are the keys to a sound golf swing.*

GRIP

There are several accepted ways to hold a golf club, but I have very little respect for any great variation from the Vardon overlapping grip. This is simply because every good player, with almost no exceptions, has used the Vardon overlap or a very slight variation during his tournament-winning days.

The Vardon overlapping grip has the club running diagonally across the left hand from the second joint of the left forefinger and coming out across the middle of the thick part of the heel of the hand. It is a combination palm and finger grip.

The left thumb runs down the shaft and about one-fourth the distance over the top of the shaft on the side of the right shoulder. Thus, the left thumb and portion of the hand above the knuckle of the left forefinger form a V. This V should point about to the right shoulder, and, if properly formed, will show two or three knuckles of the left hand when the player looks down the shaft of the club to the ball.

The grip of the right hand is a complete finger grip, with the

Reprinted by permission from Golf Doctor by Cary Middlecoff, published by McGraw-Hill Book Company, Inc., copyright 1950 by Cary Middlecoff.

little finger of the right hand overlapping the forefinger of the left. The thumb of the right hand runs down the shaft about one-fourth the distance over the top of the shaft on the side of the left shoulder. The thumb and forefinger of the right hand form a V almost exactly the same as the V of the left hand and parallel to it. This V also should point to the right shoulder.

The thumb of the right hand should be in close union with the end of the right forefinger.

All fingers on both hands should be in close union with one another, though not cramped. The club should be held firmly in both hands, though not to the point that either upper arm is tense. You might visualize the grip as similar to one you take on your knife and fork. It is a firm, definite grip, but not one you would take on the back end of an automobile to lift it.

One of the variations of this grip that is sometimes helpful is an interlocking of the left forefinger and right little finger. This is very good for people with small hands. The purpose of interlocking or overlapping is to join the hands closer together so they can work more closely in unison.

A few players have very successfully used the interlocking grip with the left thumb off the shaft of the club. Usually this grip is adopted by a player who has been forced to use it because of an injury to his thumb, or some type of deformity. The leverage and guiding ability furnished by the left thumb on the shaft of the club are almost indispensable.

There is only one grip necessary for every stroke, from a chip shot all the way through the drive. No variations are needed.

Watch your grip very closely and check it before every shot. You will find that with the left hand too far over the top of the shaft and the right hand too far under the shaft, a hooked ball is almost sure to result. Conversely, with the left hand too far under the shaft and right hand too far over, a slice is the customary result.

I believe any individual, by just letting his hands hang normally at his sides, will see they hang straight down—which is the natural way. Therefore it would not be logical to turn either or both hands off at an angle and expect to accomplish results as good as you would get by the natural position.

STANCE

The stance varies slightly with almost every club. To make sure the reader understands the terminology, "Square stance," "open stance," and "closed stance," I will describe each of them briefly.

Square Stance: This is a stance taken with the toes of both feet equally distant from the direction line of the ball to the flag.

Open Stance: This is a stance taken with the left foot farther from the direction line to the flag than is the right foot, and with the entire body partly facing in the general direction of the flag.

Closed Stance: This is a stance with the right foot farther from the direction line than is the left foot and with the entire body facing slightly away from the flag.

An open stance, with the feet relatively close together, is employed in the short irons. This gradually progresses to a wider and squarer stance and then to a maximum-width stance that is slightly closed with the driver.

With the shortest irons, there is a premium on accuracy, and most of the body movement should be eliminated. As the stance gradually gets wider and squarer, the shots are longer and, though we are still looking for accuracy, more power is a necessity. Gradually more body turn is accomplished to gain this extra power, by simply setting the feet to permit it.

HEAD POSITION

Head position is one element that cannot be left out of any educational discussion on golf.

For all shots, the head must remain on its same starting axis. I think to say that the head remains absolutely still is a fallacy, for the head does rotate slightly in most swings.

One other matter to be expected during a full swing with a

driver is that the head remains practically still from the beginning of the backswing and during the downswing until the ball is hit. After that point, the head will move slightly forward, because of the swinging momentum set up by the movement of the body.

Too much stress cannot be placed upon the importance of good head position. It is absolutely essential to the consistent success of all types of shots. Head position carries the same importance in every shot. It is the gyroscope of the entire swing, so far as balance is concerned.

CURING GOLF AILMENTS
by Johnny Farrell

Nobody needs a professional to tell him what's *good* with his game. The week-end golfer probably likes to hear that he has got good hand action in his swing, or that he is all in one piece coming back, but as soon as you comment on it, he invariably eyes you sourly and says: "A devil of a lot of good that did me today. I was slicing the ball all over the place!"

So I'm going to tell you about slicing—as well as some of the other common ailments that creep into any man's game on occasion—and try to prescribe some medicine.

What *is* the number one ailment? It is also the number one rule of golf: *Keep your head down.* I didn't say that it was "looking up." You can keep your eye on the ball and still move your head.

Anchor it, and keep it anchored from the moment you have taken your stance and decided to hit. Your head must be steady. It cannot move throughout the backswing and until the follow-through motion of your arms and shoulders brings it around in the direction of the shot.

On short iron shots, and on putts, the head *never* moves.

Your objective in golf is to groove your swing—to make it so natural that you could hit a ball blindfolded. The key to a grooved swing is an unmoving head, a sort of fulcrum around which everything else is pivoting.

Head movement changes an inside arc to an outside downswing—and that's where slices are born.

Head movement makes it impossible to wait for the clubhead at the top of the backswing—forces you into rushing the downswing because you're swaying and off balance.

Head movement destroys the natural circle of your swing—whether you come back *round* or *flat*—and makes you top a ball, stub it, or sometimes miss it completely.

Most importantly, you cannot keep your eye steady on the ball if your head is not steady.

But suppose your head *is* steady—suppose it stays down with the shot and your swing comes through perfectly . . . and still the ball does not get off the way you want it to?

Something, evidently, has happened to your timing and that something may be lack of concentration.

That word, to a golfer, means many things. Its first meaning, of course, is that you are conscious of nothing on earth but that little white ball. At that moment, you are the only human being in existence and that is the only ball ever made. It occurs every time you are ready to hit—and that can be seventy times or more than a hundred times in any round. It's your absolute concentration on the ball that provides the coordination between mind and body that must go into every shot.

But beware the common mistake of confusing concentration on the ball and becoming hypnotized by it. Most experts agree that five seconds is the maximum time you should give yourself over completely to any shot. Beyond that you may freeze on the ball or swing at it lethargically.

Too, you can be concentrating on the shot with all of your conscious mind, and yet forces are at work on your *subconscious* that steal from it and dissipate it. Golf is a precise game and you can't expect to play it successfully if your mind is worried or distracted by other things.

But there are other subconscious factors that may be working on you. In addressing the ball you may be subjecting yourself to muscular strain that you believe is necessary but certainly is not. Your left arm, instead of being firm may be locked tight.

Or you may be *forcing* your knees to bend slightly rather than allowing them to relax normally.

And oftentimes a golfer will lock his right leg at the top of the backswing just as he is about to retransfer his weight to the left side of his body in the process of unwinding. Not only does this prevent him from hitting back through the ball with a loose body, but the muscular strain sends a signal to his brain that interferes with his concentration on the ball.

Also, you may be putting your head into an invisible vise, as mentioned earlier, in an effort to force your head to remain steady. The neck, in this unnatural position, protests, and your concentration is disturbed.

This is where the practice swing becomes so important. Loosen up before you are ready to hit, and hit the ball with the same *free* swing. Stay loose, swing loose, and be comfortable.

Poor Direction: Does the shot, even though the ball flies a straight course, end up to the left or to the right of where you aimed it? If it does, then obviously there is something wrong with your "aiming."

It makes sense to say that, since a ball waiting to be hit has no motion until you give it motion—and since it is the swinging clubhead that provides the motion—then it is also the swing that determines what direction the ball will go. The swing itself is guided by your hands and body and by the position of your feet, both when the swing begins and when it ends. The rule to follow, providing you are hitting the ball well and getting poor direction, is to stand at hitting distance from the ball, place your heels together and look out to where you'd like the ball to land. Plan the shot in your mind—take a mental picture of it, both for distance and terrain—and *then* take your hitting stance. Always line up for a shot—and stand for the shot and not for the ball.

A complete follow-through will also overcome any grief you may be having about the direction of your shots. Give the clubhead every chance to make the shot. Let it continue all the way through in the direction of the hole when the shot is made.

Good direction on these comes entirely from your feet and the follow-through of the clubhead. Hand control is the secret— and practice.

The Slice. There are many reasons for a slice but there's only one way *how* it's done, and that's by bringing the clubhead across the ball—outside in—and giving it a right-way spin.

Of the ways *to* slice, the number one enemy is getting the right side into the shot too quickly. You generally do this because you *sway* on the backswing, rather than *pivoting* around on your hip.

An inside arc going back that becomes an outside downswing is another fatal slice producer, and usually is caused by losing control of the shaft at the top of the backswing.

A slice can also come from a left arm that isn't firm, and because it isn't firm, the *right* elbow strays. Tuck that right arm in, and when you unwind your left hip it will follow the inside arc naturally.

But both the loss of hand control and the straying elbow are generally the result of (a) rushing the backswing and (b) not waiting for the downswing. Hand in glove with a rushed swing is a tendency to lunge at the ball—to drive it fifteen miles. This causes you to leave your hips out of the shot entirely, so that it is the arms, and not the clubhead, that are swinging at the ball. My advice, then, is to practice coming back extra-slow—all in one piece, as explained under Fundamental Three—then unwind, keeping the right shoulder behind the shot, and let the clubhead come through the ball.

Many golfers slice, too, because they *die on the shot,* as the expression goes. They come back in one piece, wait, come back down again, and then quit completely as the clubhead strikes the ball. This failure to stay with a good swing oftentimes can be traced to the club the golfer is using. It may be too heavy to continue on through naturally, or so light that it cannot withstand the speed and power of the uncoiling pivot.

An open stance with a wood or a long iron will also produce a slice. This is usually due to the fact that the hitter is not aware he stands that way, but believes his feet are square with the direction of the shot and the ball. Line up the shot carefully, as described under Fundamental Two.

In any event, never get saddled with a slice and begin "standing for it" or facing off to the left to compensate for the curve the ball is going to take to the right. If anything, face *into* the slice—and by doing this you'll be squaring your stance.

Finally, a slice may be traced on your grip. Be certain that your left hand is around the shaft and not slipping to the left so that the palm is facing up. Check, always, that the V of the forefinger and thumb points over the left shoulder. Don't waste the power of that all-important left arm, hand, and wrist. The right hand—thanks to the overlapping grip—is meant to be nothing more that a guide for the swing. And be sure that you are holding the clubshaft in the fingers of your right hand and not palming it. You must, at all times, have *live hands* that can feel the whip in the shaft and control the swing.

The Hook. It has been my observation that the beginners do most of the slicing—it takes an experienced golfer to develop a bad hook. It's true. During the first five years that a man plays golf he tries so many things to rid him of a slice that he suddenly finds himself faced with the problem of losing a disastrous hook. But "Hookitis" is not confined to any one group of golfers, for the simple reason that a hook is most often the result of timing that has gone bad. And when the expert golfer hooks a drive or a long iron it is generally spectacular because he *trusts* his swing. He bends back and lets go—and if his timing is off, however slightly—the hook that follows is sometimes unbelievable.

But the expert knows what to do about his hook. The weekend golfer sometimes does not even realize that his timing is at fault and can be corrected without the use of drugs or yogi.

First of all, keep your left foot in contact with the ground throughout the swing. In practice, do it consciously and make yourself aware that you are pivoting all at one time and all in one piece, as described in Fundamental Three. Check the pictures again.

Your timing may also be off at the top of the backswing. You may be failing to *wait* for the shift of power to the left side and allowing your hands to come down far ahead of the hip. This gets the clubhead out *ahead* of the hands and the ball takes an impact that curves it to the left after it has left the tee. Failure to wait also causes the ball to be *pulled*—which is a straight flying ball that veers sharply to the left when hit.

A *smothered hook* results from a swing that is too flat, and this can be corrected at the stance. Stand tall and swing tall should be your reminder, with knees relaxed and slightly bent. If your back is straight, without being stiff, the arc of your backswing will be bigger. Don't crouch over the ball or you will find that you're getting too much of your caboose into the shot.

Check, too, that your left hand is not over too far on the shaft. Beware the creeping left hand! Don't let it swing to the right—as opposed to palming it for the slice—and be sure that you can see no more than the first three knuckles after you've taken your grip. If you have been hooking then you had the recent company of Ben Hogan who told me that he corrected his by allowing only *two* knuckles of the left hand to show on the grip. Other experts favor a somewhat tighter grip with the left hand to correct a spell of hooking.

A hook may also be caused by a clubface that is closed at point of impact, or toed in as the backswing starts. Hold the face of the club upright and square with the ball.

Also, a closed stance, with the left foot up, will pull a ball sharply to the left and even give it a spinning hook. With woods and long irons, play a square stance.

Skying the Ball. A common complaint, especially from the tees or with the woods, is that the ball is popped high in the air. It comes from hitting too hard from the top of the swing, which causes the right shoulder to drop and the ball to be scooped skyward by the downward force of the clubhead. You correct this by slowing down on your downswing and not *pressing* the shot. If you really want to hit the ball a long way, let the *clubhead* do the work. Never rush a shot.

Topping the Ball. On the fairway, many golfers have a tendency to try and *lift* the ball into the air, and in doing so, they lift their body on the downswing as though their arms were going to pick the ball up and send it away. But the only way to get a ball in the air is to *hit down into it.* The loft of the club, plus the down-and-through motion of the downswing, gets the ball in the air and makes it impossible to top it.

Shanking. The question always is: Do you *shank* a shot with an open or closed face? I believe that it is the result of coming down at the ball from the outside-in with a closing clubface. To correct a shank, come back straight from the ball and stay in that same inside arc on the downswing. Have the feeling that the ball must get over a high tree and you will stay back on your heels and not lunge forward on the shot and hit it from the outside.

Shanking usually develops from hooking the ball. To avoid going to the left you come too much from the inside of the line and push your hands through to avoid hooking. This causes the locking of the wrists at impact. Take the club straight back and have more action with your wrists at impact of the ball.

But always remember this: There is nothing wrong with your golf game that a good swing can't cure. Keep your head steady, control the club with your hands, and come back and down again in a one-piece swing.

TIPS ON PLAY

by Lealand Gustavson

If the clubhead meets the ball on the downswing, as it should, what is under the ball doesn't matter so much. Some "lies" are more difficult than others because they allow less room for error at contact. This does not refer to "lies" in long, tangled grass, bushes, woods, rocks, sand, etc., which require special treatment.

With normal unpleasant lies play one club longer than you otherwise need: Swing with easy control and confidence and normal grip, and let nature take its course. In rough, woods, hazards, etc., the essential thing is to get back onto good territory. Determine how you can best hit the ball, how hard you have to hit it, and then proceed without undue effort. Play the stroke a little slower and even more deliberately than an easy shot. Hold your club firmly but no tighter than normal grip. Tenseness is bad. The possible gain of a few extra yards at the risk of utter failure is not intelligent golf. Maybe even playing back toward the tee a few yards would be smart if an easier opening could be found that way. How much difference does it make to you whether you have about 10 yards more to go on a shot to the green?

Tee up a ball with a little wooden tee, whenever the rules allow you to. The very best players won't spurn this assistance, why should you?

Uphill, downhill, or side hill lies do have a special treatment: If the ball is lying on an uphill lie, or is above your feet on a side

From Enjoy Your Golf, copyright 1954 by Lealand Gustavson, reprinted by permission of Harcourt, Brace and Company, Inc.

hill, you will hook, so aim a little to the right of your desired line of flight. Play one club longer than you think you need, as the ball will go high.

If the ball is lying on a downhill lie, or is below your feet, you will slice, so aim a little to the left of your desired line of flight. Play a club with more loft than for a level lie so as to get the ball into the air. Swing easily.

Playing out of sand traps requires practice: Even if you know just how it should be done, it requires an accuracy that cannot be acquired just with the occasional (or frequent) trap shots that occur in a round of play.

The fundamental objective is to get out onto fair territory in one stroke, and the "blast" is the more certain way to do that. Play the ball back toward the right foot a little, and hit down and through.

Varying kinds of sand have varying results. Take less sand if it is soft and fluffy than if it is coarse and gravelly. The softer the sand the less effect the impact has on the ball. The length of backstroke and follow-through may be nearly the same for most shots, but the amount of sand taken will determine the distance the ball will go. "Taking sand" means the amount of sand between the ball and the clubface at impact: one-half inch, one inch, or two inches.

The clubface does not touch the ball. The sand boosts it out. The clubhead must follow through. If it stops in the sand the ball probably will too. If your ball is embedded, the same principle works. Wet sand is more solidly packed than dry sand, but take less wet sand because it offers more resistance to the club. Clean chip shots from sand are very ticklish because the slightest error at contact with the ball can be disastrous. Take a little sand and the ball dies, no sand and the ball drives across the green.

If the sand is smooth and reasonably level and there is no lip on the trap, a putter may roll you out better than anything else.

Playing out of sand on long shots will frequently result in a slice, since you don't pivot as freely because of poor footing and a slight muscle strain due to the fact that you may not heel your club. Be sure to follow through on all trap shots.

When chipping out of long grass use more arm and less wrist: If the wrists are held firm, not rigid, the stroke will have better control with less chance of being thrown off line.

A lost ball is sometimes not where you are sure it ought to be: If you have covered the ground well, with no luck, give a quick onceover look to a wide area surrounding the spot. The ball may have hit something that you didn't see and bounced out of your vision.

Play for the flag at the top of the stick on all long shots for the green: Then maybe you won't always be short. It's no greater fault to be past the hole than it is to be short, and if you did go past you might have gone in. Most players are always short, they sneak up on a hole gradually, which is not good golf.

On short chip shots to the hole, determine the spot on which you intend to land your ball: Estimate the amount of run it will take, and then "toss" it up there very deliberately. Shorten up on the grip of your club to the point where you "feel" you have a delicate control. Keep firm wrists and a firm grip; because the stroke is delicate, firmness is vital. A little sloppiness and you "fluff" the shot. The right hand brings the clubface in square with the ball. Both hands must remain ahead of the club at contact.

The loft of the club gets the ball into the air, you don't. Maybe you can get more loft by scooping it up, but the loft built into your clubs is sufficient, so let the right club do the job it is meant for. Hit down and through the ball and it will go up.

In putting, the percentage of error in distance is much greater than in direction: Putts are generally short, occasionally too hard. The miss off to the side is generally a fraction of an inch to a few inches. When short or long it may be many feet.

Putting practice might well be devoted largely to learning to stroke for distance. Good direction can be attained by simply keeping the putter blade at a right angle to the line of flight until after the ball has been hit.

Some players do this: address your putt about 4 inches back of your ball, line up your blade, and as your stroke reaches out ahead to contact the ball you thereby deliberately follow the line of the putt, which may be an aid to keeping your putter blade moving forward on that all-important visual line.

On a putt of about 3 feet or less aim for the center of the hole and stroke the ball good and firm. If you do that, drift and grain of the grass will have little effect. Have the courage of your convictions.

Grain is the way the blades of grass lie toward you, away from you, or sideways, and they push the ball accordingly.

When drift must be considered, be sure to putt above the hole on a side hill putt. The ball might drop in from above even if your judgment was a bit in error, but if it goes below the hole it can't roll back uphill.

Reading the green is very important. Study the slopes and the grain of the grass and then try to allow for their effects on the line the ball will follow to the hole.

The most important element of putting is to keep the face of the putter at right angles to the line of play as long as you can. The common error is pulling or cutting across the line.

Although putting is primarily a right-hand stroke, your left hand should be kept moving toward the hole. If the left hand stops, the right hand rotates around it and turns the club-face off line.

Another common fault that causes the same thing to happen is having your body weight forward on your toes. Drop back onto your heels, and if you have been playing the ball close to your toes, move back from it a few inches as well. That should help correct the "outside-in" effect which causes so many short putts to miss the hole on the left side.

When a green is wet the ball will slow down very fast at the end of its roll. Side drift will be less.

"Fast" or "slow" greens are only a comparative description: If you have learned what is a standard for you and can stroke for correct distance on that standard, then the "fast" or "slow" means hit a little less hard or a little harder.

In addition to the mechanics of putting, the mental approach is important. Your practicing for distance, line, and smooth stroking prepare you for the final task of dropping the ball in the hole, not just near it. Try to form an exact mental picture of just how your ball must travel to drop into the hole. Permit that mental picture to guide your subconscious efforts. That is what is meant by "touch" on the putting green. Some days it's easy to come by, and other days you couldn't generate it if your life depended upon it.

When a choice is permitted between partners of whose turn it is to putt, a little psychology enters into the play. If both partners are on the green in the same number of strokes but you are somewhat closer to the hole, putt first. The reason: it is the easier putt to make and you have less mental pressure on you, knowing that the sole burden is not on you as your partner still has a chance, even if you miss. If your partner putts first and misses, your easier putt may then look very hard, and as a result you may miss what you would otherwise have made easily.

There are no hazards in the air: You can ordinarily hit a ball 150 yards or more in the air without undue effort. That is enough to clear most difficulties that may be on the ground between you and the hole. Don't be concerned about them. Just stroke the ball properly and the troubles vanish. If you are insecure about your ability to hit over trouble, that is the real hazard. Select the club that will hit your ball high enough and far enough and then swing it normally. Applying that *extra effort* is what causes you trouble.

Pitching over sand traps is the same thing. Certainly you can pitch a ball 20 or 30 yards, so why should a nearby sand trap worry you. Pitch over it with a normal easy stroke.

Form a mental picture of going over trouble instead of into it, and your chances of going over are good.

Strong winds have a great effect on the flight of your ball: Just how much distance will be added or subtracted depends on the way you hit your ball and the velocity of the wind. Don't underrate the effects. Long, hard-hit shots will be affected less in distance than short pitches because the short pitch is a high-floating ball.

With the wind behind it, the ball will fly farther and will roll farther. Backspin has little effect.

Against the wind the ball will fly higher, almost come to a dead stall at the end of its flight, and drop straight down or actually come back a bit; consequently there is little or no forward roll. If backspin has been applied the ball will roll back toward you.

A strong head wind can cut a club down to half its normal distance: Side winds must be allowed for, too. A hard, well-hit ball will hold its line regardless of a side wind, but a slight hook or slice will be greatly exaggerated. This also holds true against head winds. Tail winds have little effect except to add distance and reduce the effectiveness of backspin.

Short, high pitches will be blown off line by side winds quite a lot, as much as 20 feet or more in 50 yards, while a low crisp chip will be affected much less.

It may be advisable under such conditions to play a straight-faced club at part strength so as to keep the ball low and allow it to roll up to the hole.

Don't play in the rain if you don't have to: It is not pleasant and you get awfully wet. But if you do play, an umbrella is the best protection. Rain jackets add to the difficulty of swinging.

Rubbers with spikes fastened in them are helpful. There are also spiked rubber shoes.

Cotton gloves are a big aid to retaining a hold on slippery grips. Undertaker's gloves do fine. Wet your hands and gloves after putting them on.

Use one club longer than you would ordinarily; the ball won't go as far in the air and it stops dead when it lands.

Pitch or chip a *high* ball to a wet green close to the hole. A low-flying shot will often skip off like a flat stone skimmed across water, or may be stopped dead by the surface water.

Lightning is a serious threat to life on a golf course: Don't take lightning storms lightly. Many deaths and injuries have resulted. Players, caddies, and sponsors of golfing events are urged to take every precaution available to them to guard against disaster. Players in a tournament may discontinue play if there is lightning or a serious threat of it.

The soundest advice is: 1. Get into a large protected building. 2. Stay away from isolated trees or small buildings and sheds, wire fences, and hilltops, or wide open spaces. Depressions, dense woods, or a grove of trees are desirable.

Raising golf clubs or metal umbrellas above your head is dangerous. Drop your bag of clubs on the ground, and wait for the storm to pass. As an added precaution, lay your bag on the ground so that the lengthwise of the clubs does not point toward you like a gun.

GETTING STARTED RIGHT

by Johnny Revolta and Charles B. Cleveland

A golf swing, simply stated, consists of swinging a golf club away from the ball and then back to strike the ball. The club head is in the same position at the start of the backswing and at the point of impact. The backswing takes the club away, the downswing brings it back to the same spot from which it started.

The club head moves away from the ball in a groove and comes back in that *same* groove to strike the ball. That's what we mean by a grooved swing.

Also—for all practical purposes—the position of your body at the time you start the swing and when you hit the ball at the bottom of the downswing are identical.

So, half the battle for a good golf swing is won if you start right.

This starting position we call stance.

There is nothing mysterious about stance. I know you have heard a lot of complicated ideas about it. Well, forget them. Most of these complications exist because some golf teachers try to build a set formula for every golfer. As a result, most beginners bend themselves into an unnatural pose trying to imitate someone's system.

There should be no ironclad formula for stance. There are a few basic rules to follow, the rest is up to you. In building your swing, take the position that is natural for you. And be comfortable. "Doin' what comes naturally" was not only a good song, but a good golf rule.

Here are the fundamentals. I'll give them to you quickly now, and then we'll go into details.

1. Your club head should always lie flat on the ground.
2. Stand with your weight equally on both feet.
3. Stand with your toes pointing slightly outward.
4. Stand with your weight back on your heels.
5. Bend your knees slightly—a sort of sitting-down position.
6. With the No. 7, 8, or 9 iron (we will start with them), stand with your heels about six inches apart. That's just a starter, we'll experiment around in later chapters until we find the most comfortable position for your feet. Stand with your left foot about an inch farther back from the line of flight (the line from the ball to the cup) than your right foot.
7. Place the ball on a line midway between your heels.
8. Stand with your left arm in a reasonably straight line with the club shaft, and bend foward at the waist so your hands are slightly away from your body.

Before we go into an explanation of the whys and wherefores, let's try the stance once.

Take the proper grip on the club with the left hand only. Place the club face behind the ball, the bottom of the club resting squarely on the ground. Now place your feet, left foot slightly farther back than the right, the ball midway between your feet. Your heels are about six inches apart, the weight evenly balanced between the two feet. Your knees should be bent and your weight back on your heels. Now complete your grip by grasping the club with your right hand.

All right. Now let's go over the stance slowly, point by point, to clear up any uncertainties. As they used to say in the Wild West when they carried a man to Boot Hill, let's go feet first. We'll build the stance from the ground up.

Balance is going to be our prime concern. Scientific tests have shown that when the average golfer swings in a drive the club head travels between ninety and a hundred miles an hour. That means you've got to be well set, firmly grounded.

If you've ever played hopscotch, you know it isn't easy to balance yourself on one foot. Nor is it easy to swing a golf club ninety miles an hour with your weight balanced on one foot. Like a sailor on a rolling deck, get your weight evenly balanced on both feet.

Remember that. Your weight should be evenly divided between your two feet. That's important because so many pupils have peculiar ideas about standing with their weight on one foot or the other for different shots. Just remember the old adage and stand on your own *two* feet.

You will also find it helpful to stand with your toes pointing slightly outward. The reason will become clear in the next chapter when you start swinging a club. Suffice it for now to say that it will help your freedom of movement during the swing.

There is another important point in balance. Most golfers— 80 per cent of my pupils—have their weight shifted forward on the balls of their feet. They are off balance and in danger of falling forward on their faces.

Your weight should be back on your heels.

Rock back on your heels so your toes are off the ground, then rock forward so they touch the ground. Feel that weight back on your heels. That's where it belongs. You can feel your weight in the back of your thighs and the calves of your legs.

For a while you will have to remind yourself of those two points, keeping your weight back on your heels and evenly divided between your two feet. It is easy to forget until you have practiced enough so that it becomes automatic.

Bending the knees slightly is especially important. The knees act as shock absorbers. If you jumped from a wall onto the ground and landed with your knees stiff, you would jar your entire body. If, on the other hand, your knees were slightly bent, they would absorb the shock.

That is one good reason for keeping your knees bent in taking your stance. Another is that the bent knees will help make your movements in the swing flow evenly.

The combination of bent knees and weight back on the heels gives you a position best described as sitting down. Your posterior protudes.

How much you bend forward at the waist is up to you. Your back, however, should be reasonably straight from waist to shoulder. Some golfers (particularly the tall and lanky ones) stand fairly erect, while the short and stock players are more likely to bend over farther.

There are only two other essentials. One, which I mentioned earlier, is that the base of the club head must lie flat on the ground. In a later chapter we'll go into the mechanics of golf when we'll discuss the fact that this position gives the best hitting area for the club and enables it to perform the functions intended by the manufacturer.

The other is that the left arm should be reasonably straight. By "reasonably" straight, of course, I don't mean rigid and locked, but comfortably straight. The left arm is the guide arm to the swing and keeping it reasonably straight will help you to develop a grooved swing.

The left arm and the club shaft should also form a reasonably straight line. This again enables the club to perform its proper function—the loft (or slant) of the club face will strike the ball at the proper angle.

Your hands, therefore, will be ahead of the ball. As you look directly at the ball, your hands will be on the left of your line of vision.

Also, it is obvious that the more you bend forward at the waist the farther away from your body your hands will be. Thus, for someone who stands fairly upright to the ball, his hands will be quite close to his body. The golfer who bends over markedly will have his hands well away from his body.

The position of the feet (about six inches apart, left foot slightly back) as I explained covers the No. 7, 8, and 9 irons.

"I've got it figured this way, if I start at the 19th hole I don't mind what kind of game I play."

The width of the stance and the relative position of the feet will vary with different clubs. But don't worry about that now. We'll take up the other positions as we discuss the other clubs.

There is another point about the stance that you have probably noticed. The right shoulder is lower than the left for the very natural reason that the right hand lies lower on the club shaft. I mention it only because some students have a tendency to thrust that shoulder forward, when actually it should merely take its natural position parallel with the feet.

Again, let me put in a word about your balance. Just a reminder that it is vital to the process of getting started right. And now, let's put that golf game in motion.

ON STANCE AND SWING
by Bobby Jones

Keynote of Address—Ease, Comfort, Relaxation

Keep Ball Forward . . . Toes Turned Slightly Outward

The keynote of the address position should be ease, comfort, and relaxation. Above all else the first posture must be one from which the movement of the swing may start smoothly without having to break down successive barriers of tension set up by taut or strained muscles. To go a bit further, the player should feel himself alert, sensitive to impulses, and ready to move in either direction.

AVOID UNCOMFORTABLE POSTURE

It is always better at this point to be one's own natural self than to make an effort to look like someone else. Any posture that feels uncomfortable is certain to produce a strain somewhere that will cause the ensuing movement to be jerky. It is well to remember that there are no forces outside of the player's own body that have to be resisted or balanced. There is no need for him to set or brace himself for there is nothing to brace against. If one could conceive that he were standing naturally, with a club in his hands, engaged in ordinary conversation, and that he then bent over enough to ground the club behind a ball not too far away, the resulting posture would be quite good.

Let's visualize a natural, comfortable position. The body is erect and is bent over just enough to reach the ball, which is near enough so that this can be done while the arms hang almost vertically from the shoulders. The knees are slightly bent so that their movement can be free and the weight is about equally divided between the two feet, which are not abnormally spread apart.

Contrast this with poor posture. A player's body is "set," tight. His knees are locked so that his legs are useless; his feet are so far apart, his legs cannot turn; his arms and wrists are as lengths of wood. He is making of his game as hard work as he possibly can.

BALL OPPOSITE INSTEP OF LEFT FOOT

Only two points which might not result naturally, would I emphasize. One is the location of the ball. The swing is greatly simplified by placing the ball far forward, about opposite the instep of the left foot, for here the player is sufficiently behind it so that he can get into position to hit without complicating his backswing by the addition of a shift to the right. Effect of placing ball too far back will appear later.

The other point, is that the toes of both feet should be turned slightly outward. This is done in order to make equally easy the turning of the hips in either direction. To point the right foot to the front or to turn it inward would tend to block or restrict the turn to the right, as a similar placement of the left would affect the turn in that direction.

FORWARD PRESS

A Short Wind-up to Start Backswing Moving Smoothly

The one idea for the golfer to keep always in his mind is that when playing a shot, his job is to SWING the club-head. If he does this, hitting the ball will take care of itself. And the place to start swinging is at the very beginning, as soon as the movement of the stroke gets under way.

From an easy, relaxed position at address, the first movement in the swings of all first class golfers is directed forward, or to the left, in the case of a right-handed player. The movement is regarded by some as a mannerism and non-essential, but there can be no doubt that it serves a useful purpose in breaking down whatever tension may have entered the address position, and in providing a sort of wind-up for a smooth take-off.

This movement is usually referred to as the "forward-press", yet it does not involve, as so many make it do, any independent movement of the hands. Because the common tendency of golfers of all classes is to swing the club mainly with their hands and arms, neglecting to make sufficient use of the powerful muscles of the waist and back, it becomes a matter of the first importance that the conception should be had that the swing originates in the center of the body, in the region about the base of the spine.

HIPS MOVE FIRST

The "forward-press" then, though it moves the hands forward, is accomplished by a movement of the hips—a short, and sometimes, very quick, turn toward the left, handled easily by the responsive legs. The hands press, or rather, are pressed, forward and relaxed wrists become flexed backward. In reality, it is a short wind-up, or backing-up so that the backswing can begin moving smoothly.

The two common mistakes, at this stage are: one, picking the club up with the right hand in a way that prevents the extension of the left arm and carries the club-head toward the outside of its proper arc; and two, whipping the club around the knees by an independent movement of the hands and wrists. The latter fault flattens the arc too much, and causes the head and shoulders ultimately to move back from their correct location.

It is very helpful to think of slinging the club to the top, to originate the movement in the center of the body, by executing a simple turn of the hips without any sidewise movement of the head and shoulders. Communicate this movement to the club through the left arm and hand, allowing the right hand to rest lightly upon the club until it is needed, half-way through the backswing, to assist in lifting the club to the top.

WHEN LEFT GRIP SHOULD BECOME FIRM

If the beginning has been made correctly, the club-head will have moved at least a third of the way back before any change in the relation of the shaft of the club to the left arm will become noticeable. As the hands were pressed forward by the slight twist of the hips to the left, now they are moved backward by the beginning of the reverse turn. The grip of both hands, and the wrist joints remaining relaxed, the hands move past their location at address before they actually pick up the weight of the club-head. In slow-motion there is produced the definite impression that the club is being dragged away from the ball. At the first tug of the club-head upon the moving hands, the grip of the left becomes firm and the club begins to move.

EXTENDED LEFT ARM REQUISITE OF GOOD FORM

Contributes Accuracy, Consistency and Momentum to Swing

Good form in any physical activity must be valued in terms of efficiency. The efficiency of a thermal engine, for example, is measured by the ratio of the work done by the engine to the heat energy supplied to it. The efficiency of a golf stroke must be measured, in the same way, by the ratio of the work done on the ball to the amount of physical energy used up in the swinging. The expert golfer drives far with little apparent effort because of the high rate of efficiency of his performance. The duffer, though he strain himself to the utmost, falls far behind because so much of the energy expended goes to waste.

EFFICIENCY DEPENDS ON THREE THINGS

A high rate of efficiency, and hence good form, in golf, depend upon three things; the development of the greatest possible club-head speed at contact, with whatever energy or power the player can supply—the production of a precisely accurate contact between club and ball, directing the blow along the line upon which it is intended the ball shall travel—and consistency in performing approximately according to these ideals.

Although these are obvious generalities, it is helpful to do a little thinking along these lines in order to appreciate the importance to a golfer of a proper use of his left arm. For it is in this particular that all duffers are most appallingly deficient, and here too that the better players most often go astray.

STRAIGHT LEFT IMPOSSIBLE FOR SOME

For some persons a straight left arm is a physical impossibility. So let us say, that an *extended* left arm is one of the prime requisites of good form. In many ways it contributes to club-head speed, accurate contact, and consistency of performance, the three components of the efficiency rate.

Just now we are interested chiefly in the backswing. The backward movement is merely the means of storing up power to be used in the hitting, but to increase the amount of this stored up energy is of first importance. We have seen that the beginning was made in the hips in order to assure that the wind-up of the body would at least be started. When this had progressed a short distance we began to force the club back with the left arm.

Now with the club having completed about half of its backward travel, the left arm has become almost straight, and is pushing the club as far back as it can comfortably go. The arc of the swing is thus made very broad so that the space and time for adding speed to the club-head coming down will be as great as possible.

THE PAUSE NO SWING SHOULD BE WITHOUT
by Jack Burke

His ability to pitch is usually a yardstick to a golfer's over-all ability. A pro can murder a top-flight amateur with the pitch. A tournament-tough amateur can tear a club player to pieces with it. And among the club players almost as many club championships and dollar Nassaus are won with the pitch as with the putter. It is the one shot which you can use to overcome a really bad shot.

In the final round of the 1952 Houston Open, a $10,000 tournament, I hit only six greens in regulation figures, yet I managed to win the tournament by as many strokes. This was mainly due to my ability to pitch the ball.

I had been spraying my irons all over Texas. The final round of a $10,000 tournament seemed like hardly the time or the place to figure out why. I let them fall where they may, and fell back on my pitch shots for support.

In importance, the pitch stands behind only the putt and the drive. Touring pros spend almost as much time and study on its technique as they do on the putt.

Technically, the only difference between the proper procedure of the pitch and that of the chip is the length of the backswing.

For maximum effect, the short pitch must be played with your wedge. Like the chip, it, too, is essentially a billiard shot.

The ball must be mashed against the turf with a downward blow.

Part of the backspin is imparted by the high loft, part by the flanged sole characteristic of the wedge. The beveled edge of this sole acts on the ball like a snap of the fingers.

As in the snap of the fingers, the wedge shot must be executed with authority—deliberately and crisply. This can only be accomplished by pausing just before you make your downswing.

On any golf shot, once you have addressed the ball properly, the most important single act you can perform is to pause between your backswing and your downswing.

Among its many other services, the pause acts as a time and place in which to muster your resolve, a last chance to reaffirm your desire to hit the ball properly.

If you don't already have a pause in your swing, go beg, borrow, or steal one. No golf swing is complete without it.

I have never cottoned to the theory that the golf swing is composed of three or more sections. Two is the most I have been able to discover. You swing the club back and you swing it down. What else can or should you do with it?

To come down to the ball after having gone back, you must shift out of reverse. And in order to keep from stripping your gears, so to speak, you must come to a complete stop before you shift. This is the pause, and it must be done deliberately.

Watch any good golfer at the top of his backswing and you can actually see this pause taking place in his mind. The deliberation will be written all over his face.

As I say, psychologically, the pause is the time and place to muster your resolve, your last chance to reaffirm the purpose behind everything else you have done—to hit the ball. But the pause has more than just psychological value.

The pause causes the slow backswing, which in turn, prevents the body from swaying.

The speed of the slow backswing and the movement of the

head, like the follow-through, are typical carts-before-the-horse in the average golfer's analysis of his swing.

You can't help but move your head back and forth. As we have pointed out, the danger is in moving it up and down, which can be prevented simply by standing erect at the address. What actually happens when most golfers think they merely moved their head is that they swayed their entire body. This is caused by taking the club back faster than the hands, arms, and shoulders can handle it as a unit.

The surest way to bring the club back in the proper rhythm is to establish a pause at the top of the swing. This eliminates the necessity or desire to hurry.

I have seen plenty of bad players with very slow backswings. Most of them end up lunging at the ball. And I've seen plenty of good players with fast backswings, notably Gene Sarazen and Tommy Bolt.

But I have never seen a bad player who paused at the end of it nor a good player who didn't.

Walter Hagen has said that he never paid any attention to this backswing. He found it unreliable in positioning himself for the downswing. Instead, the Haig used a pronounced pause at the top, often repositioning the club before he went into his downswing.

The pause is the cause of a proper backswing, not the effect of it.

YOUR SWING
by Harry Gottlieb

The golf swing has no relation to the swing in any other sport. But many of the terms and principles applicable to it are used in bowling, basketball, tennis, and other sports, especially bowling. Yet the golf swing remains in a class by itself and accounts perhaps for the disappointment suffered by many athletes of other sports when they take up the game. Golf seems so simple compared to the rugged sports in which they have participated. As they try to hit the ball the proverbial mile, they are shocked to find how difficult it is to hit it at all. Being athletic is an advantage in learning any sport but in golf the athlete soon discovers there is a lot to the game that he must learn like every other beginner. Because of his coordination and an athletically trained brain, he may learn faster, but learn he must.

The golf swing varies as personalities vary. I know of nothing that will disclose character more. If you have any defect you want to hide from friends, be careful about your golf swing. Defects in golf swings can, likewise, be traced to your character and personality. Often our faults are so ingrained that it is next to impossible to change them. Nevertheless, some people are flexible and as golfers they are able to improve. If you have been playing incorrectly for a very long time, it will be difficult to learn how to swing properly, but the sooner you begin, the better chance you have of eradicating your faults.

Golf is an exact science, involving many principles of physics.

But the basic principle is the ancient power of the lever, one of man's earliest discoveries.

Anyone who can hit a straight ball is well on his way to golfing success. The variations of that straight ball are only corollaries. I learned the "secret" of hitting a straight ball many years ago from Dave Cuthbert, a top flight golf instructor. Cuthbert, who cured a slice for me in less than 15 minutes, knew I was a slicer even before I started my club head down. He was able to diagnose my fault in my back swing. Thus, the "secret" of a straight ball is the position of the face of your club at the completion of the back swing. From Dave Cuthbert I learned to tell what kind of a ball a golfer will hit merely by observing the position of the face of his club head at the top of his back swing.

As the stance in golf has three fundamental positions—square, open, and closed,—so does the face of the golf club on the back swing: (1) a slice or open position, (2) a closed or hook position, and (3) a square or straight position. It is not enough to know this; you must be able to recognize these three positions. The club face is completely open when it is perpendicular to the ground. It is completely closed when the face is parallel to the ground, that is, when facing the sky. It is straight when midway between the open and closed positions. In other words, when the club face at the top of the swing is at an angle approximately 45° to the ground, the club is in the proper position to hit a straight ball. If you could place a six-foot carpenter square on the face of your club on the back swing, the end of the square would touch the line running through the ball to the hole. If the face of your club is not in the square position, adjustments have to be made. Before describing a foolproof method of getting it in the proper position, I think it might be helpful to review briefly the history of the golf swing.

Before we developed our own players in America, starting with Francis Ouimet and followed by our own homebred professionals and amateurs, the golf swing was entirely different from today. In Scotland and England, it was built upon the principle of the pivot. Everything turned: the player pivoted or turned his body; he "pronated" his wrists (a term borrowed from the medical profession, meaning, in golf, any turning of the wrist, whether forward or backward). It was truly an arduous task to hit a ball with everything turning backward and forward. It is amazing that those old-timers in Scotland and England scored the way they did. It was almost impossible to be consistent because the ball had to be struck with a flush club face at the moment of impact, which meant that the turning had to be perfectly timed. They had one out of a dozen or so chances to accomplish this, because it was most difficult to so regulate the pivoting of the body and the turning of the wrists to hit the ball consistently in a straight line.

American golfers in the twenties soon discovered that this turning and pronation was not conducive to accuracy. By trial and error they discovered the "straight face" theory, keeping the club face throughout the entire swing in the exact position it assumed when addressing the ball. The face of the club goes back from the ball without any turning of the wrists, and therefore without any turning of the club face. You can close your eyes and take your club back in this manner, and the club face will come back to the ball perfectly square with it.

Let me emphasize that you must not turn or pronate your wrists in a golf swing. Wrists, like hinges on doors, must open and close but never turn. If the position of your club face is being changed constantly by the revolution of your wrists, you have about one chance in twelve to hit a straight ball. With the straight face position, you have many chances to hit a straight ball, whether you are late or early. The hitting area of a pronator is only about two inches, whereas the hitting area of a straight face swinger is more than a foot. There is no doubt that the American golfers were bound to surpass their English cousins in golf once they discovered the secret of the straight ball.

There is one tip I want to give on how to insure the straight face position of your club head. You can keep your eye on the ball and still watch your club go back for at least one foot. The area of vision of your eyes covers even a greater distance than one foot, so you can watch the club head go back for at least a foot and that first foot is important. Be sure to take it back with the face still toward the ball, without any turning to the ground or to the sky. This is done by your arms without any breaking of wrists.

Now for the back swing. So far, I have endeavored to give a mental picture of the straight face principle. First, let me say that I do not advocate practice swings. To me, they are anti-climactic. In golf, you are constantly winding up your muscles to supply power, and in taking practice swings you stretch these muscles unnecessarily, diminishing their effectiveness. Save strength and muscular action for the real thing.

The waggle plays a prominent part in golf and is beneficial in setting you up for the shot by loosening your wrists. In a recent invitation amateur tournament, I observed a golfer who consistently took 14 waggles before he got ready to hit. What a pest! No one should take more than two or three waggles.

Some golfers waggle in a long sweeping movement of the club head, permitting it to swing as far past the ball as behind the ball, causing a break in the wrist. This destroys the radius of the arc of your swing, which should be maintained in a straight line from your right front shoulder down through your front arm, wrist, and hands, as though they were an extension of the club shaft itself. Therefore, to waggle past the ball is getting yourself into a bad habit of breaking that requires radius. In waggling, never let the face of the club pass the ball. That is your objective and that is as far as you should go in loosening your wrists.

After a few waggles and just before the club starts on the back swing, there is a motion, typical of golf, that many professionals and low handicap golfers seem to have acquired naturally and without effort. It is in a way the badge of a good golfer, and I have hardly seen one who did not possess it. Called the "forward press," it is a forward movement of the body, knees, and hands, with the club head remaining on the ground where it has been dropped behind the ball after the waggle. It is sort of getting yourself attuned to the swing. In it the back swing is actually set up by a forward motion. It may be described as being a twitch of the knees, and gives the golfer a flowing motion to his back swing, and seems to set the club head in motion gracefully and without effort. It is one of the eccentricities of the game which I doubt exists in any other sport.

If you don't possess a forward press, don't think that your game is hopeless. Many a fine golfer plays without it. Perhaps the finest exponent of the forward press was Bobby Jones, and it is no wonder he is considered to have the most graceful golf swing. This does not mean you can't try it, but I warn you, if you are not a low handicap amateur, do not attempt to add more woes to an already difficult problem. Try it, however, and you may improve your back swing.

Whether or not you try a forward press, eventually you start the club on its back swing. It should be taken back with the club head as low to the ground as possible, as this reaching back will automatically shift the body weight to your back leg and insure a wide, flat arc of your club head. This will also create a certain firmness in your hands, wrists, and back leg. Cream puff hands will not drive a ball 225 yards. There must be firmness in every part of your body. I don't mean poker stiff; you can be firm and relaxed without being stiff and strained.

While power in golf is definitely in the back hand, there is special work for the front hand in the back swing. The back hand in left-handed golfers is the left hand, and in right-handers, the right hand. Nevertheless the front hand is by no means a helpless appendage. It has a definite and important job which it cannot perform without a firm grip of the club.

The right hand of lefties is the hand that controls and guides the plane of the club in the back swing. It is important because any variation in the back swing is bound to have an effect upon the down swing of the club. Once the swing is started wrong, there is little or no chance of ever making allowances for the error. The front hand, also, must guide the club head back to the ball, and in doing so it must act as a brake for the power of the back hand. Regardless of what you may think you are doing, your back hand is the powerful force that you are always using at work or at play, and unconsciously this force takes command. If it is permitted to go unrestrained, it usually will get you in trouble. If you don't watch the back hand, it will carry the front hand with it past the ball, without delivering the punch that is necessary. Therefore, the third reason the front hand should be firm is to stop the swing, momentarily, at the instant the club head comes in contact with the ball. You do not stop your swing. You only stop the right hand for a fleeting second at impact and this is the secret of the "follow-through," about which more will appear later.

The club head is taken back slowly, with a positive effort and with a feeling that someone is holding on to it and restraining you from completing your back swing. It is not a loose fleeting sensation, or a motion lightly taken, but definitely a sensation of tension, the sensation you get if you try to straighten out a coil spring. This slow and synthetic build-up of power is necessary to put the muscles of your arms, legs, and body in spring-coiled condition. In fact, the whole swing, especially the waist of your body, should give you the feeling of pulling against a resisting force. This is the only way you have to store up power in your muscles in order to release that power and hit the ball. If you can't get that sensation, ask a friend to hold your club head and lightly resist its back swing. You will see what it means to have muscles tightened for the job at hand. It is the only answer to power in golf, but not necessarily true of golf alone. The baseball player, tennis player, boxer, bowler, and many other athletes also store this power.

Taking the club back slowly and feeling that resistance, notice that the club head goes back as far as you can reach behind the ball. But don't raise the club head abruptly. If you want to find out how to do this, ask your friend to stand about four feet behind the ball and then try taking the club head back as though you were going to hand it to him. You will find, in doing this, that there is absolutely no bending of the wrists, and that the club head is taken back solely with your arms. Only after it starts to rise above your waist do the wrists take any part in the back swing.

In it the club head has been taken straight back from the ball, and as it reaches the belt line, it moves around the body, by the knees and with a partial turning of the body. Notice, however, that the back leg is perfectly straight and has formed an axis with the body. The knee of the front leg is bent toward the back leg and the heel of the front foot has been raised. Note, too, that taking the club head straight back has automatically shifted the weight of the body to the back leg, where the weight should be on the back swing. The body has only slightly turned back, but it is surprising how much my shoulders are turned at this stage of the swing. The front shoulder has not turned in a plane parallel to the ground, but has started to turn by going under the body. Observe that my head is inclined fully toward the ball.

Up to this point, all I did in the back swing was to take the club head back as though actually handing it to someone behind the ball. I did not purposely straighten up my back leg, bend my front knee inward, raise my front heel from the ground, nor turn my body or shoulders. These actions were the natural consequence of taking the club back properly. The basic cause was the way the back swing was started, and all the other things were the natural effects of this action. It is, of course, impossible to think of each integral movement but it is necessary to think of primary causes. The rest will follow.

There are three things I think about when standing before a golf ball, the first of which is to take the club face straight back without turning it away from the ball and until it has traveled at least one foot in this manner. The other two will fall into their proper niche as we discuss the swing. At present, let us continue with our back swing.

A great deal has been written about keeping the head down and your eyes on the ball. It is a good habit to tilt the chin away from the hole and look at the ball with your front eye (the one nearest the hole), which I hope is your best eye. By putting your head back in this fashion, you accommodate your body on the back swing and allow the head to move to a vertical position in the foreward swing, before the head is able to raise itself to see the ball. Just that distance between these two positions of the head, from the cocked back position to the vertical position, is enough to let the club head hit the ball before your own head is raised. It is a good trick and will usually work. Cocking the head back is good form, too.

Now, back to the wrists. You will notice that they have bent back as far as they can go. Wrists are exceedingly important in golf, and if you can bend your wrists at a 90° angle to your forearms, you should be a powerful golfer. But if you don't have fully breaking wrists, then in order to accommodate the full back swing you will have to bend your forearms a little, as I have done.

Most great golfers have their front arms as straight as ramrods on the back swing. It is truly a beautiful sight, and undoubtedly a great aid in hitting consistently. It is a fine thing to be able to maintain an unbroken radius, even though the arm is only part of that radius. I especially admire the straight front arm of Sammy Snead, who is one of our greatest stylists in golf, but then Bobby Jones, Craig Wood, Ben Hogan, Lawson Little, George Von Elm, Tommy Armour, Jimmie Thompson, and many others have perfectly straight front arms in their back swing. There is no gainsaying that it is fine golf form, and probably the best one can possess. If you can imitate it without loss of your efficiency, you should do so by all means.

But there are others who have attained great heights and have been singularly successful without that front arm. Byron

Nelson, from an examination of his pictures, appears to have a very slight bend in his front arm. So, too, with Lloyd Mangrum, Patty Berg, the old stylist MacDonald Smith, Horton Smith, and even Walter Hagen. Yet, Jimmie Ferrier, one of the best of the recent group of golfers, who has burned up many a golf course here since his arrival from Australia, has a most pronounced bend in his front arm. My own back swing resembles his more than any other professional. But I do not advocate a break in your front arm on the back swing. If you do it, don't feel it is hopeless to improve your game. A front arm bent on the back swing straightens itself out and puts the club in the right path before the club reaches the halfway mark on the down swing. So, if you cannot get your club back more than halfway without bending your arm, go ahead and bend it. I will tell you how to overcome any disadvantage in a moment.

At the top of my back swing the situation is this. The shaft of the club has not reached a parallel line to the ground, which is the accepted position of the long clubs. Our great golfers have been going back even farther than this parallel line in order to reach prodigious distances. They are able to do this and still maintain control. I sacrifice distance for control, yet get 225 to 235 yards under normal wind conditions. Professionals get 265 to 300 yards but if you can average 225 yards on your drives, you can score in the 70s on any course, and that is good enough for an amateur who doesn't intend to make golf his vocation.

Some strong golfers can average 260 yards on their drives with less than a horizontal position of their club on the back swing. Horton Smith did it and Lew Worsham is doing it today, with less than a three-quarter swing. But what he lacks in swing, he makes up for in muscle power. Bobby Locke didn't reach the horizontal position the first year he played in America. However, this South African, who was discovered by Sam Snead, found that he was being outdistanced by American players. The next year, I noticed that he was reaching farther back, past the horizontal position, adding quite some distance to his shots without losing control. If you can do it without losing control, you should.

Let us go back to the picture. Notice that there has not been a complete turn of the waist or shoulders. You can still see my belt buckle, and you can also see my back shoulder. American golfers long ago abandoned the English system of turning the body and shoulders. They used to pivot the body completely so that their back was to the hole and early American golfers did likewise. But the modern American golfer of the last 20 years no longer takes a complete turn of the body in the back swing. Instead, it is shifted to the rear by sliding the hips back. Don't confuse this with swaying; they are not the same. The hips are shifted without the entire body moving off the center of the centrifugal force. This shifting flattens out the arc at the base for at least a foot, and makes it easier to come into the ball on the down swing. Byron Nelson, I believe, is the greatest exponent of this form, and no one can deny that he was the most accurate golfer of all.

Don't overlook the position of the hands. The fingers and thumbs have not relaxed their grip on the shaft one iota. The back hand is under the shaft and supporting it. The shaft has not been permitted to fall down in the base of the **V** of the back hand.

The front hand is properly on top of the shaft. The angle of the top of the hand is on the same plane as the face of the club, which is on an angle to the ground about 45° also.

The second of the three things I think about during the swing (the first was taking the club face straight back from the ball) is the path my club is to take on the back swing. Actually, I trace the path of the club head until it reaches the extreme position of the back swing. When I don't do this, I have a tendency to stop with half a swing. If you have any trouble taking a full swing, just get this mental picture of tracing the club head back until it reaches the horizontal position. Be sure, however, that you stop it at that horizontal position and don't overswing.

Again, I don't think of the position of my hands, arms, wrists, or the club face. I think of my swing, and the rest has to follow naturally. These are the effects, not the causes of a good golf swing.

Slow Back Swing

The golf swing is the longest in any sport and consequently takes more time to execute. Because of this, you have to wait longer to complete the swing. This is only a matter of seconds, but to some golfers it seems like an eternity. Anxiety overcomes them and they hurry their back swing, unable to wait. This slow taking back of the club is a suspenseful thing, like the calm before a storm, and is more akin to emotion than reason. In today's golf, slow back swing cannot be emphasized too much.

In the beginning of my golf career all pros talked about dragging the club head back from the ball, even leading with their hands in the back swing in order to accomplish this dragging-back action. Actually, they created a loop of the club head while it dragged across the ground. The wrists were loose and pliable. To me, it was a most unsatisfactory way to maintain accuracy, but everybody tried to emulate the pros. Because of the loose and pliable wrists necessary to drag the club back, the swing itself was loose, and usually resulted in just slapping the ball.

The "drag back" has long been forgotten, and in its place we now have the firm and slow back swing. The hands no longer lead the club head, but maintain the same relative position as they did in the address. If anything, they are placed ahead of the ball by use of the forward press. It has therefore been definitely established that the club head must lead the procession, and precede the hands, the arms, the shoulders, and the body. The wrists are immovable until the club head reaches the height of your hips. You are trying to build up power, and the only way to do this is to firm up your arm muscles with a very slow back swing. A fighter does not draw his hand back quickly

before punching his opponent; a baseball player doesn't pull
back his bat with a fast jerk before hitting a baseball; a basketball player doesn't take the ball back quickly before shooting a
basket; nor does a good bowler take his ball back hurriedly before rolling it down the alley; and the same thing applies to
many other sports. All athletes sense this build-up of power. In
the golf swing it is more evident. It is a winding up, coiling up
process in order to gather power in your muscles to deliver a
ball or strike one. It is easy in some sports to build up this
power, but in golf there seems to be a psychological reason why
the participant often is unable to do it.

A fast back swing invariably ruins the down swing. You cannot go in opposite directions at the same time, but that is
exactly what the golfer with the fast back swing attempts to do.
He tries to hit the ball before his back swing has been completed. Unable to stop the club head in its backward arc before
he starts his hands and arms forward he usually loses his balance
and is unable to execute the shot. Some teachers advocate a
pause at the top of the back swing in order to change its course
of motion. This can be accomplished by taking a mental picture
of the path of the back swing and making a conscious effort to
stop it as the shaft of the club reaches a parallel position to the
ground. But the only real way to stop the habit of a fast back
swing is to get the feeling or sensation of winding up your arms
as you would the mainspring of a large clock. You wind up all
your muscles as though they were all a part of a large spring,
and then let fly. The result will be the longest ball you ever
hit! So be sure to take the club head back real slow exagger-
ating the slow action if possible. It is not easy, and some get the
impression that they are hardly moving their club back. It won't
feel natural, but you must practice until it does.

Note that the hands are pulled straight down. The body
weight has not as yet been transferred to the front foot. The
back foot is still carrying the load of the body, and the front
heel is still off the ground. Many writers advocate slapping that
front heel on the ground, but it is more natural to let the heel

go down when it comes its turn to move. It should go down
when the weight of the body is shifted forward to the front leg.

There is a tendency to hit from the top of the back swing and
to hurry the motion to strike the ball. If you can develop the
habit of holding back on the down swing, you will find that the
club head involuntarily gathers momentum as it reaches the
height of the hips, that it will be lashed into the ball by your
wrists with all the force required. The position of the hands in
front of the club head will whip it into the ball more than
otherwise. Don't worry that the arms and hands are not in a
straight line. From the position of the hips until the club head
strikes the ball, the wrists will straighten with the arms, and
this straightening will cause an increased acceleration of the
swing from the position of the hips until the club head strikes
the ball. This is a natural tendency, and will be brought about
without any effort on your part.

When a first class pro hits an average drive for 265 yards, his
club head, just before it strikes the ball, is traveling about 125
miles an hour. Bobby Jones, in 1938, had his drives tested by a
super-speed lamp, and he was found to be swinging his club at
114 miles an hour. The amateur, hitting 200 yards, has obtained
a velocity of about 90 miles an hour. When you consider the
speed of the club head which must be obtained in order to get
these distances, it is easy to understand why golf is such a difficult game and why golfers—even good golfers—miss some of
their shots.

There are several things that should be observed at the moment of the ball's contact with the face of the club. The front
leg and the body form an axis. The shaft of the club is in the
same relative position as this axis. The front leg is straight and
firm, and is braced for the blow, while the back leg is starting
to cave in to accommodate the forward swing. Both feet are
solidly on the ground. Note the position of the shoulders. The
front shoulder is hiked up, while the back shoulder is considerably below it. This is vitally necessary because, fundamentally,
the golf swing is an "underhand" shot. The club head does not

go around the body in the back swing nor in the forward swing; it goes up behind the ball, and it goes forward under the ball. This is the only way to insure hitting the ball straight, as it permits the club face to remain with the ball for a long time. Notice, too, that the front arm has become firm and straight, even though that elbow was broken on the back swing. As for the back, note it is in the proper position to apply the power. There is still a break in the back elbow, as the full force of the arm has not yet been applied in hitting the ball. I didn't realize until I re-thought this problem that I, too, have developed the "cock back" of my head. Say I'm looking at the ball with my front eye, my head definitely to the rear. This is certainly going to insure not lifting my head before the ball is struck. Before leaving this picture, note that the **V**s of my hands are in the same relative position as in the address, pointing over my back shoulder. The important left thumb is still holding on tenaciously to the shaft, with the thumb nail straight out.

After the ball is struck, the club head has moved at least two feet in the line of flight and the back leg has moved forward more to accommodate the forward motion of the club head. My own head, however, is still in the same position it was when the ball was struck. Note that the hands have moved only a few inches past the front leg but have not turned over at all for you can see the thumb nail of the back hand. And the club face is definitely still pointing toward the hole, the club head still leading the hands.

The Follow-through

The follow-through is a natural consequence of the speed of your club head and one of the most graceful movements in golf. No benefit will ensue from a conscious, premeditated attempt to bring it about. You will get a follow-through when you hit a good shot. By the same token, if you have a good follow-through, you usually have a good shot. But what brings about a follow-through?

Acceleration of the club head before the ball is struck is

virtually necessary to obtain distance and a real follow-through. Some authorities refer to this action as hitting past the ball as though it were not there. Others call it throwing the back hand into the shot at the bottom of the swing. All of this is true, but it is not the whole answer. The follow-through is the action of the club head pulling the hands through and up after the ball has been struck. The club head, and not the hands, takes control of the swing. The power transmitted to the club head becomes greater than the hands because they no longer can carry the power forward. The hands have reached the extent of their power.

I have already mentioned two of the three basic things I think about in my golf swing. That third thought, the only important thing I think about in my down swing, has to do with the follow-through and the straight ball.

In my opinion, the secret of the follow-through lies in your front hand. It may sound strange but I think one try will convince you that I am right. *The secret of the follow-through is the ability to stop your front hand momentarily at the instant the ball is struck.* This is probably contrary to anything you have heard. To stop your front hand completely would be like trying to pull down the walls of Jericho. The stopping is only a momentary action, more a sensation of trying than actually stopping the front hand, but there must be a definite, conscious effort to stop it. There are two valuable contributions of this to your golf swing: it will cause a greater acceleration of the club head at the moment of impact with the ball, and it will guarantee a perfect follow-through. Stopping your hands at the impact of the ball is like the sensation you get from cracking a whip. With a whip you pull your hand back over your shoulder and bring your arm down and just before the tail of the whip reaches your belt, you stop your hand suddenly and the whip cracks. If you just pull the whip down, there is no crack at all for the whip simply hits the ground.

This stopping of the hand at the point of impact is done in baseball, tennis, bowling, and even boxing. If the hand just continues without a stop, the result is a puny push, with no pep and no power. This stopping puts "authority" into your shot.

Don't worry about stopping your back hand by stopping your front hand. The power of the back hand, although momentarily arrested, will continue with greater force and pass the front hand. This application of power is based upon the principle of the fulcrum, known to man since ancient times. There must be a fulcrum so that the lever will work to its maximum effect. Your front hand acts to give the back hand lever a chance to do its maximum task.

If you continue your hands in the position they were in at the point of impact, they will continue for a short distance after the ball and then be stopped, because there is nothing to carry the club head any farther. The club head, however, by proceeding in its path in front of the hands, creates a force that pulls them up and above your front shoulder. It is the same sensation you get if somebody grabs your club head and tries to jerk it away from you. Try this stopping of the club several times until you get the feeling. Actually, the club head can pull you off your feet. But in order to get your maximum power, the club head should not stop a few feet off the ground, or even waist-high or shoulder-high, but should travel on and on until it has assumed the same position over your forward shoulder as it did in the back swing over your back shoulder. This is the formula for obtaining a follow-through, and is the only way it can be accomplished.

So we come to the finish of a full swing. You will note that the front side is still braced and the left side is completely relaxed. The front foot is solidly on the ground, while the back foot is balancing on the toe and a portion of the ball of the foot. The head is still inclined and is not perpendicular to the ground. In fact, it is best never to raise the head to a full vertical position. After I hit the ball, I want my head to be on the left side, toward the ground; eyes at an oblique angle to the ground, with the left eye almost underneath the right eye. It is as though you were sleeping on your left side with the left side of your face on your pillow. The head only is turned long after the ball has been struck. I don't believe in keeping the head down longer than necessary, and there certainly is no reason to keep looking at the spot where the ball rested, long after the ball is in flight. While this is an exaggeration of keeping your head down, it certainly does not accommodate the turn of your body.

Not all shots are spoiled because heads are lifted. Too many things in golf are blamed upon lifted heads. This is another illustration of the confusion of effect and cause in golf. Head-lifting is not the cause but the result of a bad shot, indicating that something has previously gone wrong. Lifting the head is, in 99 out of 100 cases, the effect of an error in the golf swing itself. Indecision or lack of knowledge is enough to cause your head to lift in order to see the disastrous results. If you lift your head, look for some deep-seated cause other than the mere lifting. If all is well in your swing, your head will stay down long enough to let the ball go on its way, and then it will come up naturally to see where the ball settles. It will help you to look at your ball with your master eye, and keep that master eye on the spot where the ball rested for a split portion of a second. I hope that your master eye is your front eye. It will help in your golf.

THE SWING
by Cary Middlecoff

I think it is necessary to begin tying in the stance, grip, and swing. Let me reiterate that with the proper grip and stance, the proper swing is practically sure to follow.

A brief outline of the fundamentals of the swing reveals first a relatively straight left arm—though I know that in cases of middle-aged people taking up golf for the first time, it might be almost impossible to swing with a perfectly straight left arm. However, at least some semblance of this should be attempted and worked at until mastered as nearly as possible.

By means of a straight left arm, one movement—that of the elbow joint—is eliminated, and this allows the left arm to act as a fulcrum in the movement of both hands when hitting the ball. The more troublesome phases that can be eliminated from a golf swing, the more simple the process of hitting the ball correctly will become.

The next item we will consider is that of balance, which ties in directly with a proper stance. First, observe yourself walking. Are you slightly slue-footed? Are you pigeon-toed? Or do you walk with your feet pointing straight ahead?

About 90 per cent of all men are slightly slue-footed. That is, their toes point in an outward direction normally.

Your feet should be placed in a golf swing in the same position they assume when you walk. If you walk naturally with your toes pointed slightly outward and you started to pick up a heave weight, or to run, or to hit somebody with your fist, you surely would not assume a stance different from the one that is natural for you. If you take an unnatural stance, you are sure to lose leverage, and the result will be lack of power in your swing.

This little personal reminder of what comes naturally to you will follow through your entire golf game. For instance, if you take your stance at a golf ball and discover either foot is pointing in an unnatural direction, correct it immediately. Otherwise you will invite trouble and almost surely come up with one of the common faults—either a slice, hook, pull, or push.

A faulty stance almost invariably will force your shoulders and the entire line of your body to cut the swing of your club across the ball.

Your ankles will bend in only one direction when standing, so to speak, and that is up and down. If you set your feet and ankles in a direction that throws your body off line, the swing of the hands and arms will naturally follow and be off line. The swing of the golf club itself is executed merely with the hands and arms and will definitely follow the pattern set up, starting with your feet.

The key to the whole solution is to set what we will call the immobile part of the body—the feet, legs, hips, and shoulders—on the proper line to your objective. Then the mobile parts—the hands and arms—which you actually think about moving, will naturally follow the correct pattern.

Item three to be considered is the plane of the swing—upright, medium, or flat. I like to imagine my swing simulating a wheel lying at about a 45-degree angle to the ground. The club, hands, and arms all go back in one definite track, which at the top of the swing points the club directly at the hole, the objective. Then it comes back down in that same track and finishes swinging at the objective.

This can be accomplished very simply if the rest of the body is properly set before the swing begins.

BALANCE AND FREEDOM OF MOVEMENT

Proper balance and freedom of movement are essential to accomplish the desired swing.

First, a definite flexing or slight bending of the knees is necessary in all shots. Try it on yourself. Stand up and take a golf stance. Then, with your knees straight back in the sockets, try to turn your body around and look behind yourself. You'll find it mighty hard to accomplish. Now bend the knees slightly, and you will find the entire body will "give" and coordinate quite easily.

The next item to consider in the stance is the distribution of your weight.

The weight should run from the balls of the feet back to the heels. The person who lets his weight rest on his toes is very susceptible to losing his balance and moving his head forward in the direction of the hole during the swing. This can cause many faults, the worst of all being a "shank."

A shank is a shot in which the ball is struck directly on the hosel or shaft of the club. This makes the ball fly at almost right angles to the intended line. And mind you, the ball need be hit only about an inch away from the center of the club face to do this. However, you will find that by concentrating the weight back near the heels before the swing is even started, the head will not move forward at all.

Also in the stance, I like to feel that my weight is concentrated toward the inside of my feet. This is carried out rather simply in the swing by feeling on the backswing that the left foot rolls in toward the ball. Or you can feel that the left knee makes an inward movement toward the center of the two feet.

On the downswing and follow-through, I like to feel my right foot and right knee roll in toward the center of the two feet. This slight rolling movement starts, though in a very slight degree, from almost the shortest shot after the chip shot.

FIRST MOVEMENT OF THE BACKSWING

I won't attempt to say whether the body or the hands make the first movement, though I have noticed that in most good players there is a slight forward press. That means that the hands and the body—particularly the knees—seem to make a little reflex movement to the left. This simply acts to get the body out of its stable position and to start the backswing in a smooth motion instead of with a jerk.

I do not feel that a conscious effort to start either the body or the hands first is advisable, though I firmly believe a slight forward press is good. It is definitely a relaxing, tension-removing motion and seems to allow everything to start back together as a unit.

The one conscious effort that I make at the beginning of my backswing is an attempt to start the arms back without any cocking or even movement of the wrists. I like to take my hands past my right knee on the backswing before I allow any beginning of the cocking of the wrists. I can count on one hand the players that I have ever seen—good or bad—who were forced to make a conscious effort to cock the wrists. I definitely think cocking the wrists is a natural thing to do and should not be thought of once the swing is well under way.

I definitely believe the path of the arms should be considered when trying to groove the golf swing. If the arms follow the proper path, the wrists will take care of themselves. The best guide that I know to a well-grooved backswing and a downswing is to keep the right elbow close to the body going up and coming down. In a full drive, of course, it is impossible to get the hands above shoulder height and still keep the right elbow pointing to the ground at all times. Without the elbow against the body, the backswing can go almost anywhere. It has no guide. However, with the right elbow brushing against the right side on the backswing and downswing of all shots, it becomes quite simple to swing exactly the same way every time.

One thing I advocate strongly is a firm grip with the left

hand. Very few people can form less than a right angle with the shaft of the club and the left forearm at the top of the swing *if the club is held firmly in the left hand.* There are some very few exceptions—people who are extremely agile and limber. However, that right angle at the top serves as a good check. Whenever I look at the top of my swing and see the club shaft and my left forearm forming less than a 90-degree angle, I know I am not holding the club firmly enough in the last three fingers of my left hand. That is most important. Remember, too, that *the length of your swing is determined by how high you get your hands on the backswing,* not by the position of the club head.

POSTURE

In placing your club behind the ball and taking your stance, posture is extremely important. I recommend the rather erect stance, though some slight crouch cannot be prevented.

The most certain and simplest way to make sure you are standing the proper distance from the ball is to sole the bottom of the club flat on the ground and then step up to the club. With the arms fully extended but not rigid, the club itself will force you to stand correctly.

At the point of contact with the ball during the downswing, it is almost essential that both arms be practically straight. As a result, it is much simpler to start out at the address with the arms well extended and keep them that way, rather than try to correct the bending of the arms during the swing.

THE PERFECT GOLF SWING
by Johnny Revolta and Charles B. Cleveland

The other day I came across an old yellowed newspaper clipping that quoted from the *American Medical Journal* of 1928. "Golf," it said, "is what letter carrying, ditch digging and carpet beating would be if those three tasks had to be performed on the same hot afternoon by gentlemen who require a different implement for every mood.

"Each implement has a specific purpose and ultimately some golfers get to know what that purpose is. They are the exceptions."

This humorous definition is unfortunately true for many golfers. All too few do know exactly what happens when their club strikes the ball. Until you understand some of the mechanics involved, you will have trouble leaving the beginner's class.

In the early days of golf every club was made by an artisan and each was a little different. Today, manufacturers have standardized their clubs so that each club of a particular model is just like the next. In addition they have spent a lot of money in research to design clubs to fit the needs of today's golfers.

The club is designed to do your work for you.

Let me repeat that. The club is designed to do your work for you. A sand iron is designed to get a ball out of sand traps. Your job is simply to swing the club so that the club face hits under the ball; the club does the rest.

Let us now look at the various clubs to see what each can do. We will learn the whys and wherefores of a good shot and the reasons behind a poor shot.

Each club has a different hitting surface, different because each club has a different function. The main difference is the amount of angle on the club face. A driver is practically straight up and down. Its function is to carry the ball as far down the fairway as possible.

The other woods are designed to play the ball off the grass and are built with more slant to the face to get the ball into the air. The irons have more and more angle to the club face as the number increases. The No. 1 iron is practically straight up and down; the sand iron, on the other end of the scale, is slanted way back.

The more slanted the club face the less distance the ball will travel in the air, the higher into the air it will go, and the less distance the ball will travel after it lands.

With the short irons great slant results in a high lob shot to the green. This is the system used by Bobby Locke, the South African, and by most British golfers.

American golfers, however, use a lower-flying ball with plenty of backspin. That was the system I taught you earlier in the book. Here is the reason that, even with an angle to the club face, the approach shots with the No. 7 iron travel low.

A golf club, when swung properly, moves in an arc. With the driver the bottom of the arc coincides with the spot where the ball is teed. The ball is literally swept off the tee. With the irons, however, the club is still traveling downward as it hits the ball. The bottom of the arc lies anywhere from a fraction of an inch to an inch or so in front of the ball.

That is the reason you "take turf"—your club cutting into the grass—ahead of the ball on the properly executed shot. This downward hit puts a spin on the ball—a backspin—which helps get the ball into the air and which causes it to "grab" when it finally strikes the ground. The greater the slant the club face has, naturally, the more backspin it will put on the ball.

But there is another factor in the swing that produces back-spin. With the driver, your feet are well apart and your club, entering the hitting area, comes in low. As your feet come closer together and the length of the club shaft gets shorter, the arc of your swing will be sharper. Thus with the sand iron on a chip shot, your feet are very close together and your club shaft is shorter. The result is a small, sharp arc to your swing.

Let's take another look at the clubs. Pick up your driver and place it so the bottom of the club head is flat on the carpet. Now place a golf ball on the floor squarely in the middle of the hitting surface of the club. Now do the same with your fairway woods and each of your irons, finally ending up with your putter.

This is the exact position at which each of the clubs should strike the golf ball when you swing properly.

Notice, too, another point which **Ralph Guldahl**, twice National Open champ, made at a recent golf clinic—how large the golf ball looms against the club face. Not much room for error.

One common golf error is to have the club tilted back, thus robbing the club of part of its hitting surface. This also increases the possibility of striking the ball with the heel of the club, resulting in a wild shot.

Now, while you have a golf ball out, take a look at it. Notice that it is covered with tiny holes—or dimples. Their function is to catch the wind and make the ball turn; in a sense they are tiny windmills. They have both a good and a bad function. Their good function is to cause the ball to travel farther and straighter. Scientific tests have shown that perfectly smooth balls travel only about a third as far. The turning motion of a golf ball is similar to the function of rifling in a pistol which causes a bullet to revolve and hence fly straight to the target.

The bad function of those dimples on the golf ball is that an improperly struck ball will spin sideways and curve out into the rough.

As the club is swung, there are three ways in which it can contact the ball. It can strike from straight behind. Or it can hit the ball inward or outward. Let's see what happens in each instance.

Hit from straight behind, squarely in the middle of the hitting surface, the ball will fly straight.

Hit inward toward the left foot, the ball will scrape against the hitting surface and begin to spin. Take your club and rub it against the ball, moving the club toward you. Notice how the ball begins to rotate in a clockwise fashion. This is the same action that results if the club head strikes the ball while traveling inward.

This turning of the ball, magnified by the wind catching in the dimples, causes it to curve in the air. Turning clockwise, it curves clockwise in the air. In other words, it curves off to the right. In golf language, a slice. Notice too that the greater the angle at which the club strikes the ball, the more the spin and, in turn, the greater the slice.

On the other hand, if the club head strikes the ball on an angle outward it will produce a counterclockwise spin and a ball that curves to the left in a hook. Here again, the greater the outward angle, the greater the hook.

The ideal golf swing is one that travels slightly inside-out. This produces a slight hook. It is somewhat better than a perfectly straight ball because it travels a little farther and the turning motion results in a longer roll when the ball lands.

To summarize: the perfect golf swing is one that travels slightly away from the left foot, crossing the line of flight on a slightly outward angle, and in which the club head strikes the ball squarely in the middle of the hitting surface.

Place one of your clubs on the carpet again with a golf ball squarely in the middle of the hitting surface. Now turn the club slightly. This slight turn, if it occurs in a golf swing, will cause the ball to fly off at an angle. In addition it will cause the club to rub along the ball and produce a spin. A club turned outward is said to be "open" and results in a slice. Turned inward it is "hooded" and results in a hook.

This illustrates the reason for the proper grip and for the

"It looks like your 126 is just too good for me, Boss."

straight-wrist exercise. Both prevent the club from striking the ball in either an open or hooded position. Let me illustrate another reason for the straight wrists in the hitting area. Place your club behind the ball, using the proper stance. Keep the club head behind the ball but move your hands forward by cocking your wrists. Notice now what has happened to the club face. It is set to drive the ball into the ground. Now move the club back to the right, so the wrists are cocked the other way. The bottom of the club face is now striking the ball. This too would result in a "topped" shot which never gets into the air.

Thus you can see that if your wrists are not straight as the club strikes the ball, your shot will be dubbed. That is why, in my instruction, I have placed so much emphasis on the straight-wrist exercise. It is the only sure way to guarantee that the club face will strike the ball squarely.

And now let's put this golf theory to work in helping to cure your faults.

TEE AND FAIRWAY WOODS

by Mildred (Babe) Zaharias

'Do as I say, not as I do,' says Babe to most women

Now that I am on the convalescent list, I realize how much I miss that old familiar question, "Babe, how can I get more distance out of my woods?"

It sure is strange how an over-worked question like that can suddenly sound like "old home week." I'm certainly glad to "get back in the ball game" to some extent by setting down a few of my thoughts and ideas on the subject.

First of all, I bet that 75% of all golfers—male and female—think that the secret of low scoring is to hit a long ball off the tee.

If this were true, few women would ever break 100. A glance at the scores in women's tournaments, even local club events, should be enough to convince anyone that distance is not necessary for good scores. The real payoff comes from keeping the ball straight down the middle for moderate distances, and being deadly on the short game—the pitches, chips and putts which anyone, regardless of size or strength, can master.

Of course, if you're not even getting moderate distance on your woods, or are having trouble with control, then you have a problem which needs ironing out.

The chances are you have an erroneous mental concept of the swing. Many golfers preparing for a drive have all kinds of strange thoughts running through their heads. As they check their grip and stance and eye the ball, some sort of golf gremlin keeps saying, "You're really going to hit this . . . just as soon as you're all set. You're going to put everything you have into the swing and really send the ball sailing!"

What happens? Well, that's why so many people ask about how they can improve their wood shots.

In getting all keyed up to this extra long drive, the golfer becomes tense and then, disregarding all rhythm and smoothness, puts an over-dose of power into the swing. The result—a missed shot, either scuffed or topped or, if hit at all, usually badly off direction.

The point of all this is that there is no percentage in pressing wood shots, particularly for women golfers. If you will just be content to let the clubhead do the work and settle for the best distance within the limits of your physical capabilities—striving always for accuracy, however—you will score much better.

As a matter of fact, if you will concentrate on this program you will soon find yourself in great demand for mixed club events, because, while your male partner will outdrive you by about 100 yards, he will be out in the bulrushes so frequently you'll find the team selecting your drive more often than you think. Also your accuracy on approach shots and finesse around the greens will be a big asset.

An even greater problem than tee shots for most women are the fairway woods. The average gal has trouble getting the ball into the air. Those grasscutters are not at all satisfying I know.

The trouble here I think is that too many women try to use a brassie in the fairway. The face of this club is quite straight and has little loft. I don't believe the brassie can or should be used in the fairway by the average lady golfer unless the ball is sitting up very well. In fact, in many cases a 4-wood should be used in preference to a 3-wood. It may not give quite as much distance, but that isn't what you're so interested in anyway, remember. It certainly will make it easier to get the ball off the ground, which will increase your confidence. At the same time your direction should improve.

I think that the new number 5 and even number 6 woods which are now being manufactured are a great boon to women's golf. These clubs can often be used by gals in place of long irons, which are almost the hardest clubs of all to master. They tend to give those, who have gained any proficiency with woods at all, more confidence and therefore better results.

You ladies may have to work on your woods a little harder than the men, but the practice will pay off when you want to use a wood on the fairway.

As for scoring, don't let your inability to hit a long wood shot interfere with your game. As long as a well executed chip shot or a good putt still counts the same as a long tee shot, we gals are here to stay on the links.

HOW TO BE ACCURATE

by Ernest Jones and David Eisenberg

Accuracy means to hit the ball in the direction intended and to make the ball land where it is intended.

To achieve accuracy you must swing the clubhead, with the hands as your medium. When you learn that, you will gain control, which means to have authority of the clubhead, the weapon with which you strike the ball. The swing will give you greater speed and greater accuracy than can any other method.

I shall illustrate by explaining the action of a spinning top. What causes the spinning top to stand on end in defiance of the pull of gravity? Centrifugal force, the rotary, or spinning motion on a horizontal plane. As long as it is strong enough to resist the pull of gravity, the top will spin. When the rotary force is spent, the top falls on its side.

Notice that the faster the top spins, the steadier is the orbit in which it turns. The top begins to wobble only when the spinning slows down.

The same is true in golf. The greater the speed developed in swinging the clubhead, the steadier and truer will be the orbit in which it swings. No matter how great the speed, a swinging action is vital if the clubhead is to move in the same path time after time. Consistent accuracy in wielding the clubhead can be achieved only by the steady, smooth application of power as expressed in a true swing.

You must make that swing a part of your subconscious.

Reprinted by permission of Dodd Mead & Company from Swing The Clubhead by Ernest Jones and David Eisenberg, copyright 1952 by Ernest Jones and David Eisenberg.

Accuracy is impossible when you consciously try to direct the clubhead which is 33 to 43 inches distant from your hands. A variation of 1 degree means the ball will be off line as much as 10 feet when it stops some 200 yards distant. A variation of 3, 4 or 5 degrees compounds the inaccuracy by that many yards.

You cannot achieve accuracy any more than can a baseball pitcher acquire control by thinking of such details as the exact instant at which to release his hold on the ball. A pitcher develops control through a muscular routine which is the result of constant practice. He instinctively releases his grip on the ball, without giving any conscious thought to that detail.

Once you develop a muscular routine founded on swinging the clubhead, you will repeatedly wield it with accuracy. You will also develop as great a speed as your power is capable of producing.

No matter how long you play, however, you will at times give in to the impulse to apply more power than you can control. Invariably, that extra effort will be applied through leverage. It will be force which recedes from the center of the swinging stroke, and it will result in inaccuracy.

When a pitcher loses control he should try to regain his normal movement by throwing rather than by tampering with his method of holding the ball. I was interested in the case of Rex Barney, the Brooklyn Dodgers' pitcher who lost his control and had to be sent to the minor leagues.

Barney had the weapons for greatness, as he proved by pitching a no-hit, no-run masterpiece a few years ago. What happened? If he were a golfer, I think I could have helped him. Obviously, he is attempting the wrong methods of regaining control. Perhaps he is over-concerned with the detail of when to release his hold on the ball. He may be trying to aim the ball at the plate. If he, instead, concentrated on regaining his normal manner of throwing, he might regain his former accuracy.

To assure accuracy in bringing the face of the clubhead

against the ball at the proper angle, you must make sure of three things:

1. Check the hold, or grip, on the club. Be sure you are holding the club properly, and in a balanced position.
2. Check your stance. Stand properly in relation to the ball and the direction in which you are aiming. There must be an even distribution of your weight, which assures balance.
3. Swing smoothly and freely.

These are the three factors which determine control. Full control over the club assures accuracy. Control means the ability to feel the head of the club during the swing. When you have that control, you sense what it is doing throughout the action of your swing, making it possible for the face to meet the ball correctly at the moment of impact.

I repeat. You cannot acquire that sense of control if you consciously are aware of other details. Swing the clubhead and forget everything else. Those other actions are purely responsive by-products of the main action of the swing.

Only smooth, easy stroking with a correct grip and stance produces satisfactory distance and accurate direction. It is not some pet device which may be attempted in desperation, nor is it consciously trying to steer for control.

Control automatically results in greater distance. Thus you have the double incentive for developing a correct swing. You will be able to increase the speed of the swing for greater distance, and you also will be accurate in placing the ball where you wish. Need I repeat that the swing is achieved through the continuous action of the hands and fingers?

A moment on the subject of the follow through. Some players appear to be successful although they abruptly halt their swing the moment the club has struck the ball. They are rareties. There are more poor players who do that.

If you carry your swinging action THROUGH the ball, continue it after the impact, you will also get greater speed at the

MOMENT of impact. This ultimate in golf stroking will be achieved more easily than if you try to "slug" the ball. Do not do anything to interfere with the swinging action of the club-head.

The very fact that there are good golfers who differ distinctly in their form is proof that their stroke basically is a swing. How they came to use those mannerisms is immaterial. Jim Ferrier, a great golfer, pronouncedly bends his right knee as he completes his swing. He won the Professional Golfers' Association championship in 1947. That odd mannerism was caused by a knee injury suffered when he played football as a youth in Australia. I have a pupil who plays well in spite of bending his right knee quite pronouncedly. It is caused by a shorter left leg.

There are golfers who assumed certain mannerisms after various experiments. They became convinced it was best for their game. I insist that had those golfers concentrated instead upon correcting their swings, they would have corrected their faults much more easily and with greater success.

The mannerisms resulting from experiments run a wide gamut—change of grip, stance, body adjustment before starting the swing, waggling, etc. Eventually, a temporary solution may be found. Actually, the change may be mildly handicapping. But it brings temporary results because of being a great mental and psychological stimulant. With mind set at ease in the conviction that his new discovery has solved his problem, the player swings more smoothly and steadily.

I knew a business man who cut seven or eight strokes off his score by playing with a certain famous professional. He followed a simple procedure. On each stroke, the professional took the proper stance, distinctly marking his footprints. Then the businessman stood in his tracks and hit the ball.

This man has been a golfer for many years. It is ridiculous to think that he hasn't learned how to stand to the ball. But, by standing in the tracks of the professional, his doubts were removed and he was able to concentrate on stroking with a clear mind.

The above is harmless. But there are good golfers who unnecessarily complicate matters by adopting faulty grips or exaggerated stances. Although they may play well for a time, they would play better golf and, above all, BE MORE CONSISTENT IN ATTAINING ACCURACY, if they used sounder methods.

Most unfortunately such golfers, because they may be good, attract imitators who are not good players. For the latter, the adoption of freakish mannerisms is ruinous.

This approach to golf is backing into your task. You concentrate on correcting what is wrong by jumping from the frying pan of one error into the fire of another.

You should from the very beginning learn that which is correct. No matter how hard you work, you are doomed to failure if you attempt any plan which supposes that control can be gained in any way other than by smooth swinging from a sound base.

A leading golf writer once wrote about Bobby Jones: "He trusts his swing to a higher degree than any other golfer I have ever seen. If he is off line on a shot, he may be off 30 yards. Some of the other stars appear to sense that something is wrong, and make at least a partial correction in the hand action as the clubhead is brought against the ball. But once Jones starts his swing, he goes right through with it without any attempt at correction."

The great Jones, in short, was primarily concerned with swinging the clubhead, to the exclusion of all distractions. His record proved he was right. He was the only grand slam champion in golf history. He played in eleven U.S. Open championships without once scoring as high as 80.

His record testified to his success in achieving accuracy by striking the ball through trusting his swing, as compared to others who attempted to introduce corrective measures by conscious manipulation while making the stroke.

THE SHORT GAME
by Johnny Farrell

Golf is played from tee to green, but golf is *won* with the shots you make twenty to sixty yards from the pin. A golfer who pitches dead on the pin and gets down with one putt is never concerned that his drives and brassies don't eat up two hundred yards-plus each time. He knows that ninety per cent of the game is concentrated on or near the green—and he is the fellow who spends a good part of his practice time working on his short game.

Compactness is the word for all approach shots. I didn't say stiffness. Being compact is being closely knit, harmonizing your muscles and your reflexes and your thinking. Two hundred yards from the green you are swinging *free* with a long shafted club. Half that distance you are *compact*—with the feeling that your arms, wrists, hands, and club are controlled through every inch of the swing. But through it all, while being compact, you are never *tense*.

Pitching from seventy-five to one hundred and twenty-five yards. This is one of golf's most important payoff shots. To make it, I advise no major departure from the basic one-piece backswing. But for the sake of compactness you may do well to *shorten* the swing—to back about three quarters—so that your hands and wrists have a surer sense of controlling the shot.

You are, after all, seeking a sharpshooter's accuracy and not power. If you find that a shortened swing is affecting the distance you want, then go back a number in the club. Many a

From If I Were in Your Golf Shoes by Johnny Farrell, copyright 1950 by Johnny Farrell, by permission of Henry Holt and Company, Inc.

one hundred-yard shot from a level surface can be handled with far more precision if you swing a seven iron three quarters than with a full swinging eight or nine. Always be sure to take a few practice swings with the club to make sure that your wrists are firm but yet flexible. Do not let them collapse as the clubhead comes through the ball.

Since this shot is going to travel a comparatively short distance there is an even greater tendency here to watch its flight. You can't do it! Your head must stay down until long after the shot is completed and your eyes should actually *see the moment of impact* and the divot being taken. Not until the clubhead is resting at the opposite end of the arc can you take your eyes from the ground. I can't state this strong enough: *Stay with it!*

Within the hundred-yard radius you will want the majority of your shots to strike the green from the air and *bite,* rather than roll up. A biting ball comes from getting in front of it and hitting into it. The amount of bite depends on the control you have over your wrists at the moment of impact. Because I have always concentrated on the short game, just as Bobby Locke does today, I have always been able to make the ball do more tricks on the green than most other experts. It comes from practice. And after you have it down, practice some more.

Pitching from twenty to sixty yards. The shorter the distance between you and the green, the more delicate the shot becomes and the more compact your swing must be. There are two *pitches* to be faced from this short distance—the low flying ball when there are no obstacles and the green is fairly level with the shot, and the arcing ball when there is sand or water to get over, or a tree, or the green is raised.

The *low pitch* is accomplished by never letting the clubhead get past your hands. *Drag* your hands through the shot and hit it with your weight forward on the left foot as you swing. What you are trying to do is meet the ball on the downswing and give it the necessary bite to make it slide up to the pin. On these shots take an eight or nine iron, or a pitching wedge, and close the face slightly.

On any pitch within fifty yards of the green, open your stance. This gives you a feeling of *pointing* the clubhead toward the cup as though you were throwing the ball underhand or bowling it.

Most importantly, concentrate on *swinging* the clubhead. Don't stiffen up or try to lift the ball from the turf. And don't jab at it. Just swing the clubhead on pitch shots and feel your hands swinging through to the hole.

The high arcing pitch. Many times you are within forty yards of the green and have to get the ball high in the air and over something that lies in the way. On this shot keep your hands rather firm and take a very *lazy swing*. This is what I call the "floating shot." By this lazy swing you will give the ball enough backspin to make it stop abruptly on the green.

The "floating shot" is a genuine pitch, with a full follow-through that lets you control the flight of the ball. Its opposite is a "punch shot," which gets the ball away fast; and I wouldn't advise a punch shot from this distance unless you have an up-hill lie and must make the ball roll forward on the green. This calls for a seven or eight iron.

The Chip Shot. From five to fifteen yards off the green, *chip* the ball in. A chip shot is a crisp hit with the clubhead stopping at the ball and not following through. Open your stance, place your weight on the left foot, and hit down on the ball. The ball shouldn't drag as soon as it strikes the green when you chip, and you accomplish this by taking a lofted iron and closing the face a trifle. Some golfers feel more at home on a short chip shot with a two or three iron, but I think your wisest club is one with more loft, such as a six or seven iron. Control the chip shot with your *right* hand, and practice diligently to perfect the distance you need. It is better to land the ball on the green with the lofted club. This eliminates a bad kick from an uneven fairway.

If the fairway in front of the green is even and true a run-up shot with a four or five iron is okay. A putter could also be used if the fairway is burned out and very fast. It would be a safer shot under these conditions.

Chipping Out of Heavy Rough—Twenty to Thirty Yards Off the Green. This is a very common shot on a championship course or one whose greens are closely guarded. Grip the club *firmly,* for it is your wrists, and wrists alone, that will make this shot. You must feel more break to your wrists as you descend sharply *into the turf directly at the ball.* Don't try to follow through on this shot or the clubhead will be thrown off line by the rough grass in front of the ball. The basic idea is to get the clubhead down into the ball while encountering as little of the rough as possible. A firm cocking of the wrists and no follow-through does the trick. Use a nine iron or pitching wedge on this shot.

PUTTING AND SHORT APPROACH SHOTS

by Joe Novak

To achieve the final objective of getting the ball into the cup, the same two requirements that are present in every other golf shot—direction and distance—are also basic requirements in putting. In putting the golfer must not only gauge the speed or distance of the putt but must also control the direction with finer precision than in the long shots.

A good golf swing in putts, as in the longer shots, is a matter of organizing oneself into a rhythmic continuity of motion wherein the body turn or pivot supplies the power while the hands impart this power to the club. This formula, whereby the player gauges his power or distance by the extent of his body turn, and controls the direction of the shot by setting or cocking the club in the desired position, will work on the putting green just as it works on the long drives.

Much of the bewilderment about putting is caused by failure to apply some elementary reasoning: "If it works on the long shots it ought to work on the short ones, or vice versa." The putting stroke is fundamentally no different from any other stroke in golf except that it is done on the most delicate scale—and when you have a downhill putt on a fast green you know what I mean.

BODY IN PUTTING

The idea of body motion in putting may at first sound rather startling but that great master, Bob Jones, subscribed to the idea and no one can deny that Jones was highly efficient on the putting greens. In Bob's own words he described putting: "First get a comfortable position with feet close together then sweep the club away from the ball, keeping the club low on the backswing. Follow through the same way. If there is any feeling of movement in the body let it move!"

I would like to have had Bob recommend controlling the putting stroke power with a body movement which of course is a true pendulum movement.

Another great player who definitely employed this body control in putting was Leo Diegel. So pathetic were Leo's efforts on three- and four-foot putts that he discovered in experiments that by locking first his right arm against any movement at all, and then his left arm, and eventually both of them, his putting improved. With this locked arm position Leo had to use his body to swing the club back and forth and he correspondingly kept the putter in a set position throughout the stroke so his putts were very accurate.

Take also into consideration the young caddies or other youngsters who practically swing and sway all over the green in a carefree way, yet roll the ball into the cup with uncanny accuracy.

PUTTING ROUTINE THE SAME

So the logical and effective plan in putting is to adopt the same routine that has been suggested on the drives and the irons.

Take your position at the ball with the same four moves:

(1) Place the club closely behind the ball with the left hand;
(2) Adjust the feet, left foot opposite the ball, toes on a line. Keep heels very close together;
(3) Relax right knee to bring the right hand to the club but when the right hand comes to the club overlap with two fingers instead of only one. This will develop a more delicate feel and control in the hands;
(4) Turn the right heel out.

Now for the swing:

(1) A slight forward press;

(2) A reverse press;

(3) Start club with right hand. This will automatically develop an opposing downward action on part of the left hand (this downward thrust is felt and applied principally with the left thumb). This action of the hands kicks or lifts the clubhead off the ground slightly. At this point the body takes control and sweeps the club back and forth in a perfect pendulum movement while the hands keep the club steady.

The club is swung from the shoulders instead of being powered by wrist action. Notice how the consistently good putters among the tournament stars keep the wrists out of the putts, except for positioning the club, and you'll see how the principles of power and direction control I have set forth apply effectively in putting just as in the longer shots. And you also will see that most of the short putts—from four feet and less—are missed by depending on the wrist action rather than body action after the wrists correctly position the club.

Another thing you'll find by experience is that using body action for the "touch" or power of the putt minimizes the ruinous element of nervous "yips" when there is a particularly important and delicate putt to be made.

PLAYING SPECIAL SHOTS

Much emphasis has been placed on the fact that the easy way to play golf is to "let the club do the work"—in other words, "use the same swing on all shots."

However, on the undulating terrain of the golf course there are numerous and varied positions in which the ball comes to rest. This is all a part of the game. There are no dull moments. There may be side-hill, down-hill, up-hill lies. The ball may land in a sand trap or in deep grass.

Again let me repeat, the player is still interested in "distance and direction," and the same fundamental requirements of the swing must be applied and adhered to, even though it may be rather awkward to perform because of the difficulty of the lie.

A slight adjustment of foot position and a slight adjustment of club position can in such cases work wonders, and here are some helpful hints.

Weight shift determines contact point in swing: Practically everybody has been told that the experts all play the ball at a point approximately opposite the left heel. This is the proper thing to do in all normal shots, wood or iron.

Obviously, it is difficult if not practically impossible to move or swing the club away from the ball if the player keeps his weight on his left foot, and again if the player shifts his weight as required to the right foot for the backswing, it is impossible to swing down or through if the weight remains on the right foot. The rule is, then, that while the player assumes a position to the ball wherein the weight is on the left foot, the first thing he must do before the backswing can be started is to shift the weight to the right foot—then in order to swing through, the weight must be again reshifted to the left foot so the club can be brought down and through the ball in a full free movement.

Why ball is played opposite left heel: The player is therefore always balanced if his weight is on his left foot as the ball is being hit. The natural place then to have the ball is at a point directly opposite the left heel and, as previously explained, *this is how direction is "lined up" or how "aim is taken" for a shot.* The ball is always opposite the left heel and the shot will fly at right angles to this line.

When to play ball opposite the right foot: However, if the ball is lying in a cuppy lie, in a depression, in long grass or sunk or half-buried in sand, then the above procedure of playing the ball opposite the left foot would result in topping the ball.

In all of the above cases, the proper thing to do is to place the club in an abnormal position. The club should be placed so that the shaft is tilted forward and the club is deliberately turned down on the ball.

This placement of the club creates the effect of playing the ball at a point more nearly opposite the right heel—in other words, the ball is played farther back with hands in normal position at a point ahead of the ball. The swing is then made as usual with all the weight shift, pivot, and hand action to keep the club in line, and the net effect is that the ball is contacted earlier in the swing. The clubhead contacts the ball and then continues on down to the lowest part of the swing, taking out a divot or piece of the turf after the ball is struck.

HOW TO REGULATE DIVOTS

The farther back the club is played the deeper the club digs and the larger the divot.

It becomes therefore simply a matter of determining how far back off center (how far back off the left foot) it is necessary to play the shot, and the thing that determines that is how bad the lie is. The deeper the depression, the deeper the grass, the more the ball is sunk in the sand, the farther back the ball must be played so that the club is automatically set to go down after the ball. The above information should prove invaluable in getting the player out of the bad lies.

(But on good lies on the fairway it is not necessary to play the ball back and many needless divots can be avoided.)

Chip shots: In addition to bad lies, the above procedure of playing the ball back off the left foot will prove invaluable on chip shots or all short shots around the green. By so placing the club to the ball, the clubhead will nip the turf ahead of the ball. This will also automatically create a nice pickup of the ball and definitely insure one against topping, which of course is bad at any time but fatal on the short approach shots.

Cure for topping the ball: While on the subject of topping, which incidentally is one of the commonest faults of beginners and high-handicap golfers, it can be explained that topping is generally caused by the failure of the player to shift his weight to the left foot soon enough in the downswing.

Special effort and practice must be concentrated on this phase because all of us are more or less right-handed and we are prone to stand and balance ourselves on our right foot most of the time, if not always.

However, by following the procedure suggested, the player will soon learn to slide over to the left foot; only in that way can proper contact be made with the ball. However, the most difficult thing for some high-handicap golfers to learn is that uniformly good results cannot be had in golf unless the player learns to hit or swing down onto the ball instead of trying to scoop it up.

If such topping is a consistent fault, the practice of playing the ball back will prove very helpful.

The push shot: The above procedure, which so easily gets a ball up and out of a bad lie, has been often referred to as a "push shot," a shot that is used to play low shots into a wind. It has been presented as something that only experts should attempt, when in reality it is a certain, sure way to get out of a tight spot, provided of course that the player is reasonably well grounded in the fundamentals of the swing, to wit: weight shift, pivot, and hand control of the club.

In all such shots it is best always to keep the face of the club slightly closed because of the emphasis that has to be put on following through so that the full effect of the club can be had on the ball.

Sand trap shots: Nine times out of ten, playing the ball back more opposite the right foot will automatically get the ball out of sand traps or bunkers. However, the player who finds his ball in the sand should determine two things from the way the ball lies and decide before he plays the shot just what to do about these factors.

The first consideration is just how the ball lies—does it lie on top of the sand or is it partially or totally buried?

The second consideration is to decide whether to play the club in the regular, closed position or whether circumstances necessitate the use of the open-face club position or a "cub shot" to produce a quick rising shot.

When necessary to get distance from the sand, play the ball clean because any sand between the club and the ball diminishes the impact on the ball. Taking a lot of sand or taking just a slight amount of sand is used by good players as a definite means of controlling the distance of trap shots around the green.

Quick-rising shots: While the ordinary trouble shot procedure, that of playing the ball back opposite the right heel, is recommended for trap or sand shots because this method will get the ball up and away and also give the player a chance to control the amount of sand taken on any shot, there are times in a trap or bunker when this type of shot will prove ineffectual because it does not raise or loft the ball quickly enough.

There may be a steep bank or sand wall which may stop such a low-flying shot. In such a case, the player should reverse the procedure and play the ball forward off the left foot. Also in this case the player should deliberately "open" the club at the outset of the backswing so it is possible to deliberately cut across the ball and lift it sharply with a slice action.

The shot which is known as a "cut" shot is very effective out of deep grass which is close to the green, although the regular procedure of a trouble shot, wherein the ball is played back opposite the right foot, will be found to be an easy and effective way of actually pulling or dragging a ball out of a deep grass lie which borders some greens. This procedure, using a niblick or sand wedge, will give a most delicate control when needed near the green. In fact, on all short *chip* shots, where a pitch and run effect is desired, the ball should be played as suggested in this trouble shot procedure, that is, opposite the right foot.

Hooks and slices: There are, in effect, only three kinds of shots in golf: high-flying shots which tend to break or curve off to the right, and when exaggerated, become slices; low-flying shots which tend to pull or draw to the left into hooks; the in-between shot, the straight shot, which as a rule is perfect in flight and trajectory, being neither too high nor too low.

No player can really feel that he has mastered the game of

golf until these hooks and slices can be played at will. From the ability to hook or slice, by being able to play first one of these shots and then the other, the player can strike a happy medium and drive them straight. There is no great art or skill required in order to hook or slice. If a player is properly grounded and trained in the fundamentals of a golf swing so that he knows why and how to shift his weight, also knows why and how to use his body to swing the club through the pivot action, *then it is a simple matter "to rock and set the club" so that the corresponding hook or slice can and must be executed as desired.*

Whether the ball is to go high with a backspin or low with a "run," whether the ball is to slice off to the right or hook to the left, is something that can be definitely controlled and determined by knowing how to "set the club" before the body takes it off into the swing.

The rules that govern are these:

(1) If the club is cocked or set in an open position the law of physics, "The angle of reflection is equal to angle of incidence," will apply and the ball will turn off to the right.

(2) If the club position is reversed, i.e., closed, the ball will be met "from the inside" which of course will make it turn or fly to the left.

(3) If the club position is in between the above two, or square to the line of flight, then the ball will fly true and down the middle.

This principle of club position governing the flight of the ball is just as positive and elemental in golf as the positioning of the cue in the hands of a billiardist whereby he produces follow or reverse english on the cue ball.

If there is any phase of the golf swing that savors of sleight of hand artistry it is the part of the swing wherein the club is "positioned," "cocked," or "set," for the shot (these three terms are used interchangeably). And this so-called cocking of the club is the very essence of the shot.

Instinct vs system: Many fine golfers will wiggle and waggle the club, and purely from instinct maneuver the club to a position from which they can hook or slice at will, but it is my hope that the following outline will give you a definite plan to play your hooks and slices and from that learn to keep them down the middle all the time.

SLICES

In the slice the ball starts off to the left of the intended line of shot and then curves out to the right. This is a high flying shot which drops dead and, as a rule, has very little roll. It acts like a boomerang and if it were hit hard enough would almost curve to a point where it would start back to the player. A player who slices cannot get any distance on his shots because of this tendency of the ball to come back to him rather than to go forward and away from him. This is a common fault in golf.

Why slicing is common: The reason that slicing is such a general fault among golfers is that many golfers do not understand the importance and the necessity of shifting weight. Because they fail to shift their weight, they cannot pivot or use their body to swing the club. They are forced to start the club away from the ball with their hands and arms and the natural result is that they roll the club away from the ball with a pronating movement of the left arm which carries the club back to an open position—that is, the club face is rolled away or turned up toward the sky. Now unless the club is rolled back on the downswing (which of course would be one fault added to another) the club must be brought down across the ball with the club in an open position and a slice must occur.

Cause of shanking: No weight shift and no pivot, which produces a slice so readily, leads to another fault. Often as a player takes the club back with hands and arms only, there is a strong tendency for the weight to list to the left foot as the club is raised on the backswing. Weight on the left foot and club in an open position at the top of the swing almost invariably produces a "shank," the most sickening shot that befalls a golfer. In this shot the ball is hit with the heel or socket part of the club and it slides off to the right in an uncontrolled manner.

This "shanking" disease generally occurs in short approaches where the player is very apt to be hesitant to pivot.

How to slice: To deliberately and intentionally play a slice the procedure is as follows:

1. The ball should be played at a point slightly ahead of the left foot.
2. The club is placed so that the toe is turned in slightly and the shaft is perpendicular, not tilted forward.

From this position of the club the left hand is more or less in front of the shaft, not on top of it. The knuckles are not showing as suggested in the regular grip where three of the knuckles of the left hand are showing. This position also makes it more natural to put the right hand more on top of the shaft rather than under the shaft.

This emphasis on grip and club position is required, because the way a club is placed and gripped has a lot to do with how the club is going to be cocked or set for the shot in mind. In addition it is helpful also to assume a foot position or stance which lends itself to a slice or hook.

Stance for slice: In the slice shot it is best to bring the right foot slightly nearer to the imaginary line between the ball and the hole. This projected foot position places the body at an angle which makes it easier to bring the club across the ball as desired in a slice shot.

Now, after the club grip and stance have been taken as suggested above, a normal routine will automatically produce a slice.

The procedure is as follows:

1. Rock the club forward—this is done with a slight forward action of right knee.
2. Reverse the club position—that is, rock the club back. This is done by reversing the knee position which of course shifts the weight to the right foot. Then. . . .

3. Start the club from the ball with the right hand but as this is done be sure to let the left hand turn in toward the body sharply so that the club is cocked "open"—that is, tilted so that the face is turned away from the ball and the shaft of the club is thrown out away from the player to a point outside the line of the shot.

From this point with weight on the right foot and club cocked or set with "face open" and shaft outside the line of the shot, the body turn on the right foot carries the club up to the top of the swing. Then. . . .

4. A reverse shift of the weight to the left foot and reverse turn of the body pulls the club down and across the ball and a natural slice shot, that is, a curve of the ball to the right will occur.

PROCEDURE FOR HOOK

To hook the ball, that is, curve it to the left, the procedure is the same except that the club must be set or cocked in a closed position, that is, the clubface must be turned to the ground and the club shaft must be set on the inside of the line of the shot. The club is set in a position exactly the reverse or opposite of the slice position.

Whereas in a slice the club face is open and the shaft pointed out or across the line of the shot to the outside, in a hook the club face is closed (turned toward the ground) and the shaft is pointed in toward the right toe so that it is on the inside of the line of the shot.

Stance for hook: For the slice the club was placed out forward, in front of the left heel. For the hook the club is placed back towards the right foot more like the position for a "trouble shot." The clubface is kept square with the ball and the shaft tilted forward as the club is placed to the ball.

The left hand, instead of being in front of the club handle with no knuckles showing, is now well on top of the shaft with fully three knuckles showing. The right hand is well under, not on top of the shaft.

The right foot is drawn back away from the ball so that the body is turned away from the intended line of shot and the shoulders are pointing to the right of the line of the shot.

The regular procedure is followed in the swing.

1. The first move is the forward press.
2. The next move is the reverse press wherein the club is rocked back, the position of the knees is reversed, and the weight is shifted to the right foot.
3. Now comes the move which is critical in all golf shots, the positioning of the club. For the hook, the club is started the same as it is in every shot in golf, with a sharp pick-up action of the right hand while simultaneously the left hand with a downward thrust positions the club. In this case of positioning for a hook the left hand rolls out and away (counter-clockwise) from the body (reverse of the slice action wherein left hand at this point rolls in toward the body) and the clubface is turned toward the ground. At the same time, the shaft is tilted in toward the right toe so that the club is set on the inside of the line of the shot.

   The turn of the body on the right foot brings the club up to the top of the swing, then. . . .
4. A reshift of the weight to the left foot is made so the body turn can be made on the left foot. This body turn swings the club down onto the ball. From the way the club was set the club swings out over the line of the shot and a natural hook or turn of the ball to the left takes place.

SIDE-HILL LIES

It has been emphasized, and properly so, that direction in a golf shot is determined entirely by the hands through the manner of positioning the club. Also, that distance or power is a direct result of body turn or pivot as it makes the club swing through the ball. This system or formula is correct and when positively applied will produce positive effects.

However, a faulty or negative effect of the hands will not

only affect the direction but in turn influence or affect the distance. For example, if a player makes an otherwise perfect swing but through a faulty hand action permits the club to drop to an open position, then not only will the ball slice but it will fall short of the distance the ordinary shot would produce. The reverse effect would be true if the club were faultily closed.

In the same manner, a faulty action of the body not only affects distance but also affects direction. For example, if a player reaches the top of the swing perfectly, and then fails to shift the weight to the left foot, naturally a distorted action will occur in the downswing which would most likely turn or roll the club over into a hook motion. Likewise, an exaggerated slide to the left foot would make the club drag through and across the ball and thereby tend to produce at least a fade, if not a slice.

So it is then, that if a player finds the ball in a position where it is higher or lower than the level on which he is standing, a subsequent torque is produced in the body turn and consequent hooks and slices will occur.

Whenever the ball lies on ground higher than that on which the player is standing, the natural tendency is to hook or pull the ball to the left; when the ball is below the player the tendency is to slice. The best procedure to follow is to allow for the above results and deliberately aim to the left or the right as the case may require. That is to say, if an expected hook or slice would prove disastrous, that is, put the ball out of bounds or into a bad lie, then the player must and can compensate for it by deliberately "opening" or "closing" the club at the outset of the backswing in order to control the direction of the shot.

A helpful suggestion in the case of all side-hill, up-hill, or down-hill lies is for the player to keep his knees more relaxed, bent so that freer movement can be had in both directions of the swing in the matter of weight shifting. If one does not shift weight both ways he is bound to lose balance and dub the shot. Don't take too big or too long a swing in these lies; use a stronger club wherever the situation permits. For instance: if the lie is good, instead of a full swing with a No. 7 iron use a one-half or three-quarter swing with a No. 5 iron.

Study the situation and be governed by whether the green can be reached in one shot—whether it is wise to try to reach it in one shot—or whether the desired score can be secured by playing surely and safely.

LEFT-HANDED GOLF

While this may not be the best place in the book for this chapter, nevertheless I do not feel that this book would be complete without some reference to left-handed golf.

There is no reason why left-handed golfers cannot play as well as or better than right-handed golfers. Golf is in effect a two-handed game, and a two-legged game. It has been explained that it is necessary to establish a working arrangement of both right and left hands in positioning the club and that both hands are necessary in order to keep the club in control throughout the swing; also it has been demonstrated that a golfer must shift his weight to the right foot for the upswing and back to the left foot for the downswing. So the player has to learn to use both feet and both sides of his body.

To play left-handed golf just reverse the 1-2-3-4 outline for position and the 1-2-3-4 outline for the swing. In my work at the University of California at Los Angeles, after the students thoroughly understand the form and the count, I make them reverse the form and swing left-handed. This gives them a look at the swing from the other side and naturally gives them a better understanding.

Any good golfer can, when the occasion requires it, reverse his grip and play a good left-handed shot if the ball is up against a tree or fence which prevents a right-handed swing.

Just to prove this point let me relate an experience of many years ago. A friend of mine and I, dressed in street clothes, were strolling down the street while visiting in a distant town. Neither of us was recognized when we entered a golf school on the street level. I stepped up on the mat from which they drove the golf balls and using a right-handed mashie I assumed a left-handed position to the ball and began to make a motion to strike the ball with the back of the club.

By this time the person in charge came forward and said, "You can't play golf that way."

I said, "Why not?"

"Why, you are trying to play left-handed," was the answer.

"Yes, I understand that," I said, "but this club seems rather awkward; nevertheless this is the only way I'd like to play."

"Well, it can't be done," came the answer.

"Why do you say that?" I insisted.

"Well," answered the man, "golf courses are not built for left-handed players."

With that, I turned the club upside down so that the toe of it was pointed down to the mat, making it a left-hand club. Then I swung it up in a big swing and came down on the ball with a solid resounding smack. I dropped the club and we walked out, leaving the confused man to figure his own way out.

All of which proves that golf can be played both ways, right- or left-handed, and in fact both ways with either right- or left-handed clubs. Try it.

COMMON FAULTS AND THEIR CURES

Topping: The first fault generally suffered by beginners is topping. They're told they don't "keep the eye on the ball." They don't, but that's a result, rather than a cause.

Actually what is by far the most frequent cause of topping is lack of footwork and proper weight-shifting, which is the only way the proper body turn can be developed.

Check up on the position of the ball with relation to the feet. Make sure you get the forward and reverse "press" details of the swing routine and be sure to get back to the left foot on the downswing. That way you'll cure topping.

Hitting behind the ball: This is also usually the result of improper weight-shifting, especially failure to shift weight to the left foot at the start of the downswing.

Slicing: Clubface is in an open position. Often this is caused by a very tense grip with the left hand which forces the left wrist to turn in toward the body on the backswing. This rolls the clubface open so the clubface is drawn in and across the ball and a slice must occur. In gripping the club the left hand may be too far in front of the shaft and the right hand may be too much on top of the shaft.

Failure to shift weight to the right foot at the start of the backswing also produces this open position of the clubface, with a slice the result.

Hooking: This often is caused by failure to shift weight to the left foot at the start of the downswing. When the player keeps his weight on the right foot as the club comes forward on the downswing the club may turn over as it comes through and pull the ball off to the left in a smothered hook. By pausing for an instant at the top of the backswing you encourage the tendency to make a correct shift of weight subconsciously as the initial action of the downswing. That good habit (pausing at the top of swing) greatly reduces the hooking and slicing that results from improper transference of weight.

In curing the hook also check up on the grip. In hooking the right hand may be too far under the shaft and the left hand too much on top.

Shanking: Shanking is in reality an exaggerated slice.

A tense, tight grip with left hand and weight on *left* foot at the top of the swing will produce shanking (hitting the ball with the heel of the club).

Lack of pivot, a common fault on short approaches, also causes shanking.

TRAP SHOTS

by Cary Middlecoff

At one time or another you are sure to press the wrong button and end up in the average golfer's most dreaded territory—the clammy, white, sand trap with those ugly jutting jaws which frequently grab a perfectly hit shot as well as the bad ones.

The sand trap shot does not differ from the normal shot in the actual swing, although it does vary in its method of sending the ball on its way. Whereas with the normal iron shot you attempt to strike the ball first, with the semi-explosion shot from a sand trap—which I use at all times within 20 yards of the flag—the object is *never* to strike the ball first.

The first objective for any player approaching a sand shot is getting out of the trap. Great accuracy definitely can be expected from a master sand player; still, even the best players realize that getting out of the trap and onto the putting surface is a very satisfactory result in itself.

TECHNIQUE OF THE SHOT

A semi-explosion or explosion shot, played with a sand wedge, never allows the club to touch the ball. I have a rather short-shafted sand wedge which I grip exactly on the end of the club every time from a normal lie in a sand trap. If you choose to hold the club farther down the grip, the one essential thing is to hold it in exactly the same place every time.

I take a stance about as wide as that which I use on my No. 2

Reprinted by permission from Golf Doctor by Cary Middlecoff, published by McGraw-Hill Book Company, Inc., copyright 1950 by Cary Middlecoff.

or No. 3 iron. I definitely attempt to stand exactly the same way every time and play the ball off my left heel. I take a slightly open stance because my actual swing is a little bit more upright—and from the outside in. Then I cut very slightly across the line to the flag with my swing. The swing is like a lazy, loose practice swing, not a hard one.

After taking the correct stance and grip, the next thing is to be sure the club face is as wide open as possible. In other words, the club should be turned back so that it has more loft than normal. With this open position of the club, the flange or sole on the bottom of the club is set at such an angle that it will not dig deeply into the sand but will hit the sand and almost bounce.

If your ball is buried, of course, you will have to close the face of the club enough so that you're sure of digging deeply enough to blast the ball out of its position and up onto the green.

During the swing proper, I concentrate my weight on the left side. By doing this I have a better chance of striking the sand with the club exactly at the spot I desire.

Having taken a stance and a grip—the grip being the same as in all other golf shots except putting—we are now ready to begin the shot. I try to hit approximately the same distance behind the ball every time, which is about 3 to 4 inches, and hit a little harder on longer shots.

Finally, the other part of the shot which cannot be neglected is the follow-through. The follow-through is the one item which will assure you of getting out of that sand trap.

For a buried lie, I play the shot exactly the same as for an unburied one, except that then I close the face of the club, or toe the club in. By this means, the angle of the flange on the bottom of the club is such that it digs sharply into the sand and once again gets under the ball.

This, together with the follow-through, brings the ball up and out. It is impossible to prevent a buried trap shot from rolling after it hits the ground. The other shot, the semi-explosion from a good lie in the trap, will invariably have a good deal of backspin. They must be played accordingly.

UPHILL AND DOWNHILL LIES IN SAND TRAPS

I have discovered that the best way of playing sidehill trap shots is by taking my stance in the trap and sinking one foot or the other farther into the sand until I come as close as possible to having a normal, flat stance. Then I merely play the shot the same way as if the lie were flat. With an uphill lie, sink the left foot deeper in the sand than the right one; with a downhill lie, just the opposite.

CHIP SHOTS FROM SAND TRAPS

Chip shots are, for the most part, to be avoided from sand traps. The first necessary prerequisite for a chip shot in a trap is a perfect lie, with the ball sitting high and almost out of the sand. The next absolutely necessary element is not to hit behind the ball. Even half topping the chip shot out of the sand is much, much better than hitting the slightest fraction of an inch behind it. If you have ever tried this precarious shot, you know that hitting the least bit behind the ball will leave it in the trap.

I never try a chip shot from any sand trap which has a bank more than 1 to 2 fee high. As a matter of fact, I never chip out of sand traps bordering the green.

The one time chip shots out of a sand trap are recommended is when a trap lies 20 to 30 yards or more from the green. Then you actually get into the pitch-shot class. However, once again, the prime requisite is to hit the ball first.

When I do find it necessary to chip from a trap, I plant my feet firmly in the sand with the same stance I use on any chip shot around the green. Next, I make it a definite point to stand a little more upright and to extend my arms to the fullest without being too rigid. Then I try to eliminate all body movement from the shot, and merely hit it with my hands and arms—striking slightly downward and hitting the ball first.

The selection of the club to be used to chip out of a trap doesn't make too much difference, as long as you can clear the edge of the trap. However, I never would use a sand wedge, a pitching wedge, or even a No. 9 iron when chipping from a sand trap.

THE WEDGE AS PLAYED BY AL CIUCI

by Oscar Fraley and Charles Yerkow

This is the club which the professionals call the greatest advance in golf since the invention of the gutta-percha ball.

This is golf's trouble shooter.

If you are in the sand or in heavy rough, whip out the wedge and you're on the green—and in all probability very close to the hole.

It is true that most trouble shots out of traps or rough can be played with the eight or nine iron. But the wedge is a far more certain conqueror of those treacherous spots. Its heavy head cuts through easily where the eight iron or nine iron might have to be forced.

Playing the wedge as explained here by veteran Al Ciuci, one of the game's greatest teaching pros, can move you from a deplorable lie to within one-putt distance of the flag in one stroke. It is that kind of a club, and one which every player should add to his bag.

That's the advice of the entire tournament set of teachers like Ciuci, a head professional since 1914 who tutored Gene Sarazen to the heights of golfing greatness. From traps, it's great.

TRAP SHOTS A LA CIUCI

There are several ways to play a shot from the sand trap, but the best way is the explosion shot. This is a different shot from almost any other in golf. That is because here the object is to hit the sand and not the ball.

Thus the stance is open and the ball is played off the left heel. The club is gripped fairly low on the shaft and the clubface is open.

All of this helps to make certain that you will strike the sand first, for it is the force of the sand exploding against the ball which pushes—or explodes—the ball up into the air.

There are three important points in hitting the trap shot— the lie, the distance required, and the texture of the sand.

Distance is determined by the length of the backswing and the rhythmic force put into the shot. Only practice can tell you how much force is required for given distances.

The lie and the texture of the sand in the trap tell you how far to hit behind the ball. For instance, if the sand is loose and dry you must hit farther behind the ball than if it is wet and packed. Many players hit too far behind the ball in playing this shot. For the ordinary trap shot, you do not need to hit more than a half inch to an inch in back of the ball.

If the ball is partially buried, however, you may have to hit as far as an inch and a half in back of the ball. In this case it also helps to close the face of the club a trifle.

Grounding the club in a trap before hitting your shot is, of course, against the rules and calls for a penalty. But you can determine the texture of the sand as you walk to your shot or as you set your feet well in the sand. A firm foothold is essential in playing the trap shot, so wiggle the feet in tight and comfortable.

"As for hitting the shot," explains Ciuci, "just remember to slow the action for timing and swing through the shot."

That lazy timing of the trap shot is one of the secrets of the professionals. For this is not a brute-force shot, but one of finesse.

You will note that there is little leg action to the shot. The club is taken back with the straight left arm, and the hands rarely go much above the waist line. From that point the action is in the wrist cock.

The left arm is straight and the right elbow in close to the

"Well, you said I had to make a choice—didn't you?"

body as the arms come down. Then the wrists unleash their power in a smooth-flowing motion which explodes the sand out from under the ball. You will note, in the front-sequence pictures, that the club is past the ball, which is rising from the impact of the sand.

Notice, too, the complete follow-through. Most players make their greatest mistake out of traps by quitting on the follow-through once the club has driven into the sand. Don't just bury the clubhead. Remember you are trying to drive under and through the ball.

Neither is it necessary to try to "lift" the ball. The loft of the club will do that. Just swing on through the sand.

When playing out of a trap, there are times when you will be tempted to chip out. It is possible, but the ball must be sitting high on the sand and must be picked clean. However, it is a dangerous shot, particularly if there is a bank in front of you. Your best bet is still the explosion shot.

However, if the sand is not too loose and heavy, and if you have the right kind of a lie with no lip on the trap between you and the green, you can use a putter advantageously. This shot is hit much in the manner of a long putt.

When using the putter out of a trap, a flat arm motion is always best for the stroke. This brings the blade of the putter into the ball parallel with the sand. If you use a putter and hit the ball on either the upswing or the downswing, you are likely to drive the ball into the sand.

Getting back to the wedge, you will find it a fine club from heavy rough as well as from the sand. In this instance, the ball is played more off the right foot so that contact will be made with the ball before the clubhead strikes the grass.

THE CUT SHOT

It is in playing out of deep rough, particularly when you are near the green and must make the ball stop quickly, that the cut shot is of great value. It also is desirable when extra height is needed.

When playing the cut shot off solid ground, the ball should be positioned just inside the right foot. The stance is opened so that the body is almost facing the hole. This is to make certain that the club cuts across the ball, as in hitting a slice. The clubhead should be opened wide, and the ball must be struck before taking the divot.

The cut shot also is invaluable in playing out of traps when a quick stop is needed. Here, however, it is played off the left foot, so that a thin cushion of sand will be taken before the ball is hit. The stroke is the same, upright and down across the ball.

This is not a shot which is mastered easily. It requires a great deal of practice. But it is a valuable one to have when and where you need it.

The wedge, as you can see, is not overrated as "the golfer's best friend." Used properly, it will save you a lot of shots. Just remember:

DO . . .

Slow the action and hit with loose arms and wrists.

Hit under and through on trap shots.

Hit the ball first out of the rough.

Open the club and stance on cut shots and come down across the ball.

Let the wedge do its own lifting.

SOMETIMES THEY ARE UNPLAYABLE

by Byron Nelson

Lower your scores by recognizing unplayable lies, using proper club in hard sand, utilizing runup, knowing rules

"If there's one thing I've learned on this tournament tour," commented an itinerant pro recently, "it is that I know now I *can* hit the ball where I can't play it."

What the man was saying was that he had finally pounded it into his sun-backed cranium that it is possible for a golfer to knock a ball into a position from which no mortal can extricate it in less than six to 10 strokes, if at all. In short, it would be unplayable.

This was exactly the position in which Conrad Evans of Anywhere, U.S.A., found himself after he had hit a tee shot from No. 3, a par-4 dog-leg hole at his home club. The difference between Evans and the tournament pro was the amateur didn't realize the ball was unplayable.

The ball had settled between a couple of tree roots. A low branch frustrated his backswing. Twenty-five yards ahead of him was a lake. With admirable courage but with highly questionable judgment, Conrad armed himself with a wedge and attacked the problem. Let's try to follow his strategy in detail.

His first swipe tangled in the branch, bounced off the tree root and missed the ball by six inches. The second, a premeditated chop, nicked the top of the ball and rattled it back and forth between the roots enough to give Evans hope that the third try might get results. It didn't. On No. 5 Conrad finally went commercial and nudged a gentle chip 15 feet out into the fairway.

To add to the evidence that this wasn't Evans' day, the ball settled in a divot hole. Our man, figuring aggressive play might salvage the prestige that goes with being a 15-handicapper, whacked at the ball with a spoon—and dumped it into the lake.

Being a persevering character, Evans refused to pick up. He dropped back two club lengths from the lake, the necessary procedure—he thought. His drop left him on an undesirable downslope lie, from which he was partially stymied by more trees. He did manage to move an iron shot through the trees, en route to the green.

The pin was on the back of a two-level green, and Evans, trying to cozy a shot onto the upper level with the new triple-duty wedge he had just bought, dunked the shot into the sand trap. The sand resembled a freshly-poured section of sidewalk more than a golf course hazard, for the night's watering had left it wet and hard. But Evans knew just one trap shot—the full explosion—and play it he did. The heavy-flanged iron bounced off the wet sand and the ball finished over the green.

Evans finally chipped back and knocked in a 10-footer for a 13. To say that it could have been less, even without making any improvement in Evans' swing, is not an observation made merely to soothe the discouraged, confused and disgusted hordes of high handicappers. I've said before in this series, and I'll repeat it for emphasis—a little bit of know-how about shot-making can save you as many strokes in a round of golf as hours on the practice tee. You can often learn more in one "playing lesson" from your pro than you can in several hours of labor on the practice range.

Needless to say, Conrad Evans committed a number of errors, both mechanical and strategic, in blowing to his 13. Let us examine them and figure out what to do about them. It might help salvage a few strokes for yourself.

It is important to know whether you can hit a ball out of a

difficult spot in less than the two strokes the rules assess you for calling it unplayable and dropping out. It isn't often that we hit a ball into such a position, but the situation should be recognized—like death and taxes, it happens.

How can you tell if a ball is unplayable? First, you must determine if you can negotiate a backswing. The rules allow you a trial backswing, if you don't disturb the foliage. If you can't swing, you're dead. If you can take a backswing, the next question pertains to the ball. Can you get at it? Evans couldn't, not with roots in front and back. You can use as a rule of thumb the stipulation that you must have at least eight inches of clear ground around the ball in order to get it out. I wouldn't advise trying a shot from a more restricted area.

DON'T SCOOP

The subconscious desire to scoop the ball is the bugaboo here. Using enough loft in the beginning may help. If you have never shaken hands with that real friend of the duffer, the No. 5 wood, ask your pro for an introduction. The 5-wood is to your long game trouble shots what the wedge is to your short game difficulties.

Play the ball further to the right when you hit out of a divot hole. This is a difficult maneuver for the best of them. If you are using a spoon, play the ball three or four inches inside your left heel. It is vital you hit down on a shot like this. To help in this venture, cock your wrists a bit from the beginning of the backswing. Then, to avoid complicating the matter, just continue with your ordinary swing.

When you hit into a water hazard which crosses the fairway, you may drop your ball anywhere on the line on which the ball went into the water, choosing a level lie as far back as you desire. Evans got his downslope lie when he dropped the ball two club lengths behind the hazard. The two club lengths rule applies only to *lateral* water hazards. This is a case when not knowing the rules can cost strokes.

It isn't a bad idea to use a 3- or a 4-iron on short chips such as

Evans faced when he tried his wedge shot. Evans used his wedge —and with poor results.

You no doubt have become acquainted with two-level or built-up greens (where the apron is lower than the putting surface). There are two choices for an approach to one of these greens: If the pin is far enough back you can get the job done with a high pitch; if the pin is fairly close your best bet is a run-up.

The run-up is a most valuable shot, one least often recognized by the average player. Play the shot just as you would a long chip shot—ball back, wrist break from the start of the backswing, and a firm, crisp downswing.

It is best to putt or chip the ball out of a wet and/or hard sand trap. Evans tried his sand wedge, and with disastrous results. The wedge is designed with a large flange to bounce a bit in soft sand. It bounces too much off wet sand.

TRY A CHIP

If you can't putt out because of a lip and the bank is not too formidable, you might be able to chip out with a 5-iron. If there is a steep face to the trap, use a 9-iron. To get loft, play the ball a little left of center, aim about an inch behind it and use the same swing you'd employ for a pitch shot of the same distance. Try to have a feeling that you are going to "take a divot" on the shot—in other words, take a bite of sand from under the ball. This is no easy shot, but it's almost impossible to pull it off with a sand wedge.

But perhaps the soundest advice I can pass along is this:

For every six lessons you take on the practice tee, write yourself into the pro's appointment book for one playing lesson. A good pro and an alert pupil can make this lesson one of golf's best learning experiences.

SCORING

by Lealand Gustavson

After each hole the marker shall check the score with you. You should be able to keep an accurate count of your strokes on each hole; if not, your friends will surely help you. You shall check the final score for each hole at the end of the round, settle any doubtful points, then sign the card and make sure that the marker has signed the card. Then turn it in to the tournament committee or handicap committee.

You are solely responsible for the correctness of your score recorded for each hole. The Committee is responsible for the addition of scores. No alterations may be made on a card after you have turned it in to the committee.

If you return a score for any hole lower than actually played, *you shall be disqualified.* A score higher than actually played must stand as returned.

The player whose name is entered above that of his opponent on the tournament draw sheet has the honor on the first tee.

TERMS USED IN ANNOUNCING OR DISCUSSING SCORES

1 up, 2 up, 3 up, etc., indicating the numbers of holes ahead of an opponent in match play, or 1 down, 2 down, etc., the number of holes behind an opponent.

Strokes ahead—Number of strokes *less* than opponent has at the end of a prescribed number of holes (stroke play).

Dormie—A player is the same number of holes down (or up) as there are left to play in a match.

From Enjoy Your Golf, copyright 1954 by Lealand Gustavson, reprinted by permission of Harcourt Brace and Company, Inc.

EXAMPLES:

2 down and 3 to go	A player is down the number of holes first mentioned, with the holes left to play mentioned last (matched play).
3 down and 8 to go	
4 down and 6 to go, etc.	

4 and 3	A player has beaten his opponent by the number of holes first mentioned with the number of holes left to play mentioned last (match play).
6 and 4	
2 and 1, etc.	

FOUR-BALL SCORING

This is the form of competition most frequent on all golf courses. Four players play together, each playing his own ball but forming partnerships so they play 2 against 2. They can play either stroke or match play.

EXAMPLE:

Players	A + B	vs	C + D	
Score on a hole	4	5	5	5

Match play—better ball:
A and partner win the hole on A's 4
Stroke play—better ball:
A and partner score 4
C and partner score 5

EXAMPLE *of low ball and low total* (*or aggregate*) *score*—match play:

A + B = 9—low ball is 4—total is 9
C + D = 10—low ball is 5—total is 10
A & B win 2 points, one for each of low ball and low total.
2 points are at stake on each hole so both players must play their very best on every hole and must hole out their own ball on every hole.

COMPUTING PAR

by Lealand Gustavson

Par means perfect play under ordinary weather conditions, always allowing two strokes on each hole for putts. NOTE: Putting is always 36 strokes, which is nearly always half or more than half of par. This emphasizes how important putting is.

Distance is the guiding factor, but some allowance may be made for difficult or unusual conditions. Each hole should be measured horizontally from the middle of the tee area to be used to the center of the green, following the planned line of play.

Men's Par	*Ladies' Par*
Par 3—Up to 250 yds. inclusive	3—Up to 210 yds. inclusive
4—251 to 455 yds. inclusive	4—211 to 400 yds. inclusive
5—456 to 600 yds. inclusive	5—401 to 525 yds. inclusive
6—601 yds. and over	6—526 yds. and over

"Birdies" or "birds" are 1 stroke under par.

"Bogey" is 1 stroke over par. "Double Bogey" 2 strokes over par.

"Eagle" is 2 strokes under par.

From Enjoy Your Golf, copyright 1954 by Lealand Gustavson, reprinted by permission of Harcourt Brace and Company, Inc.

HANDICAPPING; HOW YOUR HANDICAP IS COMPUTED

by Lealand Gustavson

Handicaps should be based on "course rating" rather than on par.

"Course rating" is generally computed by a qualified member or members of a state or regional committee, who tour the course and estimate its rating.

You receive a handicap by turning in your score cards. A minimum number of 5 are often demanded by a club handicap committee. Your 18-hole totals are added together and an average taken. This average figure is the figure on which the handicap is taken.

The U.S.G.A. system provides that the lowest 20 per cent of the scores turned in are those on which your handicap is figured. If you turn in only 10 cards the two lowest cards are all that count. If 50 cards, the 10 lowest count. It is to your advantage to turn in many cards, as your handicap is then a truer reflection of your ability. You won't be stuck with that one super-duper round you had and be paying your opponents forever after, because you can't play up to it again. But turn that one in, too.

This method is the only one recommended by the U.S.G.A. Some clubs have adopted other methods which they continue to use, so it would be advisable to ask your club's handicap committee chairman what system is being used in your club.

From Enjoy Your Golf, copyright 1954 by Lealand Gustavson, reprinted by permission of Harcourt Brace and Company, Inc.

Some clubs keep a fluctuating or current handicap system. At regular intervals during the season members' scores will be averaged, and if you have been scoring better, your handicap goes down; if scoring worse your handicap goes up. Others base the handicap on the last season's play and only lower it if better scores are made.

State handicaps are established by a state committee. It is advisable to have an established handicap, as practically all competitive play from social club activity at your home club to when you are a guest at major state events, is based on handicaps. Without a handicap you generally would have to enter at scratch, meaning no handicap. In social play you would have to guess at your average which can be very wrong in either direction and consequently unfair.

HANDICAP EVENTS

Before starting in any handicap competition you should check your handicap from the official list and then inform yourself of the holes at which strokes are given or taken. These holes are indicated on the club score card. There is a column on the card marked "Handicap" or "HDCP."

In a competition where there is a Committee, that Committee is responsible for the application of the correct handicaps.

The net difference in strokes between opponents' handicaps is the figure to consider.

Example: The difference is 8. The holes on which the numbers from 1 to 8, inclusive, appear on the card are the holes on which one stroke each is given. All other holes are played even.

The placing of these handicap numbers varies on every course, as they are determined by the difficulty of each hole. The hardest hole on the course is the first hole on which a stroke is given, and so on throughout the 18. This is adjusted so that each 9 holes has its proper proportion of handicap holes.

How to decide ties in handicap events shall be determined by the Committee, and the decision shall be published in advance of the playing of the event.

A halved match shall not be decided by stroke play. A tie in stroke play shall not be decided by a match. This means, qualifying round or tournament ties should not be decided by "sudden death" play-offs or matching cards, etc.

A handicap match tie should continue to play hole by hole, starting where the match began and strokes allowed as in the prescribed round.

A handicap stroke competition tie should be played off at 18 holes, with handicaps. If that be inexpedient, there may be a shorter play-off with an equitable percentage of handicaps.

HOW VARIOUS TYPES OF PLAY ARE HANDICAPPED

Example: (.05 or over counts as 1. Players are letters. Numbers are their official handicaps.)

A	B	C	D
4	13	8	12

Singles—85% of full difference

A *vs* B difference is 9—85% = 7.65, or 8 strokes.

Four-ball stroke—75% of individual taken as they come on the card.

A	B	C	D
3	9.75 or 10	6	9

Four-ball match—Low handicap is reduced to scratch and all others are reduced a like amount. 66⅔% of resulting difference is taken as they come on the card.

A	B	C	D
—	9	4	8
—	$2.66 - \frac{2}{3} = 3$	$5.33 - \frac{1}{3} = 5$	5

Reduced by A's 4—stroke handicap to scratch

Foursome match—

A + B	C + D	
4	8	20
+ 13	+ 12	− 17
17	20	3

(40% of full difference is 1.20 or 1 stroke.)

When selective drives—30% of full difference is .09 or 1 stroke.

$20 - 17 = 3$

Another kind of handicap is "Bisques," which are strokes given to be used at any time, singly or all on one hole if desired. If 8 strokes are generally given, 4 Bisques would be ample. Bisques are used in social golf only and are not popular because they can only be based on guess. However, they are an interesting novelty.

GOAT GETTING

by Morie Morrison

Golfers might be said to fall into six separate emotional groups. Each group has its own weaknesses, and it is those weaknesses that unsportsmanlike "friends" study. They know that opponents who add special worries of their own to regular worries about their play will be easier to defeat.

(The author assumes, naturally, that readers will refrain from using this information to further their own selfish ends, except in cases of dire emergency.)

THE BIG 6 IN GOLF WORRYING

1. The *timid* type: Fearful of attempting unfamiliar tasks, afraid of failure, shuns competition.

2. The *irascible* type: Bitter about the success of others, complains of his hard luck, always wants another chance, is touchy.

3. The *aggressive* type: Frequently tries to cover inferiority, seldom has a planned attack, does things with a "grandstand" flourish, impulsive, somewhat emotional.

4. The *egocentric* type: Supremely confident because he doesn't realize how little he knows, likes to take bows for his good play, resentful of criticism that implies he is ignorant of the rules or customs.

5. The *perfectionist* type: observes all the rules, intolerant of compromising standards, loves flattery, overreaches himself when complimented.

From Here's How to Play Money Golf by Morie Morrison, copyright 1953 by Erwin G. Morrison, reprinted by permission of Doubleday & Company, Inc.

6. The *intense* type: normally polite and considerate, prone to forget everyday golf courtesies and customs, oblivious of his golfing habits and traits that irritate others.

A golfer who likes to make wagers quickly spots the **timid** player who dreads failure and worries about competition. To the money player, the shrinking opponent is a wonderful prospect to whom he can sell worry and fear, and he loves to do it with not-too-helpful suggestions. He has in his repertoire such remarks as, "Now don't let that fast, sloping green bother you. You can roll into the trap, but I don't think you will," or "The sand in the traps is heavy, but don't let it worry you."

A timid person is easily upset when an opponent says casually, "We've got to keep moving. That foursome back there is breathing down our necks." Being a conscientious soul, he naturally becomes flustered if he thinks he is spoiling the foursome's fun. As he hurries his shots, he makes more than his normal quota of errors.

A sensitive player will fall apart completely when, after making a poor shot, his opponent gives him a look of pity. If a remark accompanies the scornful glance, such as "For gosh sakes, Harry, I don't know why you ever took up this game," it will short-circuit the duffer's entire nervous system.

A timid player will sometimes accept a higher than normal bet because he doesn't want to appear "cheap." Having made it, he will then worry about the sizable amount until he loses it.

If an **irascible** golfer is a methodical person, he will become nervous whenever his rival mixes fast play with delays. For instance, taking an extra-long time to find a lost ball will make him very impatient. Opponents who desire to dip into his pocketbook sometimes pair him with a boisterous, non-methodical partner who will exasperate the excitable gentleman so much that his stroke count will soar to the stratosphere.

When in a deep trap, an irritable player is particularly vulnerable. Because he is over-aggressive, he can be encouraged to risk a shot for the pin instead of shooting safely for the green.

As often as not, his anger or concern will cause him to swing so furiously that he will muff the shot.

When playing with women, especially his wife, an impatient player is prone to mutter, "Playing with women always ruins my game." He becomes very touchy when an opponent intimates that a lady's drive almost equals his. In trying to drive the next shot a mile, he will find himself slicing onto the wrong fairway.

A golfer who "blows his top" generally seeks a scapegoat for his troubles and frequently focuses his venom on a caddy. Unsportsmanlike rivals know this and sometimes instruct a "green" caddy to be in the wrong place at the right time. A caddy whose shadow waves back and forth across the cup has a particularly devastating effect on an irascible player.

An **aggressive** person is one who long ago acquired the habit of depending upon himself for results. Consequently he approaches every adverse situation with grim determination. If his opponent says casually, "That's a tough shot. Why don't you play it safe?" it is a distinct challenge to the aggressive player to do just the opposite. He is in the habit of thinking that he can lick any situation, and he is inclined to swing with more bravado than sense.

When a determined player is having trouble with his game, he will sometimes find himself listening to suggestions, such as "Keep your head down. You're rolling your shoulders and head before you hit the ball." This will cause him to hunch his shoulders, lower his head, and tighten the muscles of his upper body. The greens' committee will be able to trace him by the blazed trail of divots he digs.

Remarks associating the aggressive player's style with something uncomplimentary are usually disturbing to him. If a rival suggests, for instance, that he wiggles his "fanny" like a worn-out fan fancer, the aggressive type will begin thinking more about the movement of his posterior than his swing. This, too, can soon wreck his game.

The aggressive player prides himself on his ability to "take it." He thinks of himself as being physically superior to every-one else with whom he plays. He can be persuaded to hurry his play when he should be relaxing between shots.

The **egocentric** golfer is a self-centered person who thinks well of himself. An opponent can easily take advantage of the egocentric's self-satisfaction by asking him for advice. The know-it-all egotist will be flattered by this and happy to pass out his words of wisdom. He will often forget his own game and devote much of his time to encouraging his opponent.

The egocentric longs secretly to be mistaken for a low-handi-cap expert. During warm-up swings on the first tee, he will swing with so much elegance that one would think he was putting on a gala performance. In his rendition of the style-beautiful, he forgets swinging fundamentals, if he knows them, and with adequate encouragement can be persuaded to con-tinue showing onlookers how beautiful a golf swing can be. This can ruin his game before he starts playing.

When practicing, the egotistical golfer devotes ninety per cent of his time to hitting drives. He likes to be called a long hitter, and he forgets that seventy per cent of a good player's shots are of the short variety. He will accept bets on his ability to hit occasional long balls, and he will lose wagers because he goes to pieces on the greens.

Since he is interested in himself, he is naturally interested in his score. With encouragement, he will dwell on the bad luck he had on a previous hole, and this can easily cause him to try too hard to regain lost strokes. On the other hand, if he is play-ing over his head, he is easy prey for that old line of reasoning, "If you keep this up, you will break ninety." This will usually boost his score back to normal as he begins to think about how well he is playing.

When the **perfectionist** is disappointed because something didn't work out as he had planned it, he will explain in detail the reason for his failure. If an opponent chooses this opportune time to belittle the alibis and say, "Aw nuts, with that wild shot of yours, you're lucky to be on the golf course," the precise player will be exceedingly upset. Frustrated because his drive was imperfect, on his next shot he may try a tricky hook to give the boys something to talk about, and five to one he will be in further trouble.

Flattering remarks please a golfer who strives continually to perfect his game. He glories in the appreciation for his skill. If he has been getting a string of pars, flattery will encourage him to shoot for birdies. This step-up in his game can be disastrous, because it can cause him to worry unnecessarily about slight mistakes. For this reason, a player who has good luck on the first nine holes will often throw his game away on the second nine.

The perfectionist takes his game seriously and addresses his ball in a painstaking manner. He regards his careful deliberation over each shot as a sort of holy ritual. As in the case of the timid golfer, he is easily disturbed by such remarks as "Are we going to let that foresome behind us go through, or are we going to continue to hold up the whole course?" In his case, this is especially lethal and his game will suffer because it is geared to a snail's pace.

A perfectionist is easily embarrassed by any implication that there has been some slight misunderstanding about his knowledge of the rules, etiquette of the game, or sportsmanship. This is particularly true if he is trying to make a favorable impression. A flustered golfer who finds himself concentrating on being a gentleman will usually pay off at the eighteenth green.

The **intense** player usually yells at his ball after each shot and then turns to the other members of the foursome to explain what did or did not happen. A casual inquiry, such as "Why do you always have to explain each shot?" will make him realize he may have been acting foolishly, and this can easily affect his composure and confidence.

When an intense golfer hits a shot, he often starts walking immediately. In his deep concentration he often forgets that his companions also have to shoot. A pointed remark, such as "Now where are you going?" can have a bombshell effect. It will blast his composure and break his intense concentration on the game.

As soon as this happens he is a goner, because his winning instinct has been deadened.

On a putting green an intense golfer can become so wrapped up in his own problems that he is honestly unaware he is bothering others while he continually moves around to study his ball's lie. Calling him a "Jingle Foot," a "Nervous Nellie," or any other uncomplimentary nickname will surprise him so much that he will become intensely apologetic and determined to make amends. This will unconsciously change his routine and perhaps upset his timing.

A golfer who strains for perfection on every shot frequently becomes so intense that he takes an unusually long time to address his ball. Such a player can be driven to distraction by an opponent who is obviously worried about completing the round before sunset.

FLATTERY IS EXPENSIVE

As old King Henry IV of France remarked back in 1602 or thereabouts, "One catches more flies with a spoonful of honey than with twenty casks of vinegar." With a philosophy of this kind, His Royal Highness would have made a superlative week-end golfer. There is no more foolproof way to undermine a rival's game than to make syrupy and flattering remarks about his performance.

Compliments stir a person's ego, and in a game like golf they make a player acutely conscious of his swing. This self-consciousness is in itself dangerous, but a complimentary remark or two can flatter a player so much that he will be encouraged to go all out to show off his specialty and to share his pleasure with others by telling them how he does it. This establishes a one-way path to self-destruction, because as he performs, describes the reasons for his skill, and answers questions as to why he is so good, he becomes conscious of his different motions. The first thing he knows, he is slamming his shots out of bounds. As it is with a blonde cutie who flatters a butter-and-egg man into thinking he is Mr. Muscles, so it is on a golf course where an ordinary 90 shooter can be flattered into thinking he is another Lloyd Mangrum.

There are different types of flattery that work best on different types of individuals. For instance, the gregarious, full-of-personality golfer who enjoys talking continually is a sucker for any type of flattery that suggests he really knows his golf. He is secretly convinced that this is true, and when others imply that they, too, realize it, naturally he feels very good about it. Little does he know that in sharing his secret he is paving the way to the scene of his downfall. In his case, praise takes his mind off the game. It makes him conscious of his movements, which can affect the smoothness of his swing. He is vulnerable for a well-timed gibe which may suddenly shatter his confidence.

The ex-athlete is also particularly susceptible to flattery. His early training taught him to believe that he can always perform best when the chips are down. The ex-hero doesn't need much encouragement or praise to be persuaded to accept unfair odds, swing too hard, or overestimate his skill. He thinks he is still an all-around athlete and forgets that he is older and less skillful than he was in the old days. Consequently he is often inclined to hit with hope instead of skill.

A long hitter can be thrown off his game if he is asked consistently how he does it. A sensitive man who wants to look like an expert can be flattered into swinging with so much nonchalance that he sacrifices precision for elegance.

Despite the fact that flattery is pleasant to hear, it is one of the most effective tools in a clever golfer's bag of tricks. A few complimentary remarks aimed at the ear of a week-end player can revive weaknesses he has almost forgotten. It takes very little to bring them to life again.

There are a thousand and one phrases, such as "You have powerful wrist action," or "You shift your weight beautifully," that are highly complimentary but may cause a man't game to blow sky-high. They are the statements a man always wants to hear, and a flatterer uses them for bait as the housewife uses cheese to attract a mouse to a trap. A golfer is heading for trouble when he gobbles the flattery his rival proffers, because actually it is merely another form of cheese.

BEWARE OF FRIENDLY RIVALS

The average week-end golfer harbors a wee bit of legal larceny in his heart. One of the reasons he likes to play golf is that the game offers many opportunities for making small wagers. By winning more than his share of these bets he is able to prove to himself that he is really not such a dull, plodding sort after all.

The cagey money player figures that his opponent always regards the poor round yesterday as a matter of bad luck. Lack of skill had nothing to do with it. More often than not a golfer will forget the high score of yesterday and accept a bet based on what he hopes to shoot today. He never expects to three and four putt again, and he tees off determined to hit every shot down the middle and avoid the rough or traps.

Keeping all these human frailties in mind, the "friendly" week-end money player loves to offer a tantalizing assortment of bets. He does this, not because he is in need of money, but rather because money is a symbol of victory. As he sees it, the more money won from a variety of bets, the greater the victory. During the match he may be genuinely helpful to an opponent and make constructive suggestions or concede long putts; but regardless of courtesies or comradeship, he will always have his mind on the wagers he can win.

He may suggest bets on the first nine, the second nine, and the match. Perhaps he wants a syndicate at ten cents a hole, with double for birdies. He frequently recommends paying twenty-five cents to the man nearest the pin and fifty cents for the longest ball. He will offer a string of handicap bets that he knows his opponent will consider it folly to refuse. For instance, he may suggest three different wagers and offer to give his opponent one-up, two-up, and three-up for the eighteen-hole round, at fifty cents a bet. His rival will think automatically and gleefully of the highest three-up handicap and accept all three bets on that basis. This is questionable business judgment on the part of his opponent, because the money player will proceed to knock him off on the one-up bet, begin gaining ground on the two-up bet, and soon he will have his opponent fretting, and sometimes losing, the three-up wager.

The "friendly" golfer who likes to play for fair-sized stakes begins planning his strategy long before game time. He enjoys exploring ways and means of building up the amounts to be played for. In the locker room he may talk casually of sizable bets and how they help to make a good game. This is especially effective at country clubs where certain games of chance are available for members and guests. The money player uses this informal atmosphere to advantage while conditioning his prospects. Dice games such as "Ship, Captain, and Crew," "Bull," and "Liar's Dice" are typical of the sociable activities to which a player is introduced while he is being "prepared." The betting connected with these games gives a prospect the habit of winning and losing quarters and half dollars, something the prospect doesn't intend to do, he thinks, on the golf course. But it is surprising how quickly he responds to good fellowship, laughter, and a slap on the back as he shakes the dice, makes small wagers, and hears such remarks from his host as "You lucky stiff, I'll never beat you at golf today." In no time at all he may even be leaving the dice games momentarily to drop coins into a slot machine in the hope of winning a golf ball. At this point, the fact that it may cost two dollars to win a ninety-five-cent ball is not even considered of importance. The poor fellow is too full of good will toward men to worry about crass things like pieces of silver. Little does he realize that already he is well on his way toward reaching for his folding money.

From the dice tables, the prospect is led to the luncheon table for further treatment. Here an extravagant luncheon is ordered, and amid heart-warming comradeship the prospect is encouraged to eat, drink, and be merry. And then the money player comes up with a wonderful idea.

"Aw hell," he says, "let's not pay for the lunch now. Let's

settle the bill by adding it to what we play for this afternoon—
just to make the game more interesting."

And so the "lamb" leaves the locker room full of good food,
drink, and a commitment to play for an expensive luncheon
tab. He has lost any conception of the value of a dollar, and he
is willing to accept almost any further propositions these wonderful fellows have to offer. In fact, he may be so completely
carried away that he will begin offering instead of asking for a
few strokes handicap. Occasionally this preparation of the lamb
for slaughter has a reverse twist. The confidence and relaxation
acquired amid good fellowship are sometimes the underlying
reasons for a neophyte's playing over his head and hitting balls
210 yards when a 180-yard slice is normal. In this case, the lamb
becomes a lion, an unhappy turn of events for his opponent.

The path to the pro shop is another favorite location for the
money player to ply his trade. From experience he may know
that his opponent's game is erratic, and so he reasons that he
must approach today's betting problem scientifically. He recog-
nizes the fact that it is impossible to forecast his rival's score.
Like many golfers, on some days his opponent is good and
others he is terrible. Therefore, the money player concentrates
on making certain that his opponent's game will be as poor as
possible on this particular day.

One imaginative money player relies on the hot-water theory
of rejuvenation. Before leaving the locker room he holds his
hands in a washbowl of piping-hot water until his opponent
asks what he is doing. That is his cue to explain that the blood
circulation in a middle-aged athlete (he always uses the terms
"athlete" or "outdoorsman" while selling this idea) is a trifle
sluggish and should be stimulated prior to a round of golf. He
insists that the normal lack of stimulation reduces sensitivity in
the fingertips and is one of the major causes of poor golf.

As he stands there with his hands in hot water, he says, "This
type of therapy is the very latest wrinkle. I hear it is the secret
of Ben Hogan's success, and Ben is scared silly that other big-
name pros may find out about it."

The victim may not insist on steeping his own hands in scalding water, but often he does while his "friend" says, "Boy, this will make our hands sensitive. I promise you we will feel every shot."

Even if he is successful in keeping his hands out of hot water, as a result of all this propaganda the victim is so conscious of his hands that sooner or later he is more aware of his grip than he should be. This, in turn, causes him to make unconscious alterations in his playing form.

The pro shop may also be used as a laboratory in which to practice the pseudo-science of golf psychology. And the professional himself can easily become the unwitting tool of an expert bet-maker. For example, every pro is anxious to explain the merits of his stock of clubs, because that is how he sells them. Therefore, if a bet-maker introduces his victim to the club's expert and suggests that the pro explain the advantages of a new club design, the latter will need no further encouragement. If the pro is the aggressive type, he will assure the victim that the clubs the latter now owns are largely responsible for his mediocre game.

Taking a club from the prospect's bag, he may say, "With that sand iron you have, you'll never get out of a trap consistently. You will have a tendency to dig too deep into the sand, and if you try a chip shot you'll fall short." Then he will describe the merits of a new sand wedge and go into detail about design and construction.

When a victim leaves a pro shop convinced that the clubs he is using are an assortment of antique bats, his confidence will naturally be affected a bit. Later on, when he tries a sand-trap shot, automatically he will think of the pro's warnings about his poorly designed club, and he will try to steer his swing, a poor maneuver at any time.

The pro is also eager and willing to talk about other equipment. A smooth bet-maker knows this and may suggest "helpfully" that his partner get some tips about the importance of a golf glove. This will lead to a discussion about the golf grip and make the victim conscious of his hand action. Even a conversation about the merits of long and short wooden tees can confuse a neophyte.

The first objective of a gambler is to upset his rival sufficiently to insure poor play on the first hole. A man who has bet more than he can afford is handicapped by a fear of losing. Finding it difficult enough to tee off before an audience under normal circumstances, a golfer may go to pieces noticeably in the face of added money worries. He may become so anxious to excel that he will swing his club as if the ball were a cork about to pop from a champagne bottle.

Before teeing off, the money player often uses other upsetting tricks to throw his victim's game out of whack. He may suggest trick exercises to ruin co-ordination, or fancy putting contests to destroy touch, and, if his opponent is especially vain and naïve, he may ask the caddies to pay strict attention to his friend when he tees off because "this man's swing is a beautiful thing to watch."

A "friendly" money player often assumes a cloak of meekness to put over a point. By so doing, he throws his opponent off guard and makes him susceptible to later, and costly, suggestions. For instance, on the first tee he may pull his most winning smile and say, "Let's play for something small. I hate to see things get out of hand."

This sportsmanlike remark is received by the victim with enthusiasm. In fact, he is so relieved by the idea of small stakes that he overlooks the fact he should get a couple of strokes handicap.

After that, the tactics of the money player follow a regular pattern. On the fifth hole, if the money player is ahead, he assumes a surprised I'm-really-astonished-I-can-be-so-lucky look and insists that his opponent accept another bet so he can at least break even. If the money golfer is down, he will insist on another bet so *he* can break even. If the match is all square, he will say, "We're havin' a helluva match, aren't we? Whadda you say we make it more interesting?"

Also, at the proper moment, the money player may suddenly become helpful, or so the victim is led to believe. With an introductory remark, such as "I really don't care how I play today because I'm just out here for the fun," he throws his opponent completely off guard and makes himself a trusted companion. If his friend is having trouble, he offers what may at first seem to be good advice but really is sudden death to anyone who accepts it and acts upon it.

For example, the money player may be able to determine just why it is his victim has a tendency to slice. He thereupon offers a suggestion designed to make the fault even worse. If the victim is cutting across the ball, he tries to encourage an even deeper cut.

Flattery and logic are two of the basic tools in the money player's standard kit.

"Sam Snead," he may say, "keeps his wrists cocked until his hands have dropped below the level of his waist. I'll bet if you tried that you could knock the ball a mile, because I have noticed that your form is quite close to that of Sam's."

By this time, the victim is up to his neck in trouble. When he attempts to make use of the helpful tip, it fails to work and he goes to pieces. He's angry because he can't hit without slicing, and his anger is compounded because he can't hit like Sam Snead, although he likes to think his golfing form is not unlike that of the great Snead.

Money players also get excellent results by the simple but insidious device of giving unsolicited tips to an opponent who dislikes receiving such advice. As the victim strives to remain outwardly calm and tries manfully to remain a gentleman in spite of the constant flow of advice, he is unaware at first of the fluttering in his stomach. The little things have a tremendous and disastrous effect on a golfer's game, particularly if he is concerned about winning. When a player is irritated sufficiently to cause his "insides" to start churning, his whole system can go out of control before he knows it.

A chummy little device for wangling golf bets is the new

game with the innocent-sounding title of "Texas." Or, if the
player doesn't happen to like Texas, he might call it California,
Ohio, or Georgia. But the idea remains the same, and it is this:
When a side goes one-down after playing any of two successive
holes, it can seek a "Texas" for the next two holes. This means
that the bets will be doubled for the next two holes coming up.

Just to make the game even steeper, a gambler may suggest
an automatic "Texas," "just to keep things even all the way, of
course."

A neophyte who doesn't understand what this can lead to may
agree and say, "Yippee, I'm an old cow hand." Truer words
were never spoken, for he is about to be taken for a rough ride.
The automatic "Texas" can double the bet on every two holes,
and, even if the first two holes were played for a paltry twenty-
five cents, the player can quite possibly wind up playing the last
two holes for sixty-four dollars, plus everything he has already
lost.

By persuading a man to bet more than he can afford, a gambler can make his victim successively fearful, depressed, nervous,
and angry. Sometimes these reactions will lead to utter reckless-
ness, sometimes to extreme caution. There is only one sure
thing: the victim will not be any richer after the eighteenth
hole.

When teeing off for a friendly game with a "friendly" rival, it
is well for a player to realize there are two times in a golfer's
life when he shouldn't gamble: when he can't afford it, and
when he doesn't know his opponent.

YOU AND YOUR CADDIE

by Lealand Gustavson

Caddies become a very important part of golf. Carrying your bag and locating balls is the obvious part. The less obvious is that they become a legal part of your game. You incur the penalties that result from any infractions that may occur as a result of the actions of your caddie. In partnership play the partners and their caddies are part of the same side and are considered as such. You may ask for and accept advice from your caddie or caddies.

If a caddie is employed by two players (carrying double), it is *recommended* that he be assigned to the two players who are members of one side.

RULES AFFECTING THE CADDIE

Some instances in which the rules affect the caddie and the equipment, meaning clothes, bag, clubs, umbrella, etc., but not the ball, are:

Advice.

A ball in motion stopped or deflected by a caddie.

A ball moved accidentally by a caddie.

Handling the flagstick.

The specific rules covering the caddie when he is carrying double are different from those covering him when he carries single.

Carrying double in "match play" he is an *outside agency* except when he acts upon specific directions of a player, in which case he is considered to be *that* player's caddie. The

From Enjoy Your Golf, copyright 1954 by Lealand Gustavson, reprinted by permission of Harcourt Brace and Company, Inc.

specific directions is the technicality that makes the difference in rules interpretation.

On holding the flagstick he should be specifically advised what to do. If he attends the flagstick without instructions from either side, he is an outside agency, meaning he is *outside* the match and penalties do not exist. If he receives conflicting instructions, the wishes of the player who is about to play the stroke shall rule.

Carrying double in "stroke play" the caddie is always deemed to be employed by the player affected or playing the stroke.

If the caddie stops or deflects your ball you are penalized 2 strokes.

CADDIE INSTRUCTION

A good caddie has to be trained to his job, either by the long route of trial-and-error experience or by being taught by somebody who knows.

That teacher should properly be the pro or the caddiemaster. If they do not teach the boys it is up to the more experienced players to be patient and guide these boys along the way so that they can be efficient and happy in their jobs.

A simple suggestion arises here. It was first expressed by Gene Sarazen, who was once a caddie himself. "There are perhaps a million boys caddying; you as an adult can set them a good or bad example in life by your etiquette and observance of the rules of the game."

A CADDIE'S MANUAL

1. Be of every assistance to your employer while caddying for him.
2. Always be up with or ahead of your player, unless instructed otherwise.
3. Be in a position to see where the ball goes when it is hit. Move to the spot where the ball goes when it is hit.
4. The caddie for the first ball on the green is responsible for attending the flagstick.

5. While attending the flagstick, stand at comfortable arm's length to one side of the flag on the same side as the shadow of the stick falls, so as not to cast your own shadow across the hole or line of play. Stand quietly.
6. Stay out of all bunkers and hazards.
7. Stand slightly to the side where the player can see you when he is addressing the ball. Remain very quiet.
8. Permit the player to select the club from his bag that he wishes to use for his next stroke.
9. Stay with your player from tee to green unless he instructs you otherwise.
10. When carrying double serve both players equally well. If in a partnership match try to arrange carrying for two partners.

Caddying can be pleasant work for a boy, and you can help yourself a great deal by treating him as a fellow man who also enjoys the game. He wants to help you if he knows what you want. Help teach him and golf will be an even better game.

YOU AND YOUR PRO
by Lealand Gustavson

Your club pro can be your best friend and the important man
in your life, as far as your golf is concerned, because he can and
will tell you.

**Tips such as are in this book become valuable to you AFTER you
have learned the basic fundamentals of a golf swing.** Playing
friends are very generous with advice, but do they know? A bad
steer may take you a long time to recover from. Your pro may
be able to locate a fault and correct it in a matter of minutes.
If you try to find it yourself you may throw your entire swing
out of kilter, and still not have corrected the original error.

**First, learn from your pro the proper way to swing, and then
make a sincere effort to apply what he tells you.** It won't work
the first few times you try it because your brain and muscles are
not trained to function that way. But stay with it a while and
you'll be glad you did. It is not the pro's fault the instruction
didn't produce. It is yours, because you didn't do what he told
you to do, even though you may think you did. If you have an
opportunity to get some action photographs taken of yourself,
do it, but be prepared to be shocked when you see the prints.
You won't look like you think you do. That is why you should
sincerely follow your pro's advice, even though it may feel
wrong to you. He is generally a pretty fair psychologist as well,
and can quite accurately define your troubles in golf in terms of
mental errors as well as physical. Listen to him closely when he
talks to you. He is sincerely trying to get an intricate problem

simplified and put it to you in language that you can understand.

If you have children who are interested in golf or whom you want to interest, put them in your pro's hands for instruction. Don't depend on friends unless you are certain that they are fine golfers and can impart their knowledge to your children. Sound basic instruction early in life is the basis for good golf later.

In the matter of equipment you can't do better for your golf than to buy from your pro's shop. You may buy cheaper, or "get it at a discount," but unless you are qualified and certain of your own judgment, you will still do better at your pro's. He stocks only the kind of equipment and clothes that are good golf, because he knows what is good golf.

The design of practically all modern golf equipment is the result of the composite view of your club pros. They know from working closely with you what is needed and what is best, and pass that knowledge on to the manufacturers who design the equipment accordingly. Clothes for golfers have became much more attractive and comfortable because the pros have demanded it and have set the example.

When you are selecting new clubs, consult your pro first. He knows more about you and your type of swing than you may think he does. His advice and recommendations are invaluable because no other dealer can know about *your* needs, but will merely agree with any thinking you may have done, and that can be all wrong. If you buy from your pro he will probably make you a trade-in allowance on your old set, too, which is well worth considering.

Have you noted the spirit of friendliness which prevails in some clubs and not in others? You can pretty well put that friendly spirit down to the pro who makes it his business to see to it that all members become acquainted with each other and frequently arranges games for players who have no prearranged foursomes.

Tell him your troubles, put your faith in his judgment and recommendations and you'll be a happier golfer.

HOW TO TURN YOUR HOME
INTO AN INDOOR RANGE

by Raymond Schuessler

*Almost nothing's impossible for the dedicated 'divoteer'
who will put his mind to indoor practice this winter*

Bears hibernate and ducks migrate, but what happens to the golf bug during the winter?

If he is affluent enough he may migrate with the ducks to warmer climes to continue his relentless assault on par, but never will he hibernate—not the dyed-in-the-knickers golfer. He will continue his head-down, straight-left-arm and full follow-through all winter—driving the kids to bed with a putter, taking his mashie to chip ice off the steps, using his brassie on his wife's gluteus maximus every other weekend for mismanaging the budget. Pure frustration—golfing, that is.

But the wise bug is he who converts his household into a happy indoor golf course complete with a driving range and putting greens as a form of recreation for guests and for personal improvement.

Considerable practice can be managed indoors during the winter which will keep your game in constant trim. Then after the long layoff you won't have to go through the agony of polishing up your game so much in the spring. It can also be instrumental in lowering your handicap *and* keeping excess calories from porking around your waistline.

Merely swinging a club is not as beneficial as actual contact with the gutta, however, and as impractical as this may sound it is not an impossibility in the house. (Calm yourself, ma'am.) There are two methods, one with regulation balls and the other with imitation pellets. If you are a high grade bug you undoubtedly will prefer regulation balls, necessitating a driving net.

A home-constructed driving range in the cellar, attic, garage or spare room isn't too complicated a matter. There are standard driving nets on the market, sold through sporting goods stores and pros. The portable ones cost around $100.

Anyone faintly familiar with carpentry could build one, too. They are about 10 feet wide, six feet tall, and three feet deep, using sail canvas for a target or driving background and No. 16 twine, ¾ inch mesh net for the two sides and top to snare wildly-hit balls. Get four sturdy poles and some nails and screws and take off! Be sure to pad the poles unless you enjoy dodging balls which come bouncing right back at you.

A rubber mat or a thickness of cardboard can be used for the driving ground. It would be wise to anchor the mat in some manner. When using a driver, the ball can be teed if a handful of sculptor's clay (plasteline available at art stores) is pasted to the mat. The clay will retain its plasticity and hold the tee snugly. It's also a good idea to place a mirror on the floor adjusted so that you can control the immobility of your head.

In order to save your head from a bashing in, it might also be a good idea to give in and buy your wife that fur coat she's wanted all along. Then she wouldn't be too disturbed about the thump-thump-thump of the golf balls hitting the canvas.

Every form of practice one might need can be tried on this range. Of course there can be no true judging of distance, but painting targets at different levels on the canvas and pitching at these spots will develop a sense of touch.

This sort of practice can't help but improve your short approach game, which many say is the most important phase of golf. If a player can consistently land his short approaches near the pin, he'll score well.

Of course, if one could sink 40-foot putts consistently he'd be unbeatable. But putting is the most uncertain part of anyone's game. To be effective, it hinges upon a good approach. The approach can make up for a bad shot, and definitely holds the game together.

Those who are unable to find space for a driving net can still get in their share of winter practice by using imitation balls which do not require a net. These balls can be made by rolling a half-page of newspaper into a small ball and encircling it with a rubber band. This forms a firm and weighted object. You can buy cotton, plastic or rubber practice balls which are fairly safe around the house. It would be wise to protect the windows, though, just in case.

Chipping and short pitching can also be practiced with great effectiveness indoors during the winter, even if you don't have a net. Real or practice balls can be used, but be sure you have a target such as a bucket, waste-basket, pillow or something like that to shoot at. It's also a good idea to have drapes, the davenport or a big chair behind the target to stop the ones that miss.

Perhaps the most important part of winter practice is parlor putting. It is true that the resistance of a rug is less than that of a grass green, but the adjustment can be made in the spring from all that is learned now. A trick that many adopt also is to put tape on the face of the putter to compensate for the faster roll. Use any sort of "hole," including the discs on the market, but remember that the hole is $4\frac{1}{4}$ inches wide.

Ten minutes of putting before each evening meal can improve you, but it's more fun and a better form of practice to choose teams from among your family or guests and go at it in competitive style. This will lead to the important atmosphere of putting under pressure, which after all is the only effective method.

In solitary practice it is best to try putts from all distances. Many have the mistaken idea that if one can sink a 10-footer anything under that should be simple. This is hardly true for the ideal putting stroke is one that can make the ball die in the hole. Therefore not only is the line important but the feel of distance as well.

This winter practice should have the same effect on the golfing instinct of the average player as a somewhat similar type has on the ordinary club pro. Though he has little time to play an actual round during the season, the pro continually has a club in his hands. By this habit, whether he is swinging, instructing or repairing he retains his "feel" for the club and its mastery.

GOLF FICTION AND HUMOR

GOLF'S A BIG BUSINESS

by Paul Gallico

I may have got off to a worse start to work a National Open Golf Championship than the one just finished at the New Country Club in Cleveland, but I don't know when. First of all, A. R. kept me waiting three hours while he was tied up in a reorganization conference—A. R. Mallow & Co., one of the large manufacturers and retailers of sporting goods, had assimilated a couple of minor companies and was in the reorganization throes—and then he kept me two hours more, explaining how A. R. Mallow & Co. simply had to have the Open Champion this year, or else.

I knew all that; we had won the Open Champion for six straight years up to 1932, and then the Fairgreen Company took two of them with Angus MacDonough. They had stolen Angus from us. The next two years the S. A. Sampson Midwest Company had won it both times, and last year, when we had a sweet four-stroke lead with Jock McIntosh, Jock blew up on the last three holes, and Crabby Wilson sneaked through, playing the Sweetwood Company's Putt-Rite Ball, the ball with the belladonna center. It had cut into our sales like the very devil because it's that Open Championship that sells golf equipment, and we know it.

But A. R. had the jitters, and kept gabbing and repeating himself, and saying: "Ha-rumph, Fowler. Vital we get that championship this year. Stockholders raising hell. You know

Reprinted from Golf Is A Friendly Game by Paul Gallico by permission of Alfred A. Knopf, Inc., copyright 1936 by The Curtis Publishing Company, copyright 1942 by Paul Gallico.

what the sales graph looks like." It looked like nothing so much as Carl Hubbell's drop. "Don't let anybody get away, understand? If they have a ghost of a show, sign 'em up. It's up to you to get that championship for us. I can't square you with the board if you don't." And a lot more stuff like that for two hours, when I should have been under way.

And then, just as I was leaving, he called me back and said: "Ah-rumph, Fowler—I forgot. Contact C. A. Wilcoxon when you get out there; it's important."

I said: "Who is C. A. Wilcoxon?" with "the hell" left out, but implied.

"New advertising manager. Smith is fired!" I whistled. That was bad news. If they had started firing the big guys, they would get down to the little ones pretty soon.

So I said O.K., but it wasn't until eleven o'clock that night, when I should have been in Allentown, that I shot through the Holland Tunnel with a load of give-away balls and a dozen or so sample sets of mallets in the back of the car, and at twelve o'clock picked up a flat going through Elizabeth.

But that was nothing. My brakes burned out somewhere around Altoona. If I'd had any sense I would have ditched the bus and grabbed a train, but I had the equipment in the back and hoped to make it by driving all the next night. But I didn't figure to run through a cloudburst, skid and break an axle just outside a God-forsaken town called Blixville, or Wixville, somewhere west of Pittsburgh, and stay there seven and a half hours while they welded it.

And so William Fowler, Esq., representative of A. R. Mallow & Co., makers of the Thunderbolt and the Tuff-Hide Ball, not to mention Tru-Distance Irons and Far-Fli Woods, drove up to the clubhouse of the New Country Club in Cleveland at ten o'clock in the morning of the second day of the National Open Championship, exactly twenty-six hours too late. That was just lovely.

And the first person I have to run into is a guy I don't like to see even when I am feeling good, J. Sears Hammett, repre-

"*Fore!*"

sentative of the Fairgreen Company, makers of the Accu-Putt
Ball—"the ball with the genuine diamond-chip center; a guaranteed chip diamond in every center for accuracy. Your watch-
maker uses jewels for accuracy, so do we; retailing still at
seventy-five cents"—and looking very pleased with himself,
which is bad news. J. Sears Hammett is the only guy I ever
knew who could manage to look sour while he was smiling.

"Ah," he said, splitting his face just enough so that I can see
three teeth, "the A. R. Mallow Co., right on time. Why didn't
you stay home and listen to it on the radio? It'll be over tomorrow."

I passed the crack and said: "Who's leading?"

"The Fairgreen Company is out in front by three strokes. An
unknown from Milwaukee, named Dutch Steubner, had a 69.
I signed him last night. Some guy from Washington shot a 71,
but Midwestern nailed him. Too bad you weren't here."

"What's Whitey Brompton doing?" I was a sucker to keep
on leading with my chin, but I had to find out.

"He blew himself to a nice 76 yesterday. He's two over on the
first three holes this morning. Something's the matter with his
irons. I've suggested he try Fairgreens. He's thinking it over."

I ignored that one too, and said: "Those morning-glories all
fold up the second day. You can have 'em," but the grapes were
plenty sour, and he knew it. Sometimes they don't fold up,
and anyway you've got to nail those birds, and nail 'em quick,
before the price goes up.

"Uh-huh!" said Hammett, with a smile that made him look
sourer than ever. "That's right. Funny, though, how busy the
gang has been, picking those morning-glories. They must like
them. Well, you won't have to worry about that now. They're
all gone."

He turned and started to walk off, but stopped and called
back over his shoulder: "You might sign up Jet Scraggins."

When I am sore I bite bad, so I said: "Who the hell is Jet
Scraggins?"

"The funniest name in the tournament. He had an 81 yester-

day. It's the gag around here. Oh, excuse me. I forgot you just
arrived. Play Scraggins irons, a new A. R. Mallow product. A
sand wedge free with every set. You'll need it."

Yes, that was all just lovely. And when I got out on the course
and did a little grapevining and talked to some of the golf
writers, it was even worse than I expected. It looked as though
every big and little company manufacturing golf equipment
was out to bag that championship. Of course we had five top-
notch men playing for our company, none of them worse than
76; and Freddy McRae was in a good position for us with a 73,
and was playing nice golf the two holes I walked with him. But
you never can tell when some comparative unknown will come
staggering in with the title when the big shots begin to blow
on the last nine holes. And how they blow! Look at the way
Sam Parks came home at Oakmont last year. Nobody had him
tagged until it was too late.

Well, the gang hadn't overlooked anybody who appeared to
have the ghost of a show. I guess a lot of those bush-league pros
who were up in the 75 and 76 class must have figured the depression was over. The manufacturers' representatives must have
been working overtime handing out options and retainers. Of
course a lot of them would be out of it by nightfall; it looked
as though it would need better than 153 to qualify for the last
day's play, but those were the chances you had to take. Yes, that
field was sewed up tighter than a farmer in his winter under-
wear. If one of my five guys didn't scramble under the wire,
W. Fowler, Esq., was going to get some firsthand knowledge of
the unemployment situation.

I followed around in Angus MacDonough's gallery for a
while, practicing putting the evil eye on him for leaving us flat
and going over to Fairgreen, but I didn't have to, because he
was having a streak of bad putting. He had had a 74 the day
before, and it looked as though he would putt himself right out
of the tournament. But after a while they started to drop and
I saw something. When I met Joe Williamson, of the *Times-
Herald,* cutting through the woods to the sixteenth, I told him

about it. It was a dirty trick for me to do, but I was still sore at Hammett's cracks; and besides, he had stolen MacDonough away from us when we had an agreement not to swipe one another's pros until their contracts expired.

I said: "Want a good story?"

He said: "Know a good story?"

I said: "Uh-huh! Angus MacDonough has switched from the Fairgreen Accu-Putt Ball—they're paying him to play—back to the Thunderbolt. Take a look at it the next time he has a clean lie on the fairway. You'll see the Thunderbolt zigzag on it. He three-putted three greens in a row and then switched. I saw him take a new ball out of his bag on thirteen. He thinks he can hear that damn diamond chip rattling around inside the Accu-Putt, and it makes him nervous."

Williamson said: "Thanks," and walked off in the direction of the fifteenth. I felt a little better after that, and stopped by and had a look at the scoreboard and felt sick again. Dutch Steubner, Fairgreen's unknown from Milwaukee, had tacked a 73 onto his 69 of the previous day, for 142. Our star, Whitey Brompton, had treated himself to another sweet 76, and was just ten strokes behind him. McCrae wasn't playing until after lunch. Jock McIntosh, our other white hope, wasn't doing so well either. The three other pros we had under contract were back with the crowd and couldn't be figured on much unless one of them went crazy the third or fourth round, which was possible too. And there actually was a guy by the name of Jet Scraggins, from the Sorauga Country Club, playing in the tournament. He had managed to compile a fine 81-75 and would be departing for Sorauga, wherever that was, that evening.

But the name made me think of J. Sears Hammett again, which was enough to spoil my appetite for lunch; so I thought I would retire to a quiet corner in the locker room and start the attending eightball bringing me strong drink until I felt better. And by that time I had clean forgotten that I was supposed to contact a guy by the name of C. A. Wilcoxon.

There was a mob in there, of course, but there was a quiet

aisle down toward the end with only one guy sitting on the bench, looking glum, which is nothing strange in a golf tournament.

I had a Scotch and soda and another one started on the way when I took notice of the guy. He was a tall, lanky, nice-looking kid, with sandy hair and a lot of freckles, a nice mouth, and a big pair of paws on him. But he sure looked glum. From the expression on his face, and the way I felt, I figured maybe I was looking in a mirror. Finally I said: "Drink?"

He shook his head, so I said the usual thing: "Tough going?"

He said: "That course ain't giving any strokes back. Ah never seed greens like those." He spoke with a soft drawl and his voice was husky.

"Not your day, eh? Well, it isn't mine either."

"You playin'?" He looked sympathetic.

"Nope," I said, "buying." By this time I was glad I had found someone I didn't know that I could spill my troubles to. You know how it is. "Had everything that could possibly happen to a car happen to me and drove in here a day late. I've got a pocketful of dough to sign up players for our company and they're all signed up. Nice fresh money, and no place to spend it. Too late. That's my fix."

The kid gave me a funny look. Then he said: "Suh, the way I feel right now, I'd sign up with anybody for a ham sandwich."

I don't know. Maybe it was the way he said it, or maybe it was the second Scotch on an empty stomach—I hadn't eaten since the night before—but I said suddenly: "O.K., kid. You're on. You're working for me," and hollered for the eightball; and when he came, I ordered another Scotch and soda and a ham sandwich.

The kid stirred suddenly and made a little gesture, and then said: "Suh, you wouldn't make it two, would you?"

I said: "Just like a pro. Soon as you start to do business with them, the price goes up double. O.K. Make it two. . . . Bring two ham sandwiches."

"Bring 'em wrapped up," the kid added to the locker boy. "I want to take 'em out."

While the boy went to fetch them, I gave the kid one of our blank contract forms to fill out; and when he signed it and handed it back, I stuffed it in my pocket without even looking at the name on it. The sandwiches arrived. He took them, got up, stuck out his hand, and said: "Thank you, suh," and after I had shaken it he walked off.

But before I had that third Scotch half down, he was back with the sandwiches still in his hand. He stood for a moment looking at me, and then, in his husky drawl, said: "Suh, I cain't do it."

I said: "Can't do what?"

"Take these here sandwiches from you. I'm out of it. I had 156. That won't qualify."

I still didn't get it. I thought he was gagging. So I said: "Brother, I'm out of it too. Good and out of it, so that makes us even. We're square. Beat it!"

A funny look came over his face, and he turned and walked off. I don't know why I got up and followed him. Maybe I needed some fresh air after all those Scotches.

I didn't know, either, what I was going to say to him when I finally would catch up. He was striding along fast, behind the refreshment tent and past the practice tee and on down way to the end of the parking lot, so I cut a little off by walking around by the press tent; and so I came up to where his car was parked —an old, battle-scarred wreck of a job—from behind the clump of bushes back of the fourth green—where our Whitey Brompton had blown two strokes in the second round—and was just going to step out and start saying nothing, when I saw a girl sitting in his car. Yes, sir, she was a girl.

She had a fine face, that girl. Fresh and fine. She was pale, too, and had a pair of dark blue eyes big enough around to hole putts in. She had hair the color of uncut grain, and it must have been long, because there was a lot of it fastened in a big knot at the back of her head. So I thought: "Oh, oh! Amscray, Fowler," and started to check out, when I heard the kid say: "Grub, Effie! Come and get it," and the girl sigh and answer: "You eat it, honey. Ah'm not hungry." She had a voice that was just like wild honey. Just that rough and sweet. So I stayed and listened a little bit. . . . Uh-huh! Well, what of it?

The kid said: "Effie, you're a lovin' liar. Come on. I've got one too."

The girl said: "You eat 'em, honey. You got to play tomorrow. Ah don't get hungry sitting."

"Ah'll not do much playing tomorrow with 156. I won't qualify by three strokes. Look, Effie, that's genuine eighteen-karat ham and store bread. Or do I have to stuff it down your lovely throat?"

So the girl took one of the sandwiches and peeled off the paper wrapper and bit into it. "Honey," she said, "that's the best thing Ah ever tasted in my life, even if you did steal 'em. But Ah'll go to jail happy."

They sat side by side for a while, eating their sandwiches slowly and saying nothing. All of a sudden the kid said: "A hundred and fifty-six. Effie, I let you down badly, didn't I?"

The girl slipped her hand into his big paw and said: "Honey, you cain't let me down. Ah love you."

That was where I turned around quick and got back into the gallery around the fourth green, just in time to watch Jock McIntosh come up and blow a three-foot putt for the glory of A. R. Mallow & Co.

I kept thinking about those two kids. I knew there were a lot of pros tin-canning it up to tournaments in the hope of winning enough money to get back home on—depression pros. In good times they all had plenty of money, but that kid seemed to be in a bad way. And I couldn't exactly see where the girl fitted in, because she didn't have any wedding ring on her finger.

But I forgot about them soon enough when I went out on the course again to see whether I could save anything from the wreckage. I couldn't. I picked up one kid by the name of Wilmox, but the thunderstorm that broke over the course washed him home in 158. The same storm raised hell with the scores of those who had to go out in the afternoon, though our Freddy McRae managed to squeeze out a 72. The same storm likewise soaked me to the skin, so I went back to the hotel to dry out and grab a hot bath. The way things were breaking for me at that tournament, the least I could figure on was double pneumonia.

When I emptied the pockets of my suit before giving it to the bellhop to dry out, I came across the contract I had got from the kid in the locker room, and realized that I hadn't even looked to see what his name was. I did then. You guessed it. I had signed up Jet Scraggins, professional at the Sorauga Country Club, Clementine, Texas, to play the A. R. Mallow & Co. products for one year, for two ham sandwiches. If J. Sears Hammett ever found that out, I was sunk. He would spread it around among the gang and they would laugh me right out of business. He had been right. That name "Scraggins" was a gag all over the layout.

Yes, and I'll tell you another funny one. The kid qualified with 156. It was a screwy tournament all around. That thunderstorm caught a bunch of top-flight players and came close to drowning 'em, and the scores of a lot of good golfers went rocketing. There had been only a few good morning scores, and so 156 and ties qualified for the last day's thirty-six holes. There were seven who had 156, and so the kid was in. I was glad for the sake of the girl, and the kid too. Somehow I had the idea they were a pretty gutty pair.

I don't have to tell you how the Open Championship is played. Eighteen holes of medal play the first two days, and then the field cut down to the top thirty; with ties, making about thirty-seven in all, for the last popeyed thirty-six-hole scramble from the tape. Eighteen in the morning and eighteen in the afternoon. The last eighteen holes, and sometimes the very last nine holes, all the pros go completely mad. As soon as a pro finds out that all that he needs is par to win, bang! It's usually some unconscious guy who drifts through at the end.

Of course I ran right into J. Sears Hammett when I got back to the club early the next morning, and he gives me a smile that would curdle a lemon. "Hello," he said. "How's your man?"

I'm an awful sucker for that guy, which is maybe why I dislike him so. I said: "What guy?"

"Jet Scraggins."

I hope my face didn't show the vacuum created when my heart fell clear down to my spikes. I couldn't figure how he had found out so soon. The kid didn't even know who I was. I took a desperate stab and said: "What makes you think he's my man?" and was plenty relieved when he said: "Oh, I thought maybe you took my advice and signed him. A. R. Mallow & Co. ought to have somebody in this tournament."

"We've got enough to win it," I growled, leading with my chin again.

He showed four teeth and said: "Like to bet a hundred Fairgreen doesn't finish ahead of Mallow?"

Me, I don't bet in hundreds, but I couldn't let that fourflusher sit on me any longer; so I said: "Make it two hundred," though it nearly choked me. And that's where we left it, and I had the satisfaction of seeing him swallow a little on that one.

At that, with the boys just starting off the first tee, I wasn't in such a bad spot if I just stayed lucky. Dutch Steubner was out in front of our Freddy McRae by three strokes, with Angus MacDonough, of Fairgreen, three strokes behind Freddy. A lot can happen in eighteen holes. A lot did. Freddy McRae went higher than Prof. Piccard and took a 77. Dutch Steubner, J. Sears Hammett's find, didn't blow enough to stir a gentle breeze. Not with a fine par 72, which, tacked on to his 69-73, gave him a fifty-four-hole total of 214 and an eight-stroke lead on my nearest man, the aviating McRae. Steubner was a big, blond, stolid-looking German with a powerful swing that he

seemed to have grooved from that tournament. I thought, looking him over the day before, that I had detected what Damon
Runyon, or maybe it was W. O. McGeehan, once called the
"look of beagles" in his eye, but I guess I was wrong. That was
a fine 72 he fired into the teeth of that field.

I spent most of the morning at the scoreboard, watching the
results come in, hole by hole. The only thing I had to feel good
about was that just before lunchtime they came and posted a
72 for my man Scraggins. I was glad for the kid, but of course
the pardon came too late. It gave him a three-round total of
228, just fourteen strokes behind the leader, which is a lot like
chasing Gene Venzke for the mile, lugging a sixteen-pound shot
and trying to hit him with it.

But thinking of Scraggins gave me an idea. Hell, I liked that
kid, and as far as the Open and Bill Fowler were concerned
that year, the party was over; so I went out to the refreshment
tent with a pocketful of scrip tickets that I had not been able to
drink up yet and bought an armful of provisions. I got a cold
chicken and a flock of sandwiches and sugar wafers, and four or
five half pints of milk, and went down to the end of the car
park by the fourth green and did a nice job of accidentally
stumbling across the kid and his girl, sitting in their traveling
wreck.

"Hey!" I said. "What a break! Hope you haven't had lunch
yet. I'm stuck. Chet Myers and Joe Dingie and I were going to
chow in the woods back of five, because the clubhouse is
jammed. When I got back there with the grub, the marshal said
they had gone off with a couple of blondes. Nice boys! Give us
a hand. I can't carry this around all afternoon."

I guess I must have sounded convincing, because the kid
just licked his lips once and said: "That's very kind, suh. We
hadn't planned to eat very much between rounds. I don't remember your name, suh."

I told him, and he introduced me to his girl, whose name was
Effie Creighton. I broke out the rations. Neither of the two
was looking any too good, and I was hoping they would be

smart enough not to pile in too much, because I didn't know how long it was since they had eaten anything but those two ham sandwiches. The girl just took off a wing of the chicken, and when she took the first bite out of it I never let on I saw a tear gathering in the corners of those big eyes. She must have been pretty hungry.

I made them drink all the milk—the only time I am really a dope is when that J. Sears Hammett is around, I guess—and then we got talking, and the kid said they had driven up from their home town, which was Clementine, Texas, and it had taken them four days and they hadn't figured on having to spend money on having their car fixed—I knew something about that and we compared notes on car troubles—and then they loosened up a lot, and the kid said: "Effie and I are engaged. I figured I could win some money in this tournament and we could get married and drive back home in style. I didn't want her to make the trip. It was a tough one, but she came along."

Effie said: "He needed me. He could have won if—if—" She stopped.

I know my face wasn't showing shock or surprise or anything, because I am broad-minded about such things; but I guess the kid was smart enough to know what I was thinking. He smiled —and I told you he had a nice smile—and said: "We been sleeping in the car out here. And all the way up. Effie can curl up on the back seat. I can stretch out my legs better in the front."

"Do you mean to say that you spend the night sitting up in the front seat of that wreck, and then go out and play golf?"

"Well, suh, it saved hotel bills. We had about enough money for food and gas when we came away—that is, until we ran into that little trouble with the car."

"And playing without food?"

The girl suddenly said passionately: "Oh, he never had a fair chance! He can play golf better than anybody in the world! He hasn't eaten for thr—"

"Hush, honey," said Scraggins—what a name, but it was his

—and placed that big strong golf paw over her mouth and held
her that way for a moment and looked down into her eyes; and
I hope that some day I will be able to look at a dame that way
and get it back the way he did. " 'Tain't so, suh. I was plumb
careless on that first round. I figured those greens all wrong. I
deserved an 81."

I said: "You're a pair of dopes. Keep smacking 'em. You may
get into the money yet. And if you don't, I'm going to stake you
home."

"No, suh. I'm sorry, suh, but you cain't do that."

"Why not?"

"We cain't take such charity. We cain't start that way."

"Charity, hell! I signed you up. You're working for me."

The kid looked at me for a moment and then said: "You
can tear that up, suh. I was foolin', and so were you. I don't
hold you to it."

"Hold me to it! I'm holding you. You've et your sandwiches."
We started to laugh. I saw Freddy McRae getting ready to tee
off way down on the first, by his yellow sweater. He wasn't
much use now, but he was our only chance; and I had to pray
him around the layout if it was my last job for A. R. Mallow
& Co., which was just about what it was likely to be. So I said:
"Keep hitting them up to the cup, son. They might drop," and
walked off, leaving them standing there with their arms about
each other's waists. And somehow at that moment I didn't give
a damn about A. R. Mallow & Co.

You read the papers. You know who won the Open Championship at Cleveland as well as I do. Only there are a couple of
things about it that you don't know. But I'm coming to that.

That last eighteen holes of the Open is a great show. Everybody wants to come home with the winner, so you go galloping
about the course, chasing players and rumors, picking up this
one who has a chance until he blows, or getting the news that
someone else clear on the other side of the layout is burning up
the course. It calls for good legs and a sixth sense. The boys
play in pairs, and the committee is usually pretty smart in team-

ing up a leader who has a show to win with some chap at the bottom of the list who hasn't much chance anyway, so that when the gallery comes whooping and trampling on the heels of the potential champion, it doesn't much matter if they run over the mug. I noted from the pairings that they had Scraggins teamed up with Dutch Steubner, and figured, after I had done what I could to root McRae home, I would have a look at that couple shoot a few holes and then go on away and begin to think about looking for a job.

McRae shot nice golf and turned in 36, and I had a glimmer of hope, but it went bye-bye when I got the news that Steubner, playing behind him, had had a 38. That meant that he had probably got the bad golf out of his system and could come home in par, or even two or three over par and shoe in. I also heard that Scraggins had turned with him in even par, 36. He had picked up two strokes on him, but inasmuch as he had started fourteen behind, that was like landing a left jab on Dempsey just before he knocked you out. Still, I was hoping the kid could pull up and knock off a fifty- or a hundred-dollar prize.

Then I got word that Whitey Brompton had turned one under and had birdied the tenth, so I hurried over there to lend aid, assistance, and comfort where possible—although the guy who finishes second in the Open is just another agate line in the newspapers—and watched him shoot the twelfth and thirteenth in par and then go one over on the 500-yard fourteenth. Most of the gallery, of course, was trailing Steubner, but our McIntosh, who was an old favorite, had a good crowd of the faithful plodding around with him, and I was just cutting through the woods by the sixteenth to see how he was doing when I heard a roar go up from the Steubner gallery way over the hill, like no other roar I ever heard on a golf course before.

Joe Williamson, the *Times-Herald* man, went streaking by me through the woods like a frightened deer. I shouted: "Hey!" He kept on running, but threw over his shoulder something that sounded like: "Scrang! Holywa!" I didn't get it, but I started to run too. The excitement of the Open gets you like that. The fourteenth fairway was just on the other side of the woods, and the gallery, panting, red-faced, was already streaming down the sides. I found out what the yell had been for. It wasn't Steubner. It was Scraggins. On the 187-yard thirteenth, he had bounced a three iron onto the edge of the carpet, from which it took two hops and a bite—it had had plenty of back-spin—and walked into the hole. A hole in one on the last round of an Open Championship! Sure, it was blind luck, coupled with a fine shot. All holes in one are. But I was tickled to death for the kid. The publicity wouldn't do him any harm. Steubner had been bunkered, and two-putted after he got out, for a four.

The fourteenth was a 500-yard, par-five hole, uphill slightly. The kid had had a long straight drive and, as I got there, had his big mitts wrapped around the handle of a big, deep-faced brassie with a curious hump on the top of the club head. He laid into it, and from the crowd packed around the fourteenth green came another yell, backed by the crackle of applause. No, it wasn't in the hole, but from where I stood it didn't look to be more than three feet from it. Of course, when you get up closer, that stretches out a little. With a whoop the gallery was off and almost ran right over Steubner, who hadn't played his shot yet. He was twenty yards short of the green. We walked down the fairway. The kid saw me and winked. I said nothing. I knew enough not to talk to a golfer in a tournament until I am talked to.

The kid had a five-foot putt when we got to the green. Steubner's chip overran the cup by eight feet, and he rimmed it, coming back, for a par five. Scraggins went up to his ball and dropped it into the bottom of the can as though he was rolling for a bucket. The kid had picked up five strokes on the leader in two holes, and the gallery was wild.

I've seen golf explosions touched off by a lot less than two consecutive eagles, one of them a hole in one. But the fireworks that followed were worthy of the match that set them off. That was some pyrotechnical display. And they blew Mr. Dutch

Steubner's weakness wide open. He couldn't handle that gallery! Because by the time they had driven off the fifteenth, all the rest of the field must have thought it was playing a Monday-afternoon club tournament. Everybody on the course, including the marshals and the gang out of the clubhouse and the locker rooms, had come on over to have a look at Scraggins.

Golf galleries, when they get out of hand, will ruin any player who hasn't years of experience playing through them and can control himself. Once they pick a favorite to watch, his partner might just as well be playing through a herd of cattle. Steubner's partner, given to him for just that purpose—to protect him— had been a boomerang. The crowd had taken that lanky, sandy-haired kid with the screwy name right to its heart. They were galloping down the fairway, chanting: "Come on, Scraggins!" as though they liked to say it. Of course, nobody had the ghost of an idea that he could possibly win, but they enjoyed rooting for him. Steubner picked up a nice juicy six on the fifteenth, when he dumped his second over the green and into some thorn bushes, had to wait five minutes before the crowd would give him a lane through which to hack it toward the pin, was short and then three-putted. The kid canned a fourteen-footer for a birdie—oh, a nice putt—and the balloon was up.

He ran into me, walking off the green, and suddenly slipped his arm through mine and said: "Come on, walk along with me." He laid his drive smack down the middle of the sixteenth. Steubner hooked into deep rough near the brook. Walking down the fairway, Scraggins said: "Ah can play this game when Ah've got a feed under my belt. Ah'll lay this one stiff." He did, too. Four feet. It was all Steubner could do to get back on the fairway. Result, Steubner another one over par. The kid tanked his three, walked over to me, and said: "That was mighty good chicken."

The crowd suddenly realized that, throwing out the hole in one on the thirteenth, the kid had shot 3-3-3 for the last three holes, or 1-3-3-3 for four, six under par. They knew they weren't looking at golf, but a miracle, and sobered a little. All at once

I felt myself jostled away from the kid's side, walking to the seventeenth, a par-three 230-yard hole. Uh-huh! It was none other than J. Sears Hammett. He said:

"Oh, Mr. Scraggins! Hammett's my name. Fairgreen Golf Company. If you have not made any commitments, I—er—should like an appointment to see you in the locker room immediately after the match—er—if you win. I can offer you—"

If I hadn't loved that kid before, I loved him then. He said:

"Go away from me, suh. Cain't you see Ah'm playing a tournament? Ah don't know you. Ah just know this gentleman here." He slipped his arm through mine again, and we went on to the seventeenth tee, where he dumped his tee shot into a deep trap on the left of the green.

Steubner got on, about thirty feet from the pin. From the groan that went up from the crowd, you would have thought the Last Judgment was at hand.

But walking down to the green, Scraggins leaned over to me and said: "Don't let that worry you, suh. Where Ah play mah golf, it's all just one big bunker."

While Scraggins sat on the edge of the green, grinning and waiting for the marshals to organize the crowd so that he could play out of the bunker, Steubner started studying his putt, which is always a bad thing to do. It took a long while, and so, by the time that the kid strolled down into the pit and exploded the ball a foot from the cup, the German had a fine case of the jitters, and the yell that went up from about five thousand people didn't help any. Sure, he three-putted. The kid had a kick-in for his fourth consecutive three.

And then, started from the ranks of the golf writers, the way it will, the word rustled through that crowd faster than a prairie blaze that, coming to the eighteenth tee, Steubner and Scraggins were all square and even Stephen. The crowd had forgotten that while Scraggins was going under par, Steubner was going over, and handing back two strokes at a clip. Starting from the tenth, where Scraggins had been par and Steubner had slipped one over on a putt that should have dropped, the kid had made up twelve strokes, which, coupled with the two he had acquired in the first round, made up the fourteen that he owed the lead. The man who won that eighteenth hole would be the new Open Champion, or tie for it, because the others who had a chance were all in and their scores posted; and believe it or not, Mallow's Freedy McRae, by virtue of a 73, was leading with 295. Both Steubner and Scraggins had par for 294, which would win the tournament, or, if they both made it, force a play-off between them the next day.

The eighteenth at Cleveland is a brute, a 440 par-four hole, uphill all the way, with a brook guarding a trick green. Every yard of that hole was solid with people, and they were banked twelve deep around and behind the green near the clubhouse, with batteries of sound as well as still cameras waiting.

Well, I don't know why I'm putting a lot of suspense into this when you all know what happened. Scraggins laid one down, 230 yards, and Steubner passed him by ten yards. Scraggins was always behind Steubner on the tee shot. Did I say that that Dutchman could hit? He could. There were bunkers coming out from either side of the fairway on the near side of the brook, designed to catch a wood second that was rolling short. It called for a shot all right.

Scraggins pulled out a number-one iron. I just shuddered quietly and said nothing. Advice is something you don't give a pro. But I felt better when I saw how small it looked in those big hands of his. He laid into that one too. There wasn't a sound out of the crowd. He had his distance all right. Cleared bunkers and brook, but too far to the right. And then she started to come in. He had faded that iron from right to left to allow for the dip of the green. She lit, bit, and stopped. Six feet from the cup. They tell me they heard the roar that went up clear in downtown Cleveland. It was ten minutes before they could control the crowd so that Steubner could make his shot. He was badly shaken, but he showed some guts there. He pulled himself together and laid into a spoon that was as straight as a carpenter's rule. But he couldn't stop it. It hit and kicked on

up into the crowd on the edge. At that, the crowd saved him a
worse shot, because if they hadn't been there, his ball would
have gone yards over. As it was, they stopped it in the fringe
just off the green.

Steubner had to play first. He had the flag taken out, and
sighted the line, but he wasn't the man for the shot that day.
His nerves were gone. He had a downhill roll, and he chipped
too strong and rolled past the cup, three inches to one side and
three feet past.

Scraggins walked over to where I was sitting and said: "Get
ready to give me a hand, suh! There's goin' to be hell to pay
with this crowd when I sink this!"

Get it? When he sank it! So I went over and knelt down behind the official scorer, and the kid went up, took a look at the
line, and then knocked it in. Wow! Mallow & Company had the
Open Championship. My troubles were over. At least that's
what I thought. That just shows you how wrong you can be.

We hustled that kid through the hysterical crowd—I'm a
pretty big guy—and into the committee room reserved for the
champion, and shut the doors. There were three or four of the
Golf Association officials in the room, and a short, stoutish, gray-
haired man wearing glasses whom I didn't know, the kid, and
myself.

One of the officials said, "Son, do you know you shot a sixty-
five? That's the greatest golf I've ever seen."

The kid said: "Thank you, suh."

And then there was a loud knocking at the door. One of
the officials went to look and, when he opened it a little, J. Sears
Hammett pushed in. There was a flock of golf writers behind
him. Eight or nine. I took a quick feel in my pocket to see if my
contract with Scraggins was still there. It was. I noticed one of
the newspapermen was carrying a golf bag that looked like the
one Scraggins had been playing with.

The tournament chairman said: "See here. You can't come
breaking in here this way. This is a private room."

But, you know, they were in. Hammett showed two teeth and

said: "Sorry, but the press is just after a little story I suggested to them." Then he said to me: "Fowler, I heard you signed up Mr. Scraggins. Is that true?"

Boy, that was where I came in. I had been waiting for this moment. I reached down into my pocket and produced the contract with Scraggins's signature on it and said carelessly: "Why, yes. Certainly, it's true. Mr. Scraggins plays the A. R. Mallow Company products—Thunderbolt Ball and Tru-Distance Clubs, the Equipment of Champions."

"Yeh?" said J. Sears Hammett in a very nasty way. "I don't think. Boys, I promised you a good story, and here it is. An even better story than the one about MacDonough switching from our Accu-Putt diamond-center ball to the Thunderbolt in the middle of a round."

I said to myself: "Oh, oh!" I knew I shouldn't have tipped that story.

Hammett took the bag from the reporter and showed it to the kid. He said: "Is this your golf bag, Mr. Scraggins?"

The kid looked it hard for a minute and said: "Yes, suh, it is."

Hammett fished down into the side pocket and came up with three golf balls. "Are these the balls you have been playing with?"

The kid was getting mad, but there was nothing for him to do but answer. He said: "Yes, suh. They are."

"What are they called?"

"They're Skyrockets."

One of the boys said, "What the hell is a Skyrocket?"

The kid spoke up quickly and defiantly: "It's a thirty-five-cent ball. Down where I play, we cain't afford much better. I get 'em from the Reckmyer Company in St. Louis."

Hammett pulled out two or three clubs, a wood and two irons. They all had a funny little hump in the middle of the blade on the top edge.

"Ah, and your clubs. Did you buy them from the Reckmyer Company too?"

"No, suh," said Scraggins. "I made those mahself. Anything else you'd like to know?"

"No," said J. Sears Hammett. "That's enough. . . . There's your story, boys. A. R. Mallow Company products, nothing. This kid drove up here in a car patched together with string and adhesive tape, dead broke, and won the Open Championship with a record-breaking, last-round 65, made a hole in one and five consecutive threes, playing a thirty-five-cent, three-for-a-dollar golf ball"—so that was why Scraggins hadn't been getting more distance on his drives—"and a set of homemade clubs. Is that a yarn, or isn't it?"

It was, too. Several of the boys gave me a "Sorry, pal" look, but I was sunk, and I knew it. That story would make page 1 in every newspaper in the country, but I took one shot at bluffing it out.

"That's a lot of bunk," I said. "Hammett is sore because he muffed signing Scraggins. All you fellows know how those things go in the business. We bought the right to use Scraggins's name, all proper and regular." I hoped nobody knew or would find out what I had paid for his signature. "We have the right to use it in our advertising. Hammett would have done it, if he'd got there first. Scraggins will say he used the A. R. Mallow Company products and deny the other story, and Hammett can go to hell."

I looked to the kid for confirmation, but he was shaking his head. I should have known. He said: "I—I'm sorry, suh, but I cain't do that."

"Why not? It's done all the time."

"Because it ain't true, suh!"

Well, there it was. Every paper would headline that story, and if we tried to claim anything else in our advertising we would be a laughing-stock. And no business can afford to be laughed at.

J. Sears Hammett said: "How do you like those apples, Mr. Fowler?"

Me, I had no comeback. But that was where a new voice

chimed in. It was the little, stocky, gray-haired man with the eyeglasses. He said, "Ah—might I be permitted— Perhaps I can be of some service here?"

Everybody looked at him. Hammett said to him: "And who might you be?" That was a mistake. He didn't look like the kind of a guy one speaks to like that. And his answer almost jerked my knees out from under me, as though somebody had hit me across the back of the legs with a baseball bat.

"Wilcoxon is my name," he said very quietly, "C. A. Wilcoxon. Advertising manager for A. R. Mallow & Co. All these gentlemen"—indicating the officials—"know me."

Somehow I had the wild glimmer of a feeling that Mr. J. Sears Hammett was stepping into something, though, for the life of me, I couldn't see what. He showed four teeth and said: "Well, what I just told the boys goes for you too, then."

So that was C. A. Wilcoxon, the guy I had forgotten to contact. He merely said: "Thank you," and then turned to the kid and said: "Mr. Scraggins, I know you have been through a nerve-racking time, but may I ask you a few more questions?"

It was wonderful to see the kid cool right off under his gentling. He said: "Why, yes, suh, with pleasure."

"Are you sure you played with that ball—the Skyrocket?"

"Yes, suh. I'm sorry I cain't say anything different. I played with it every stroke of the way."

"That's fine, son. Don't you ever say anything else. The Skyrocket has been an A. R. Mallow Company product for the last ten days. We purchased the Reckmyer Company in our recent reorganization and expansion program. . . . Fowler, take a note: Page splash. We smash the words: 'Figure it out!' and then 'The Skyrocket. A. R. Mallow's thirty-five-cent ball won the Open Championship. What will our Thunderbolt, with the new improved gelatine inner layer, do for you?' Telegraph it to Burnett. He knows the kind of layouts I like. . . . And now those clubs of yours, Mr. Scraggins. You say you made them yourself?"

"Yes, suh."

"What is that little hump on the top of the blade for?"

The kid looked embarrassed.

"That—that's mah sighter, suh."

"Your sighter? Would you mind explaining?"

"Well, suh, I used to hit a lot of shots off the toe of mah club —my swing wasn't grooved properly—so I built a little hump right over the middle to sight on, and then practiced slow, so that I got the sighter back of the ball every time and then speeded up. It gives me confidence to know it's there now."

"And you designed these clubs for us and were trying them out?"

"Well, suh, I don't know."

"I don't quite understand, Mr. Scraggins. We are paying you ten thousand dollars a year retainer to design clubs for us, and you say you don't know. We are paying you ten thousand a year, are we not?"

The kid grinned suddenly. "If you say so, suh."

"I am saying so, in front of witnesses."

"Then it's so, suh!"

"Then all clubs designed by you belong to us and we have the exclusive rights to market them and to use your name. Hah! The Scraggins Sighter! . . . Fowler, take another note: 'Don't look at the ball; look at the sighter! The most sensational development in golf since the steel shaft. You can play any clubs, but you can't aim without a Scraggins Sighter, the exclusive design of the,' and so on." He stopped suddenly and turned to the golf writers and said very quietly: "That doesn't make your story any worse, does it, boys?"

"Hell," said Williamson, "it makes it better."

Wilcoxon turned to J. Sears Hammett and became my hero for life. "Thank you for setting it up for me, Mr. Hammett," he said. "The boys never would have believed me if I had tried to sell it to them as publicity."

The kid suddenly said: "Gee, excuse me. I have to see someone," and bolted out of the door.

I wanted out too, because I knew where he was going. Wilcoxon stopped me for a moment by putting his hand on my arm and said: "Great work, Fowler. Only a real advertising man could have appreciated the commercial value of a name like Scraggins. Congrats."

I couldn't look him in the eye, so I mumbled something about having to look after our man, and got out. Sure, they were down back of the fourth in the car. I said: "You're kissing the new National Open Golf Champion and a ten-thousand-dollar-a-year man."

The girl's eyes were wet. She said simply: "He told me."

"What?" I howled. "Do you mean to say you weren't out there, didn't see it?"

She shook her head. "It might make him nervous. He just likes to know I'm somewhere near."

The kid said: "Effie, lovely, from now on everything—everything you want—anything."

"Anything Ah want? Honey, there's something Ah want right now, more than anything else Ah've ever wanted besides you."

The kid climbed out of the car. "I'm getting it. What is it, Effie?"

"Another of those ham sandwiches."

Scraggins suddenly thrust his hand into his pocket, and his grin faded. I said: "Broke again, eh? There's a thousand-dollar winner's check waiting for you in the clubhouse, and a cup and a lot of applause. Go on in and get it. I'll stretch our contract and make it three ham sandwiches. And, anyway, I'm not paying for it."

I had just remembered that when J. Sears Hammett got through paying me our wager, I could buy two hundred dollars' worth of ham sandwiches; but I figured I'd get the Scragginses, Jet and Effie, a wedding present with that money instead.

THE PURIFICATION OF RODNEY SPELVIN

by P. G. Wodehouse

It was an afternoon on which one would have said that all Nature smiled. The air was soft and balmy; the links, fresh from the rains of spring, glistened in the pleasant sunshine; and down on the second tee young Clifford Wimple, in a new suit of plus-fours, had just sunk two balls in the lake, and was about to sink a third. No element, in short, was lacking that might be supposed to make for quiet happiness.

And yet on the forehead of the Oldest Member, as he sat beneath the chestnut-tree on the terrace overlooking the ninth green, there was a peevish frown; and his eye, gazing down at the rolling expanse of turf, lacked its customary genial benevolence. His favourite chair, consecrated to his private and personal use by unwritten law, had been occupied by another. That is the worst of a free country—liberty so often degenerates into licence.

The Oldest Member coughed.

"I trust," he said, "you find that chair comfortable?"

The intruder, who was the club's hitherto spotless secretary, glanced up in a goofy manner.

"Eh?"

"That chair—you find it fits snugly to the figure?"

"Chair? Figure? Oh, you mean this chair? Oh yes."

"I am gratified and relieved," said the Oldest Member.

There was a silence.

Reprinted by permission of the author and the author's agents, Scott Meredith Literary Agency, Inc.

"Look here," said the secretary, "what would you do in a case like this? You know I'm engaged?"

"I do. And no doubt your *fiancée* is missing you. Why not go in search of her?"

"She's the sweetest girl on earth."

"I should lose no time."

"But jealous. And just now I was in my office, and that Mrs. Pettigrew came in to ask if there was any news of the purse which she lost a couple of days ago. It had just been brought to my office, so I produced it; whereupon the infernal woman, in a most unsuitably girlish manner, flung her arms round my neck and kissed me on my bald spot. And at that moment Adela came in. Death," said the secretary, "where is thy sting?"

The Oldest Member's pique melted. He had a feeling heart.

"Most unfortunate. What did you say?"

"I hadn't time to say anything. She shot out too quick."

The Oldest Member clicked his tongue sympathetically.

"These misunderstandings between young and ardent hearts are very frequent," he said. "I could tell you at least fifty cases of the same kind. The one which I will select is the story of Jane Packard, William Bates, and Rodney Spelvin."

"You told me that the other day. Jane Packard got engaged to Rodney Spelvin, the poet, but the madness passed and she married William Bates, who was a golfer."

"This is another story of the trio."

"You told me that one, too. After Jane Packard married William Bates she fell once more under the spell of Spelvin, but repented in time."

"This is still another story. Making three in all."

The secretary buried his face in his hands.

"Oh, well," he said, "go ahead. What does anything matter now?"

"First," said the Oldest Member, "let us make ourselves comfortable. Take this chair. It is easier than the one in which you are sitting."

"No, thanks."

"I insist."

"Oh, all right."

"Woof!" said the Oldest Member, settling himself luxuri-
ously.

With an eye now full of kindly good-will, he watched young
Clifford Wimple play his fourth. Then, as the silver drops
flashed up into the sun, he nodded approvingly and began.

The story which I am about to relate (said the Oldest Member) begins at a time when Jane and William had been married
some seven years. Jane's handicap was eleven, William's twelve,
and their little son, Braid Vardon, had just celebrated his sixth
birthday.

Ever since that dreadful time, two years before, when, lured
by the glamour of Rodney Spelvin, she had taken a studio in
the artistic quarter, dropped her golf, and practically learned
to play the ukulele. Jane had been unremitting in her efforts to
be a good mother and to bring up her son on the strictest principles. And, in order that his growing mind might have every
chance, she had invited William's younger sister, Anastatia, to
spend a week or two with them and put the child right on the
true functions of the mashie. For Anastatia had reached the
semi-finals of the last Ladies' Open Championship and, unlike
many excellent players, had the knack of teaching.

On the evening on which this story opens the two women
were sitting in the drawing-room, chatting. They had finished
tea; and Anastatia, with the aid of a lump of sugar, a spoon,
and some crumbled cake, was illustrating the method by which
she had got out of the rough on the fifth at Squashy Hollow.

"You're wonderful!" said Jane, admiringly. "And such a good
influence for Braid! You'll give him his lesson to-morrow afternoon as usual?"

"I shall have to make it the morning," said Anastatia. "I've
promised to meet a man in town in the afternoon."

As she spoke there came into her face a look so soft and

dreamy that it roused Jane as if a bradawl had been driven into her leg. As her history has already shown, there was a strong streak of romance in Jane Bates.

"Who is he?" she asked, excitedly.

"A man I met last summer," said Anastatia.

And she sighed with such abandon that Jane could no longer hold in check her womanly nosiness.

"Do you love him?" she cried.

"Like bricks," whispered Anastatia.

"Does he love you?"

"Sometimes I think so."

"What's his name?"

"Rodney Spelvin."

"What!"

"Oh, I know he writes the most awful bilge," said Anastatia, defensively, misinterpreting the yowl of horror which had proceeded from Jane. "All the same, he's a darling."

Jane could not speak. She stared at her sister-in-law aghast. Although she knew that if you put a driver in her hands she could paste the ball into the next county, there always seemed to her something fragile and helpless about Anastatia. William's sister was one of those small, rose-leaf girls with big blue eyes to whom good men instinctively want to give a stroke a hole and on whom bad men automatically prey. And when Jane reflected that Rodney Spelvin had to all intents and purposes preyed upon herself, who stood five foot seven in her shoes and, but for an innate love of animals, could have felled an ox with a blow, she shuddered at the thought of how he would prey on this innocent half-portion.

"You really love him?" she quavered.

"If he beckoned to me in the middle of a medal round, I would come to him," said Anastatia.

Jane realised that further words were useless. A sickening sense of helplessness obsessed her. Something ought to be done about this terrible thing, but what could she do? She was so ashamed of her past madness that not even to warn this girl could she reveal that she had once been engaged to Rodney Spelvin herself; that he had recited poetry on the green while she was putting; and that, later, he had hypnotised her into taking William and little Braid to live in a studio full of samovars. These revelations would no doubt open Anastatia's eyes, but she could not make them.

And then, suddenly, Fate pointed out a way.

It was Jane's practice to go twice a week to the cinema palace in the village; and two nights later she set forth as usual and took her place just as the entertainment was about to begin.

At first she was only mildly interested. The title of the picture, "Tried in the Furnace," had suggested nothing to her. Being a regular patron of the silver screen, she knew that it might quite easily turn out to be an educational film on the subject of clinker-coal. But as the action began to develop she found herself leaning forward in her seat, blindly crushing a caramel between her fingers. For scarcely had the operator started to turn the crank when inspiration came to her.

Of the main plot of "Tried in the Furnace" she retained, when finally she reeled out into the open air, only a confused recollection. It had something to do with money not bringing happiness or happiness not bringing money, she could not remember which. But the part which remained graven upon her mind was the bit where Gloria Gooch goes by night to the apartments of the libertine, to beg him to spare her sister, whom he has entangled in his toils.

Jane saw her duty clearly. She must go to Rodney Spelvin and conjure him by the memory of their ancient love to spare Anastatia.

It was not the easiest of tasks to put this scheme into operation. Gloria Gooch, being married to a scholarly man who spent nearly all his time in a library a hundred yards long, had been fortunately situated in the matter of paying visits to libertines; but for Jane the job was more difficult. William expected her to play a couple of rounds with him in the morning and another in the afternoon, which rather cut into her time.

However, Fate was still on her side, for one morning at breakfast William announced that business called him to town.

"Why don't you come too?" he said.

Jane started.

"No. No, I don't think I will, thanks."

"Give you lunch somewhere."

"No. I want to stay here and do some practice-putting."

"All right. I'll try to get back in time for a round in the evening."

Remorse gnawed at Jane's vitals. She had never deceived William before. She kissed him with even more than her usual fondness when he left to catch the ten-forty-five. She waved to him till he was out of sight; then, bounding back into the house, leaped at the telephone and, after a series of conversations with the Marks-Morris Glue Factory, the Poor Pussy Home for Indigent Cats, and Messrs. Oakes, Oakes, and Parbury, dealers in fancy goods, at last found herself in communication with Rodney Spelvin.

"Rodney?" she said, and held her breath, fearful at this breaking of a two years' silence and yet loath to hear another strange voice say "Wadnumjerwant?" "Is that you, Rodney?"

"Yes. Who is that?"

"Mrs. Bates. Rodney, can you give me lunch at the Alcazar today at one?"

"Can I!" Not even the fact that some unknown basso had got on the wire and was asking if that was Mr. Bootle could blur the enthusiasm in his voice. "I should say so!"

"One o'clock, then," said Jane. His enthusiastic response had relieved her. If by merely speaking she could stir him so, to bend him to her will when they met face to face would be pie.

"One o'clock," said Rodney.

Jane hung up the receiver and went to her room to try on hats.

The impression came to Jane, when she entered the lobby of the restaurant and saw him waiting, that Rodney Spelvin looked somehow different from the Rodney she remembered. His handsome face had a deeper and more thoughtful expression, as if he had been through some ennobling experience.

"Well, here I am," she said, going to him and affecting a jauntiness which she did not feel.

He looked at her, and there was in his eyes that unmistakable goggle which comes to men suddenly addressed in a public spot by women whom, to the best of their recollection, they do not know from Eve.

"How are you?" he said. He seemed to pull himself together. "You're looking splendid."

"You're looking fine," said Jane.

"You're looking awfully well," said Rodney.

"You're looking awfully well," said Jane.

"You're looking fine," said Rodney.

There was a pause.

"You'll excuse me glancing at my watch," said Rodney. "I have an appointment to lunch with—er—somebody here, and it's past the time."

"But you're lunching with me," said Jane, puzzled.

"With you?"

"Yes. I rang you up this morning."

Rodney gaped.

"Was it you who 'phoned? I thought you said 'Miss Bates.' "

"No, Mrs. Bates."

"Mrs. Bates?"

"Mrs. Bates."

"Of course. You're Mrs. Bates."

"Had you forgotten me?" said Jane, in spite of herself a little piqued.

"Forgotten you, dear lady! As if I could!" said Rodney, with a return of his old manner. "Well, shall we go in and have lunch?"

"All right," said Jane.

She felt embarrassed and ill at ease. The fact that Rodney had obviously succeeded in remembering her only after the

"Genesis, Exodus, Leviticus, Numbers, Deuteronomy, Joshua,
Judges . . ."

effort of a lifetime seemed to her to fling a spanner into the
machinery of her plans at the very outset. It was going to be
difficult, she realised, to conjure him by the memory of their
ancient love to spare Anastatia; for the whole essence of the
idea of conjuring anyone by the memory of their ancient love
is that the party of the second part should be aware that there
ever was such a thing.

At the luncheon-table conversation proceeded fitfully. Rodney said that this morning he could have sworn it was going to
rain, and Jane said she had thought so, too, and Rodney said
that now it looked as if the weather might hold up, and Jane
said Yes, didn't it? and Rodney said he hoped the weather
would hold up because rain was such a nuisance, and Jane said
Yes, wasn't it? Rodney said yesterday had been a nice day, and
Jane said Yes, and Rodney said that it seemed to be getting a
little warmer, and Jane said Yes, and Rodney said that summer
would be here any moment now, and Jane said Yes, wouldn't
it? and Rodney said he hoped it would not be too hot this summer, but that, as a matter of fact, when you came right down to
it, what one minded was not so much the heat as the humidity,
and Jane said Yes, didn't one?

In short, by the time they rose and left the restaurant, not a
word had been spoken that could have provoked the censure of
the sternest critic. Yet William Bates, catching sight of them as
they passed down the aisle, started as if he had been struck by
lightning. He had happened to find himself near the Alcazar at
lunch-time and had dropped in for a chop; and, peering round
the pillar which had hidden his table from theirs, he stared after
them with saucer-like eyes.

"Oh, dash it!" said William.

This William Bates, as I have indicated in my previous
references to him, was not an abnormally emotional or temperamental man. Built physically on the lines of a motor-lorry, he
had much of that vehicle's placid and even phlegmatic outlook
on life. Few things had the power to ruffle William, but, unfortunately, it so happened that one of these things was Rodney

Spelvin. He had never been able entirely to overcome his jealousy of this man. It had been Rodney who had come within an ace of scooping Jane from him in the days when she had been Miss Packard. It had been Rodney who had temporarily broken up his home some years later by persuading Jane to become a member of the artistic set. And now, unless his eyes jolly well deceived him, this human gumboil was once more busy on his dastardly work. Too dashed thick, was William's view of the matter; and he gnashed his teeth in such a spasm of resentful fury that a man lunching at the next table told the waiter to switch off the electric fan, as it had begun to creak unendurably.

Jane was reading in the drawing-room when William reached home that night.

"Had a nice day?" asked William.

"Quite nice," said Jane.

"Play golf?" asked William.

"Just practised," said Jane.

"Lunch at the club?"

"Yes."

"I thought I saw that bloke Spelvin in town," said William.

Jane wrinkled her forehead.

"Spelvin? Oh, you mean Rodney Spelvin? Did you? I see he's got a new book coming out."

"You never run into him these days, do you?"

"Oh no. It must be two years since I saw him."

"Oh?" said William. "Well, I'll be going upstairs and dressing."

It seemed to Jane, as the door closed, that she heard a curious clicking noise, and she wondered for a moment if little Braid had got out of bed and was playing with the Mah-Jongg counters. But it was only William gnashing his teeth.

There is nothing sadder in this life than the spectacle of a husband and wife with practically identical handicaps drifting apart; and to dwell unnecessarily on such a spectacle is, to my mind, ghoulish. It is not my purpose, therefore, to weary you with a detailed description of the hourly widening of the breach between this once ideally united pair. Suffice it to say that within a few days of the conversation just related the entire atmosphere of this happy home had completely altered. On the Tuesday, William excused himself from the morning round on the plea that he had promised Peter Willard a match, and Jane said What a pity! On Tuesday afternoon William said that his head ached, and Jane said Isn't that too bad? On Wednesday morning William said he had lumbago, and Jane, her sensitive feelings now deeply wounded, said Oh, had he? After that, it came to be agreed between them by silent compact that they should play together no more.

Also, they began to avoid one another in the house. Jane would sit in the drawing-room, while William retired down the passage to his den. In short, if you had added a couple of ikons and a photograph of Trotzky, you would have had a *mise en scène* which would have fitted a Russian novel like the paper on the wall.

One evening, about a week after the beginning of this tragic state of affairs, Jane was sitting in the drawing-room, trying to read *Braid on Taking Turf*. But the print seemed blurred and the philosophy too metaphysical to be grasped. She laid the book down and stared sadly before her.

Every moment of these black days had affected Jane like a stymie on the last green. She could not understand how it was that William should have come to suspect, but that he did suspect was plain; and she writhed on the horns of a dilemma. All she had to do to win him back again was to go to him and tell him of Anastatia's fatal entanglement. But what would happen then? Undoubtedly he would feel it his duty as a brother to warn the girl against Rodney Spelvin; and Jane instinctively knew that William warning anyone against Rodney Spelvin would sound like a private of the line giving his candid opinion of the sergeant-major.

Inevitably, in this case, Anastatia, a spirited girl and deeply in love, would take offence at his words and leave the house.

And if she left the house, what would be the effect on little Braid's mashie-play? Already, in less than a fortnight, the gifted girl had taught him more about the chip-shot from ten to fifteen yards off the green than the local pro. had been able to do in two years. Her departure would be absolutely disastrous.

What it amounted to was that she must sacrifice her husband's happiness or her child's future; and the problem of which was to get the loser's end was becoming daily more insoluble.

She was still brooding on it when the postman arrived with the evening mail, and the maid brought the letters into the drawing-room.

Jane sorted them out. There were three for William, which she gave to the maid to take to him in his den. There were two for herself, both bills. And there was one for Anastatia, in the well-remembered handwriting of Rodney Spelvin.

Jane placed this letter on the mantelpiece, and stood looking at it like a cat at a canary. Anastatia was away for the day, visiting friends who lived a few stations down the line; and every womanly instinct in Jane urged her to get hold of a kettle and steam the gum off the envelope. She had almost made up her mind to disembowel the thing and write "Opened in error" on it, when the telephone suddenly went off like a bomb and nearly startled her into a decline. Coming at that moment it sounded like the Voice of Conscience.

"Hullo?" said Jane.

"Hullo!" replied a voice.

Jane clucked like a hen with uncontrollable emotion. It was Rodney.

"Is that you?" asked Rodney.

"Yes," said Jane.

And so it was, she told herself.

"Your voice is like music," said Rodney.

This may or may not have been the case, but at any rate it was exactly like every other female voice when heard on the telephone. Rodney prattled on without a suspicion.

"Have you got my letter yet?"

"No," said Jane. She hesitated. "What was in it?" she asked, tremulously.

"It was to ask you to come to my house to-morrow at four."

"To your house!" faltered Jane.

"Yes. Everything is ready. I will send the servants out, so that we shall be quite alone. You will come, won't you?"

The room was shimmering before Jane's eyes, but she regained command of herself with a strong effort.

"Yes," she said. "I will be there."

She spoke softly, but there was a note of menace in her voice. Yes, she would indeed be there. From the very moment when this man had made his monstrous proposal, she had been asking herself what Gloria Gooch would have done in a crisis like this. And the answer was plain. Gloria Gooch, if her sister-in-law was intending to visit the apartments of a libertine, would have gone there herself to save the poor child from the consequences of her infatuated folly.

"Yes," said Jane, "I will be there."

"You have made me the happiest man in the world," said Rodney. "I will meet you at the corner of the street at four, then." He paused. "What is that curious clicking noise?" he asked.

"I don't know," said Jane. "I noticed it myself. Something wrong with the wire, I suppose."

"I thought it was somebody playing the castanets. Until to-morrow, then, good-bye."

"Good-bye."

Jane replaced the receiver. And William, who had been listening to every word of the conversation on the extension in his den, replaced his receiver, too.

Anastatia came back from her visit late that night. She took her letter, and read it without comment. At breakfast next morning she said that she would be compelled to go into town that day.

"I want to see my dressmaker," she said.

"I'll come, too," said Jane. "I want to see my dentist."

"So will I," said William. "I want to see my lawyer."

"That will be nice," said Anastatia, after a pause.

"Very nice," said Jane, after another pause.

"We might all lunch together," said Anastatia. "My appointment is not till four."

"I should love it," said Jane. "My appointment is at four, too."

"So is mine," said William.

"What a coincidence!" said Jane, trying to speak brightly.

"Yes," said William. He may have been trying to speak brightly, too; but, if so, he failed. Jane was too young to have seen Salvini in "Othello," but, had she witnessed that great tragedian's performance, she could not have failed to be struck by the resemblance between his manner in the pillow scene and William's now.

"Then shall we all lunch together?" said Anastatia.

"I shall lunch at my club," said William, curtly.

"William seems to have a grouch," said Anastatia.

"Ha!" said William.

He raised his fork and drove it with sickening violence at his sausage.

So Jane had a quiet little woman's lunch at a confectioner's alone with Anastatia. Jane ordered a tongue-and-lettuce sandwich, two macaroons, marsh-mallows, ginger-ale and cocoa; and Anastatia ordered pineapple chunks with whipped cream, tomatoes stuffed with beetroot, three dill pickles, a raspberry nut sundae, and hot chocolate. And, while getting outside this garbage, they talked merrily, as women will, of every subject but the one that really occupied their minds. When Anastatia got up and said good-bye with a final reference to her dressmaker, Jane shuddered at the depths of deceit to which the modern girl can sink.

It was now about a quarter to three, so Jane had an hour to kill before going to the rendezvous. She wandered about the streets, and never had time appeared to her to pass so slowly, never had a city been so congested with hard-eyed and suspicious citizens. Every second person she met seemed to glare at her as if he or she had guessed her secret.

The very elements joined in the general disapproval. The sky had turned a sullen grey, and far-away thunder muttered faintly, like an impatient golfer held up on the tee by a slow foursome. It was a relief when at length she found herself at the back of Rodney Spelvin's house, standing before the scullery window, which it was her intention to force with the pocket-knife won in happier days as second prize in a competition at a summer hotel for those with handicaps above eighteen.

But the relief did not last long. Despite the fact that she was about to enter this evil house with the best motives, a sense of almost intolerable guilt oppressed her. If William should ever get to know of this! Wow! felt Jane.

How long she would have hesitated before the window, one cannot say. But at this moment, glancing guiltily round, she happened to catch the eye of a cat which was sitting on a near-by wall, and she read in this cat's eye such cynical derision that the urge came upon her to get out of its range as quickly as possible. It was a cat that had manifestly seen a lot of life, and it was plainly putting an entirely wrong construction on her behaviour. Jane shivered, and, with a quick jerk prised the window open and climbed in.

It was two years since she had entered this house, but once she had reached the hall she remembered its topography perfectly. She mounted the stairs to the large studio sitting-room on the first floor, the scene of so many Bohemian parties in that dark period of her artistic life. It was here, she knew, that Rodney would bring his victim.

The studio was one of those dim, over-ornamented rooms which appeal to men like Rodney Spelvin. Heavy curtains hung in front of the windows. One corner was cut off by a high-backed Chesterfield. At the far end was an alcove, curtained like the windows. Once Jane had admired this studio, but now it made her shiver. It seemed to her one of those nests in which, as the sub-title of *Tried in the Furnace* had said, only eggs of evil are hatched. She paced the thick carpet restlessly, and suddenly there came to her the sound of footsteps on the stairs.

Jane stopped, every muscle tense. The moment had arrived. She faced the door, tight-lipped. It comforted her a little in this crisis to reflect that Rodney was not one of those massive Ethel M. Dell libertines who might make things unpleasant for an intruder. He was only a welter-weight egg of evil; and, if he tried to start anything, a girl of her physique would have little or no difficulty in knocking the stuffing out of him.

The footsteps reached the door. The handle turned. The door opened. And in strode William Bates, followed by two men in bowler hats.

"Ha!" said William.

Jane's lips parted, but no sound came from them. She staggered back a pace or two. William, advancing into the centre of the room, folded his arms and gazed at her with burning eyes.

"So," said William, and the words seemed forced like drops of vitriol from between his clenched teeth, "I find you here, dash it!"

Jane choked convulsively. Years ago, when an innocent child, she had seen a conjurer produce a rabbit out of a top-hat which an instant before had been conclusively proved to be empty. The sudden apparition of William affected her with much the same sensations as she had experienced then.

"How-ow-ow——?" she said.

"I beg your pardon?" said William, coldly.

"How-ow-ow——?"

"Explain yourself," said William.

"How-ow-ow did you get here? And who-oo-oo are these men?"

William seemed to become aware for the first time of the presence of his two companions. He moved a hand in a hasty gesture of introduction.

"Mr. Reginald Brown and Mr. Cyril Delancey—my wife," he said, curtly.

The two men bowed slightly and raised their bowler hats.

"Pleased to meet you," said one.

"Most awfully charmed," said the other.

"They are detectives," said William.

"Detectives!"

"From the Quick Results Agency," said William. "When I became aware of your clandestine intrigue, I went to the agency and they gave me their two best men."

"Oh, well," said Mr. Brown, blushing a little.

"Most frightfully decent of you to put it that way," said Mr. Delancey.

William regarded Jane sternly.

"I knew you were going to be here at four o'clock," he said. "I overheard you making the assignation on the telephone."

"Oh, William!"

"Woman," said William, "where is your paramour?"

"Really, really," said Mr. Delancey, deprecatingly.

"Keep it clean," urged Mr. Brown.

"Your partner in sin, where is he? I am going to take him and tear him into little bits and stuff him down his throat and make him swallow himself."

"Fair enough," said Mr. Brown.

"Perfectly in order," said Mr. Delancey.

Jane uttered a stricken cry.

"William," she screamed, "I can explain all."

"All?" said Mr. Delancey.

"All?" said Mr. Brown.

"All," said Jane.

"All?" said William.

"All," said Jane.

William sneered bitterly.

"I'll bet you can't," he said.

"I'll bet I can," said Jane.

"Well?"

"I came here to save Anastatia."

"Anastatia?"

"Anastatia."

"My sister?"

"Your sister."

"His sister Anastatia," explained Mr. Brown to Mr. Delancey in an undertone.

"What from?" asked William.

"From Rodney Spelvin. Oh, William, can't you understand?"

"No, I'm dashed if I can."

"I, too," said Mr. Delancey, "must confess myself a little fogged. And you, Reggie?"

"Completely, Cyril," said Mr. Brown, removing his bowler hat with a puzzled frown, examining the maker's name, and putting it on again.

"The poor child is infatuated with this man."

"With the bloke Spelvin?"

"Yes. She is coming here with him at four o'clock."

"Important," said Mr. Brown, producing a notebook and making an entry.

"Important, if true," agreed Mr. Delancey.

"But I heard you making the appointment with the bloke Spelvin over the 'phone," said William.

"He thought I was Anastatia. And I came here to save her."

William was silent and thoughtful for a few moments.

"It all sounds very nice and plausible," he said, "but there's just one thing wrong. I'm not a very clever sort of bird, but I can see where your story slips up. If what you say is true, where is Anastatia?"

"Just coming in now," whispered Jane. "Hist!"

"Hist, Reggie!" whispered Mr. Delancey.

They listened. Yes, the front door had banged, and feet were ascending the staircase.

"Hide!" said Jane, urgently.

"Why?" said William.

"So that you can overhear what they say and jump out and confront them."

"Sound," said Mr. Delancey.

"Very sound," said Mr. Brown.

The two detectives concealed themselves in the alcove. William retired behind the curtains in front of the window. Jane dived behind the Chesterfield. A moment later the door opened.

Crouching in her corner, Jane could see nothing, but every word that was spoken came to her ears; and with every syllable her horror deepened.

"Give me your things," she heard Rodney say, "and then we will go upstairs."

Jane shivered. The curtains by the window shook. From the direction of the alcove there came a soft scratching sound, as the two detectives made an entry in their note-books.

For a moment after this there was silence. Then Anastatia uttered a sharp, protesting cry.

"Ah, no, no! Please, please!"

"But why not?" came Rodney's voice.

"It is wrong—wrong."

"I can't see why."

"It is, it is! You must not do that. Oh, please, please don't hold so tight."

There was a swishing sound, and through the curtains before the window a large form burst. Jane raised her head above the Chesterfield.

William was standing there, a menacing figure. The two detectives had left the alcove and were moistening their pencils. And in the middle of the room stood Rodney Spelvin, stooping slightly and grasping Anastatia's parasol in his hands.

"I don't get it," he said. "Why is it wrong to hold the dam' thing tight?" He looked up and perceived his visitors. "Ah, Bates," he said, absently. He turned to Anastatia again. "I should have thought that the tighter you held it, the more force you would get into the shot."

"But don't you see, you poor zimp," replied Anastatia, "that you've got to keep the ball straight. If you grip the shaft as if you were a drowning man clutching at a straw and keep your

fingers under like that, you'll pull like the dickens and probably land out of bounds or in the rough. What's the good of
getting force into the shot if the ball goes in the wrong direction, you cloth-headed goof?"

"I see now," said Rodney, humbly. "How right you always
are!"

"Look here," interrupted William, folding his arms. "What
is the meaning of this?"

"You want to grip firmly but lightly," said Anastatia.

"Firmly but lightly," echoed Rodney.

"What is the meaning of this?"

"And with the fingers. Not with the palms."

"What is the meaning of this?" thundered William. "Anastatia, what are you doing in this man's rooms?"

"Giving him a golf lesson, of course. And I wish you
wouldn't interrupt."

"Yes, yes," said Rodney, a little testily. "Don't interrupt,
Bates, there's a good fellow. Surely you have things to occupy
you elsewhere?"

"We'll go upstairs," said Anastatia, "where we can be alone."

"You will not go upstairs," barked William.

"We shall get on much better there," explained Anastatia.
"Rodney has fitted up the top-floor back as an indoor practising
room."

Jane darted forward with a maternal cry.

"My poor child, has the scoundrel dared to delude you by
pretending to be a golfer? Darling, he is nothing of the kind."

Mr. Reginald Brown coughed. For some moments he had
been twitching restlessly.

"Talking of golf," he said, "it might interest you to hear of a
little experience I had the other day at Marshy Moor. I had
got a nice drive off the tee, nothing record-breaking, you understand, but straight and sweet. And what was my astonishment
on walking up to play my second to find——"

"A rather similar thing happened to me at Windy Waste last

Tuesday," interrupted Mr. Delancey. "I had hooked my drive the merest trifle, and my caddie said to me, 'You're out of bounds,' 'I am not out of bounds,' I replied, perhaps a little tersely, for the lad had annoyed me by a persistent habit of sniffing. 'Yes, you are out of bounds,' he said. 'No, I am not out of bounds,' I retorted. Well, believe me or believe me not, when I got up to my ball——"

"Shut up!" said William.

"Just as you say, sir," replied Mr. Delancey, courteously.

Rodney Spelvin drew himself up, and in spite of her loathing for his villainy Jane could not help feeling what a noble and romantic figure he made. His face was pale, but his voice did not falter.

"You are right," he said. "I am not a golfer. But with the help of this splendid girl here, I hope humbly to be one some day. Ah, I know what you are going to say," he went on, raising a hand. "You are about to ask how a man who has wasted his life as I have done can dare to entertain the mad dream of ever acquiring a decent handicap. But never forget," proceeded Rodney, in a low, quivering voice, "that Walter J. Travis was nearly forty before he touched a club, and a few years later he won the British Amateur."

"True," murmured William.

"True, true," said Mr. Delancey and Mr. Brown. They lifted their bowler hats reverently.

"I am thirty-three years old," continued Rodney, "and for fourteen of those thirty-three years I have been writing poetry —aye, and novels with a poignant sex-appeal, and if ever I gave a thought to this divine game it was but to sneer at it. But last summer I saw the light."

"Glory! Glory!" cried Mr. Brown.

"One afternoon I was persuaded to try a drive. I took the club with a mocking, contemptuous laugh." He paused, and a wild light came into his eyes. "I brought off a perfect pip," he said, emotionally. "Two hundred yards and as straight as a whistle. And, as I stood there gazing after the ball, something seemed to run up my spine and bite me in the neck. It was the golf-germ."

"Always the way," said Mr. Brown. "I remember the first drive I ever made. I took a nice easy stance——"

"The first drive I made," said Mr. Delancey, "you won't believe this, but it's a fact, was a full——"

"From that moment," continued Rodney Spelvin, "I have had but one ambition—to somehow or other, cost what it might, get down into single figures." He laughed bitterly. "You see," he said, "I cannot even speak of this thing without splitting my infinitives. And even as I split my infinitives, so did I split my drivers. After that first heavenly slosh I didn't seem able to do anything right."

He broke off, his face working. William cleared his throat awkwardly.

"Yes, but dash it," he said, "all this doesn't explain why I find you alone with my sister in what I might call your lair."

"The explanation is simple," said Rodney Spelvin. "This sweet girl is the only person in the world who seems able to simply and intelligently and in a few easily understood words make clear the knack of the thing. There is none like her, none. I have been to pro after pro, but not one has been any good to me. I am a temperamental man, and there is a lack of sympathy and human understanding about these professionals which jars on my artist soul. They look at you as if you were a half-witted child. They click their tongues. They make odd Scotch noises. I could not endure the strain. And then this wonderful girl, to whom in a burst of emotion I had confided my unhappy case, offered to give me private lessons. So I went with her to some of those indoor practising places. But here, too, my sensibilities were racked by the fact that unsympathetic eyes observed me. So I fixed up a room here where we could be alone."

"And instead of going there," said Anastatia, "we are wasting half the afternoon talking."

William brooded for a while. He was not a quick thinker.

"Well, look here," he said at length, "this is the point. This is the nub of the thing. This is where I want you to follow me very closely. Have you asked Anastatia to marry you?"

"Marry me?" Rodney gazed at him, shocked. "Have I asked her to marry me? I, who am not worthy to polish the blade of her niblick! I, who have not even a thirty handicap, ask a girl to marry me who was in the semi-final of last year's Ladies' Open! No, no, Bates, I may be a *vers-libre* poet, but I have some sense of what is fitting. I love her, yes. I love her with a fervour which causes me to frequently and for hours at a time lie tossing sleeplessly upon my pillow. But I would not dare to ask her to marry me."

Anastatia burst into a peal of girlish laughter.

"You poor chump!" she cried. "Is that what has been the matter all this time! I couldn't make out what the trouble was. Why, I'm crazy about you. I'll marry you any time you give the word."

Rodney reeled.

"What!"

"Of course I will."

"Anastatia!"

"Rodney!"

He folded her in his arms.

"Well, I'm dashed," said William. "It looks to me as if I had been making rather a lot of silly fuss about nothing. Jane, I wronged you."

"It was my fault."

"No, no!"

"Yes, yes!"

"Jane!"

"William!"

He folded her in his arms. The two detectives, having entered the circumstances in their note-books, looked at one another with moist eyes.

"Cyril!" said Mr. Brown.

"Reggie!" said Mr. Delancey.

Their hands met in a brotherly clasp.

"And so," concluded the Oldest Member, "all ended happily. The storm-tossed lives of William Bates, Jane Packard, and Rodney Spelvin came safely at long last into harbour. At the subsequent wedding William and Jane's present of a complete golfing outfit, including eight dozen new balls, a cloth cap, and a pair of spiked shoes, was generally admired by all who inspected the gifts during the reception."

"From that time forward the four of them have been inseparable. Rodney and Anastatia took a little cottage close to that of William and Jane, and rarely does a day pass without a close foursome between the two couples. William and Jane being steady tens and Anastatia scratch and Rodney a persevering eighteen, it makes an ideal match."

"What does?" asked the secretary, waking from his reverie.

"This one."

"Which?"

"I see," said the Oldest Member, sympathetically, "that your troubles, weighing on your mind, have caused you to follow my little narrative less closely than you might have done. Never mind, I will tell it again."

"The story" (said the Oldest Member) "which I am about to relate begins at a time when——"

OPEN WARFARE

by James E. Gunn

*Tournament testing had made Jim a machine golfer
—but he faced a player with no nerves at all!*

The tournament hadn't been conceded, exactly, but everybody agreed that Jim was the man to beat. Everybody—the
professionals, the fans, the sportswriters . . .

> Slim Jim Pearson, the hard-luck boy with the velvet swing,
> is finally going to cop that U.S. Open crown. Look up these
> words five days from now.
> He's no longer the Jim Pearson who swung eight times at
> a ball buried in a sand trap in 1957, or the Jim Pearson who
> four-putted a green and picked up in disgust in 1960 when
> he could have parred in to win. He's the Jim Pearson who
> has won ten major tournaments on the winter circuit, the last
> five straight, and collected $25,000 with a sparkling perform-
> ance of cool, steady golf . . .

The Open didn't pay off anything close to $25,000, of course.
The extras made up the difference. Fame was negotiable—
testimonials, articles, books, sporting goods contracts.

Fifty thousand dollars . . .

And the money didn't mean a thing. It was just the price tag
on a girl named Alice Hatcher, who was no different from any
other attractive young girl except that Jim Pearson happened to
love her, and her father happened to have uncountable millions

of dollars. Like the marching Chinese, while you were counting them, more millions were born.

Pudgy Sam Hatcher, who would never break ninety, concealed his steely mind behind a soft face. Only after he was trapped, had Jim recognized the inflexible purpose and the wily cleverness behind it.

"You're a good golfer, Jim," Hatcher said, easing off his spiked shoes with a sigh, "even if you can't teach me anything. We've been good to you at the Country Club. I want you to do something for me."

"Yes, sir?"

"Stay away from Alice!"

"But, Mr. Hatcher!"

"I won't have her marrying a man who has nothing but coordination and muscles. When I was only your age, I was making $50,000 a year. It takes brains to do that. Brains get more valuable. Muscles deteriorate. There's nothing muscles can't do that a machine can't do better."

"You don't think I could make $50,000?" Jim said angrily.

"I know damn well you couldn't," Hatcher said. "You haven't got the guts. If you ever got within sight of it, you'd blow up —like you did in St. Louis."

Before Jim had known it, he was wrapped up, sealed, addressed and—he feared—headed for the dead-letter office. If he could make $50,000 in a year, he could have Alice—if he could get her—with Hatcher's blessing. If he failed—well, he wouldn't see Alice again.

Jim had had a long time to think about it—the better part of a year—and to admire the way he had been outmaneuvered. Fifty thousand dollars—a shrewd figure. Right at the top of the possible. Not impossible, but so close to it as to be practically indistinguishable.

There had been side effects. Touring the tournament circuit had kept him away from Alice as effectively as walls and armed guards. And somehow—Jim had a good idea how—Alice had learned about the bet. A few days after Jim had won his first big tournament, he got a note.

I won't be bought and sold. Al.

That was that—or was it? For a few days, Jim had been angry with a blind anger that cost him $5,000. And then he saw a picture over a caption that read—

Industrialist Samuel Hatcher bids bon voyage to his daughter, Alice, who will spend the next six months studying in England.

Jim studied Hatcher's expression of bland triumph. Suddenly, his anger became something else—something cold and determined. Nerves? Temperament? He didn't have any.

Each long, low, flat drive was a fist in Hatcher's face—each sure putt a dagger in his back. The prize money rolled in. The tournaments dropped behind, conquered, forgotten. And then it was Open time. The bet was almost won. And if Hatcher thought he couldn't lose, Jim had a surprise for him.

He would take the whole fifty thousand, Jim thought, and lay it in front of Alice and say, "I wasn't buying you, I was buying the right to tell you that I love you." And if that didn't work, he would set fire to the putting greens at night—all 18 of them.

Maybe Hatcher knew finance—but he didn't know golf, and he didn't know the way of a man with a maiden.

All it took was the U.S. Open. And nobody else could keep up the pace for four rounds. Jim grinned—it was going to be that easy.

And then Saul showed up.

The first hint of disaster came at the practice tee. Jim was methodically sharpening up his No. 1 woods when the spectators deserted him. The appreciative murmurs died away. Jim looked up. The mob had clotted around another tee, several hundred feet away. Jim waved the caddy in and sauntered toward the attraction that had taken the crowd away from the man picked to win the Open. Not annoyed, not upset—just curious.

From a knoll behind the other tee, Jim got a good view of the big, tall golfer. The tanned, impassive features were unfamiliar. And then the driver came down in a glittering arc.

Jim pursed his lips in a soundless whistle. He knew all the professionals and most of the top-notch amateurs. No stranger should have a swing that good, that effortless, that grooved.

But the real shock came when Jim followed the smooth arc of the glistening ball. Jim's eyes were good, or he might have lost it as it dwindled in the distance. The caddy stood at least 280 yards down the fairway, with a ball bag in his hands. He didn't move—and the ball dropped right in the middle of the sack.

Accident, Jim thought shakily. But it happened a second time and a third, and so so on until Jim lost count. Every club in the bag was used with the same incredible accuracy. The caddy had a snap job—he didn't have to stoop once.

Trick-shot artist, Jim told himself. *Wait until he gets in competition.* But there wasn't anybody that good. Not even old Joe Kirkwood.

"Quite a spectacle, eh, Jim?"

Jim knew that brisk, businesslike voice. He turned. "Hello, Hatcher." He tried to keep his voice friendly.

Hatcher was as fat as ever. "Must be unnerving to watch something like that."

"I can stand it."

"But will you be able to stand it when the going gets rough?" Hatcher asked solicitously. "Or will you blow up like you always do? It would be too bad, just when you're so close."

"You haven't forgotten our bet, then?"

"Of course not, Jim." He chuckled. "I never forget anything."

"You've kept close track," Jim said steadily. "What about Alice? Has she kept track, too?"

"I haven't the slightest idea. She's in England, you know. I suspect, however, that she has forgotten all about you."

"She'll remember. The next four days will remind her."

"I suppose so," Hatcher said thoughtfully. "Sadly, I'm afraid. Saul will see to that."

"Saul?"

Hatcher nooded toward the golfer on the tee. "Saul."

Jim's eyes narrowed. "You know him?"

Hatcher was enigmatic. "I brought him here—my own personal entry. His first tournament was the qualifying round, and he's going to beat you out of the Open."

Score up another one for Hatcher. "Then he's got something to learn," Jim said confidently.

Hatcher turned to watch Saul. The clean, crisp smack of club against ball came with clockwork regularity. "Just a dumb, country boy," he said. "Never saw a golf club until a few months ago. But I think he might teach you something, Jim."

Jim's gaze drifted irresistibly to the golf balls soaring down the fairway into the canvas sack. That was what he would have to beat.

Jim's threesome teed off early in the morning. Jim felt good. A night's sound sleep had brought back his self-confidence. He was going to enjoy winning.

From the moment he drew his driver out of the leather bag, he knew he was going to have a good day. The grip fitted snugly into his hand. His flat, thin muscles rippled without a twinge. His practice swings were loose and effortless.

The crowd was sympathetic. That always helped. They wanted to see him burn up the course. He had another rooter, too, and there was another thousand in the bank. An eager young man from a sporting goods company had talked him into using a new golf ball. The company had planned a big campaign to advertise it. *Guaranteed to add twenty yards to every drive.* They would like to add, *Used by Jim Pearson when he won the U.S. Open.*

They'd have that chance, Jim thought firmly. He knelt to tee up his ball.

"Don't tighten up yet," said a voice he was coming to know too well. "Give the crowd a show for its money."

Jim turned. "You can't have much confidence in your champion, Hatcher, if you have to try psychological tricks like this."

"All the confidence in the world, Jim," Hatcher said breezily. "I just don't take chances. *You* take chances. That's why you always lose."

"Don't be too sure. I haven't lost yet."

Hatcher shrugged. "You haven't seen Alice, have you?"

Jim forced himself to take three deep breaths. When he stepped up to his ball, he was calm. He took a few experimental waggles. The crowd sighed as his deceptively easy swing sent his first drive soaring down the fairway. It was long and straight. The slightest hook would send the ball scooting down a slope to the left behind a clump of trees on the 530-yard par-five hole.

It wasn't too tough a birdie. The next four dropped in par. Cameras clicked and whirred. The crowd applauded, held its breath or groaned in sympathy.

On the par-five sixth, Jim relaxed and lit a cigarette. It was a good day to be playing. The sky was an improbable blue— the fairway was green and springy. Jim took a deep breath and smiled at the crowd. They liked that. They applauded.

Jim got his second shock.

The white flash of a girl's face, the arch of a slim body in a cool summer dress . . . Jim started toward her.

"Al," he said, then stopped. He cursed silently. He was beginning to see things.

He tossed his cigarette away and ground it into the turf. The sixth fell, nevertheless, in birdie figures. Three more pars made him 34 for the first nine. Not brilliant golf, but the kind that won tournaments. And two putts might have dropped, but hadn't.

The second nine was even better. Jim played smoothly, confidently. The crowd, that had been tense and excited over his four birdies and three pars, began slipping away at the sixteenth. That didn't bother him. A roar of approval drifted faintly over the fairway from time to time. On the last two holes he got a birdie and a par.

He glanced quickly over the card. A 34 and a 32, for 66 on the eighteen. Six birdies—twelve pars. Three more like that should win easily.

The crowd around the eighteenth green opened in front of him as he walked toward the clubhouse. Strangers reached out to shake his hand and pound him on the back. Jim smiled for them.

"How was the golf ball, huh?" It was the eager young man.

"Fine," Jim said.

"I'll leave a couple of dozen with your caddy."

"Fine," Jim said.

Jim watched his score being posted on the big board. Most of the field was still out, but he was ahead of the closest competitor by three strokes. As he turned away, the crowd at the eighteenth green roared.

That usually meant a hot round. Jim waited. Maybe some joker had tied his 66.

A big, tall, bronzed golfer plodded silently through the crowd. Nobody shook his hand. Nobody pounded his back. But they looked at him with awe. Jim watched him for a moment and frowned.

He turned to watch Saul's score go down on the board, but two men were talking behind him. One of them was a syndicated sports writer.

"*Wow!*" the columnist said. "Clockwork—precision! There's never been anything like it. Nerves? He never opened his mouth."

The other man mumbled something.

"Yes, I said it and I'll take it all back," the writer replied. "Saul's the man to beat, not Pearson."

Jim flushed, but the other man spoke up. "I'll still bet on Pearson."

"And I'll take all you can scrape together. This Saul's a machine—every shot just where he wants it. Let me put that down before I forget it—Silent Saul, the Mechanical Man."

Jim looked back to the scoreboard. His eyes flashed quickly across the row of precise figures:

$$4 \ 3 \ 4 \ 4 \ 3 \ 4 \ 3 \ 4 \ 3—32$$
$$3 \ 3 \ 4 \ 4 \ 4 \ 3 \ 3 \ 4 \ 4 \ \ 32—64$$

That tied the course record and beat him by two. The procession of threes and fours was fantastic.

"What's the matter, Jim?" Hatcher said from behind him. "You don't look well."

Jim turned, smiling. It was an effort, but he made it. "One round isn't a tournament," he said casually.

Hatcher sighed. "Comfort yourself while you can. Saul's just getting warmed up. He's that mythical thing, the perfect golfer, but he's dumb. No brains, Jim—no brains at all."

Jim stared at the sports-page headline and lost all appetite for breakfast.

SILENT SAUL

THE MAN TO BEAT

Pearson's 66
Places Second
To Record-Tying 64

Jim Pearson, the fair-haired boy of the tournament circuit, rolled up a sparkling 66 for yesterday's first round of the U.S. Open. But only a few minutes later, Silent Saul, mystery man of the tournament, blazed in . . .

Jim set his jaw firmly and forced down his bacon and eggs. The Open wasn't over yet. There was a lot of golf yet to be played. He glanced through his mail. An English stamp! *England*. He ripped open the letter.

A girl can change her mind. Win the Open—for me.

Al.

Jim waited until his breathing slowed. He got up, stuffed the note in his pocket, sauntered to the practice tee.

So she *was* in England. But if she loved him, why did this one tournament matter? What difference did $50,000 make? He tried to see the situation from Alice's viewpoint and shook his head. Maybe Hatcher was right. Maybe he wasn't so smart. But there was one thing he *was* good at, one thing at which, when he was feeling his best, he was unbeatable.

An hour's practice went well. His hands felt good today, slim and strong. That was always a sign of readiness. He strolled over to the starting tee.

The crowd was small. When he stepped up to his ball, there was only a smattering of applause. His drive was as straight as the day before and longer by almost 20 yards.

Jim played grimly and accurately. From ahead, as regularly as a pulse, came roars of approval. That was Saul, he thought. His game became, if anything, crisper.

The crowd was larger as he teed off on number 10. The underdog, he thought—they always pull for the underdog if he's making a game fight. But if he appeared to be certain to lose— well, they were human. They liked to be on the winning side.

His second nine was a duplicate of the day before—another 32. But the applause, as he dropped the putt on the eighteenth, was perfunctory.

Jim puzzled over it as he handed the putter to his caddy. He had equalled Saul's record-tying score of yesterday. Surely Saul hadn't repeated. His luck had to run out.

It was worse than that. It was—

$$4 \ 2 \ 3 \ 4 \ 3 \ 4 \ 3 \ 4 \ 4—31$$
$$4 \ 4 \ 3 \ 3 \ 3 \ 4 \ 4 \ \ 31—62$$

He had broken the record and beaten Jim by two strokes. Jim was four strokes down. He turned away, his face set and hard. He wasn't even surprised to find Hatcher behind him.

"What have you got to say, Jim," Hatcher inquired.

What Jim wanted to say was unprintable. After a moment, however, he forced a smile.

"That's better," Hatcher said. "The good old American tradition. Good sportsmanship—that sort of thing. Bushwash! They pay off on winners."

"You haven't seen anything yet," Jim said.

"You know," Hatcher said, "I was just going to say the same thing."

Jim brushed past him and walked toward the clubhouse. There was something terribly wrong with the whole setup. In real life, things didn't happen like this. People didn't pop out of nowhere and break all records to win the Open. Men didn't take up the game and become perfect golfers in a few months. Hatcher had said either too much or too little.

Saul had a weakness. There was no perfect golfer. But how could Jim find that weakness and take advantage of it!

"*Dave,*" Jim said. He caught the scurrying tournament manager by a sleeve.

"There's some dispute about a penalty," Dave said, trying to get away.

"When am I supposed to go out tomorrow?"

"Afternoon."

"And Saul?"

"A little later. What *is* this?" Dave scowled.

"Let me go out in the morning," Jim said.

"Well, I don't—"

"It means a lot," Jim said quickly. "I've got an appointment in the afternoon."

"Well," Dave said, "I don't see how it can hurt . . ."

"Thanks, Dave. You won't regret it." And, as the official broke into a trot Jim added under his breath, "But someone will."

Hatcher hadn't been content with a simple bet, not even with all the odds in his favor. He had played all angles and, when he was about to lose, had pulled a rabbit out of his hat. Any way to win. That was a two-sided game, also.

The out nine bowed for Jim in 32 again, as he missed his usual birdie on the first hole and got it back with a 2 on the second. On the back nine, he slipped a stroke to a 33. But he refused to blow up under the pressure of Saul's four-stroke lead.

His 195 total broke several fifty-four hole records. And yet Saul could drop to a 69 to tie. Jim had a hunch Saul's game wasn't going to break. Not today.

He shook off the reporters, gobbled a sandwich and returned to the starting tee almost unnoticed. He was lost in a crowd of thousands, gathered to see Silent Saul blaze to new heights.

Saul's effortless swing belted the ball over 300 yards down the fairway, straight as the shortest distance between two points. Jim wasn't watching. His eyes were half-closed, studying the mental picture of that swing.

There was something wrong with it, something naggingly suspicious about it. Jim couldn't pin it down. It seemed—familiar —and yet Jim felt he'd never seen it before that first mad day.

Jim tramped the fairway with the rest of the spectators, drawing close enough to hear anything Saul might say to his caddy or Hatcher. There wasn't anything to hear. Saul was silent as a mute.

Saul sent one sweeping glance toward the green, 240 yards distant, selected a club from the bag, took a few oddly-familiar waggling gestures before he set his driver behind the ball and swung. The ball lit on the front edge of the green and bit.

Saul's putt rolled straight for the hole until an unruly blade of grass deflected it an inch to the right of the cup. A birdie.

That was the pattern. The only luck Saul was playing in was bad. It rode his shoulders pickaback, spoiling the incredible accuracy of his shots. A gust of wind caught a lofting seven-iron pitch—a bad bounce called up a brilliant recovery—a spectator stopped the ball short of the green with his head.

Jim smiled ruefully. Against this combination of bad breaks, Saul had whipped the front nine in 32.

What would he do when he was lucky?

And still those familiarities of swing plagued Jim's memory. Wild ideas flitted through his mind—disguise—mass hallucination. He pushed them away. This was real. And there had never been anyone this good.

The only inconsistency about Saul was his unnecessary preparatory movements. The sports writer was right. Saul was a golfing machine, tuned to perfection for just one thing. And he did nothing else. He didn't even talk.

At the start of the eleventh hole, Hatcher caught sight of him. "Ah," he said, "come to take some lessons?"

"I hope to learn something," Jim said quietly.

"Watch Saul—you will." Hatcher smiled. "Of course, the papers will eat this up. 'Pearson watches Saul spike hopes for Open.' "

Jim didn't answer. He was watching Saul again. His drive cleared the trees to roll to a stop close to the green.

"Where did he learn to drive like that?" Jim mused.

"Saul?" Hatcher laughed. "Why, he's a natural born golfer!"

Jim left him laughing and puffing far behind.

He got his first clue on the sixteenth green. Jim scowled as Saul drew back his putter in a smooth, wrist-powered arc. And Jim had part of the answer.

It might have been Tod Winters putting—Tod who was the most brilliant putter of the last ten years. Frowning, Jim's narrowed eyes obscured the physical difference, and the form leaped out at him. Saul had patterned his putting on that of Tod Winters.

No—that wasn't quite it. It was like a picture of Tod, every idiosyncrasy duplicated without reason, superimposed on Saul's massive frame.

The putt rimmed the cup and was dropped for a par. Jim walked dazedly with the crowd to the next tee. Watching Saul's drive, something sprang into his mind, then was gone before he could grasp it.

Jim shook his head and watched the long-iron shot arch beautifully to the green. That one was obvious. George Potter, who would have been a great champion if all his shots had been as well played as his long irons, was the model this time.

But again, the things that were duplicated were variations that added nothing to the success of the shots. No golfer in his right mind would have duplicated those. The waggles and twitches were Potter's way of preparing himself psychologically for the stroke.

Why had Saul duplicated everything? How had he done it so faithfully?

The crowd's roar brought Jim scurrying to the tree-embraced tee to watch Saul's last drive. This time the nagging thought leaped again—and stayed.

He might have been looking in a mirror. He should have realized it before. Of course, Saul would duplicate Jim's driving form. *He* was the boy with the velvet swing, the controlled drives that no one had outdistanced before Saul came along.

He didn't even have to watch the approach shot. Saul might be the golfer, but it would be Gordon Brown's technique. And then, as he watched Saul putt twice for a par, the answer came, the answer that was incredible but, somehow—inescapably— true.

As Jim expected, Hatcher was at his elbow with a few well-chosen comments. "A 63—you're six strokes behind with one round to go. Do you want to give up now?"

"I don't think I will," Jim said evenly. "You see, Hatcher, I did learn something—something I wasn't supposed to learn."

Hatcher was amused. "Yes? And what is that?"

"I think we'd better talk about it privately."

"Oh, that won't be necessary."

Jim shrugged. "It doesn't matter to me." He leaned closer to Hatcher and added softly, "But I know that Saul is a robot."

From the clubhouse dining room, came sounds of carefree confusion—plates and silverware clinking, spiked shoes clomping across shredded floors, loud voices describing this one that rimmed or that one that dropped. Inside the little private room, where Hatcher stood looking out the window at the rolling, green fairway, there was silence.

A smile curled the corners of Hatcher's mouth. "So you think Saul is a robot."

"Isn't he?"

Hatcher chuckled. "Of course he is. How does it feel to be beaten at your own game by a mindless machine."

"You haven't won yet," Jim said. "A golf ball takes some funny bounces."

"How did you find out—about Saul?"

"Saul is a lot of things," Jim said slowly, "but none of them is Saul. Saul is Tod Winters, George Potter, Gordon Brown and me. Take us away and there's nothing left."

"Nothing human," Hatcher said. "Just a memory, a power source, a lot of wires and a lot of motors."

Jim shook his head. "How did you do it?"

"Money can do anything. All it needs is a purpose. Someone has developed a colloidal memory bank? That's a brain—get it? The new miniature atomic power plant is ideal. Use it. Make thousands of tiny motors to serve as muscles. Throw in some sensory mechanism, some relays, then feed in an analysis of a slow-motion pictorial study."

"And you have a golf machine."

"Exactly," Hatcher said.

"It must have cost hundreds of thousands of dollars," Jim said bitterly.

"Closer to a million." Hatcher was cheerful.

"A million dollars to keep me from winning twenty-five thousand," Jim said. "Don't you think that's unfair?"

"Unfair?" Hatcher echoed, smiling. *"There's* a machine response for you. That's what the loser always says. Be a little better, a little smarter, a little stronger than your competitor, and he runs to the government, yanks on its apron strings and screams, 'Unfair competition. Unfair competition!' Understand this, Jim—nothing's unfair that doesn't break the rules. And the only rule worth remembering is this—the best man always wins."

"You mean the best machine," Jim said sourly.

"A machine is only an extension of a man, like your driver. I don't happen to be endowed with golfing muscles and responses. You do. Those—and your golf clubs, Jim—let you hit a ball farther and straighter than anybody else. Saul lets me hit a ball farther and straighter than you do. It's as simple as that."

Jim said, "That wasn't the bet. The bet was that I couldn't make $50,000 in a year. Not that you couldn't spend twenty times that to keep me from making half as much. That was obvious from the start."

"Maybe that was *your* bet. It wasn't *mine*. I bet that I could beat you at your own game. I didn't think you were good enough for Alice, not smart enough, not man enough. Maybe you didn't have a chance anyway—*I* don't know. But she was spending too much time at the Country Club, and it wasn't just to improve her game. Should I let a few well-distributed, well-trained muscles blind her to what you really are?"

"And what's that?"

"Why, you're a quitter, Jim. You can't stand pressure. You're no competitor. You've proved that time after time. Maybe Alice couldn't see it. I had to keep her from a foolish mistake."

Jim frowned. Maybe it *had* been true. It wasn't true any

more—if he could only prove it. "And yet I was going to win—until you threw your millions against me," he said.

Hatcher shook his head. His jowls wobbled. "Could I let luck give away what I value most? Of course not. Alice deserves the best, the smartest, the strongest. I knew you were a weakling. If you couldn't win at your own game, you couldn't win at anything else. At least I gave you that chance."

"Chance!" Jim's eyes studied the floor moodily.

"Have you ever played poker, Jim?"

Jim looked up. "Sure."

"Then maybe you know that, over the long run, the smartest player always wins. *Over the long run.* You have to give luck time to even out. That means the winner is the man who can stay in the game the longest, the one with the most chips. There's a moral in that. Poor men should never play poker. Rich men should play nothing else."

"So you made sure I couldn't win," Jim said. "All because of a preconception that I'm a quitter. One ninety-five for 54 holes. I don't call that quitting."

Hatcher shrugged heavy shoulders. "What will you do tomorrow, Jim? Or next week? What will you do when it's more than just a game, when the going really gets rough? That's what it is now. This is for keeps. And it isn't enough just to come close. You've got to have the will to win. Everything is unacceptable but victory."

"According to my standards, Hatcher," Jim said grimly, "you haven't played fair. Suppose I should lose—through no fault of my own—and try to win Alice anyway?"

Hatcher's voice was just as grim. "Then I'd know that you are a welsher besides a quitter. And I'd act accordingly—without compunctions."

Jim knew what Hatcher could do if he wanted to. "And suppose I should win tomorrow?"

Hatcher's face relaxed. "Six strokes back? Playing against the perfect golfer?"

"Suppose!" Jim said firmly.

Hatcher sobered and studied Jim's face. "Then I'd have to admit I was wrong. You have my word on that. And you could have Alice—if she wants you."

There was a small sound from the doorway. Jim turned. She was standing there, cool, slim, desirable.

"Al . . ." he said, and knew that he loved her more than ever.

How long had she been there? Hatcher turned. "*Alice!* But I got a letter from you this morning—from England."

Her voice was low and musical, as Jim remembered it.

"I left them with a friend to mail for me." She walked forward slowly. "I wanted to keep myself out of this. I was afraid I might disturb something."

"But you should know," Hatcher said affectionately, "that you could never disturb me."

"I was thinking of Jim," she said slowly.

Jim straightened up. He looked intently into the face he loved.

Alice's red lips twisted ironically. "That's funny, isn't it? And it's funny to stand here like this and talk coldly about something that was never put into words before. And the funniest part is that I wasn't really in love with Jim—not then, not really."

"Al . . ." Jim began, and stopped. There was nothing he could say. Alice's blue eyes turned toward him, and Jim told himself that they held a warm promise.

"It probably wouldn't ever have come to anything, Dad," Alice said quietly. "But then you let me find out about the bet. I was mad at first, but then I started to think. The bet told me something. It told me Jim was in love with me, enough to make a crazy bet like that on the wild chance that he might win. That was something I had never been sure of before, with any man. And then you kept us apart. That was more. It's worked for thousands of years. It worked this time. I fell in love."

Jim swallowed hard. In a moment he would break out singing.

"Put back the #2 iron, instead I'll use the 22 Winchester."

"You don't know how I prayed and fought every one of his tournaments with him. And, when he got so close, I had to be here. I had to be near him, even if I couldn't let him know, for fear that it would upset his game."

Hatcher nodded. "I can see why you'd be afraid of that."

"You're wrong, Dad," Alice said earnestly. "He's not a quitter. He's proved that. Anybody but you would admit it. Sure he's human. He's not a machine and I love him."

"Love?" Hatcher shrugged his shoulders. "It comes and goes. The only thing that doesn't change is character."

"You can't prove that with a machine," Alice said firmly.

"It's his own game. Remember that. If a machine can play it better than he can, he should lose. Take away his one ability and what have you got? Nothing!" He turned to Jim. "The bet still stands." He smiled gently at Alice. "I won't let you throw yourself away on a childish whim."

And he stalked out of the room with all the delicacy and refinement of a bull elephant.

Jim stared at Alice for a moment, then took two giant strides and gathered her in his arms. Eventually, they drew apart.

"Did you mean that?" he asked. "About loving me."

She nodded, her eyes glistening with unshed tears.

"What can we do?" he continued.

"Nothing," she said hopelessly. "You heard what he said about not letting me throw myself away. He meant it. He could do it, too."

"Then I've got to beat Saul," Jim said bravely. But he knew, while he said it, that he was whistling in the dark. He wasn't playing against another golfer. He was playing against himself —and Tod Winters and George Potter and Gordon Brown, the best of each. Against perfection, he had only his own fallible, erratic skill. Against machine judgment and nerveless metal, he had to pit the illusioned human senses and nerves that could, he knew only too well, turn to quivering jelly.

"Somewhere," he said slowly, "Saul must have an Achilles

heel. The prime fact about man is his adaptability. An imitation would have to have built-in limitations."

"That's *it!*" Alice said excitedly. "They had to build in at least one constant, if not more. If we can find it and alter the conditions . . ."

"Judgment?" Jim suggested. He tossed the idea away. "No—judgment has to be flexible. They couldn't know when he'd meet up with wind, rain, sunbaked courses, slow greens, fast ones, wormcasts . . ."

"He does it, too," Alice said. "I've watched him. Maybe we could find where he's kept. Tinker with him—smash him!"

"That wouldn't be fair. I could probably have him disqualified, of course. But that wouldn't be fair either."

"*Fair!*" Alice exploded. "Has *Dad* played fair? This isn't a game, Jim. We've got to win."

Jim smiled at the essential amorality of women and sobered. "That isn't what I meant. I mean your father wouldn't accept it. According to his lights, he's played fair with me. He could have had me crippled, poisoned or taken out of action in lots of ways—and gotten away with it. But he's beating me on my own ground. And that's where we've got to beat him."

Alice shook her head. "All that skill and energy—wasted on something like this."

"And it could be such a wonderful thing," Jim said. "Profitable, too. Think of the things that machines could do, if they had memories and self-contained power! Not man-shapes, like Saul. That's useless. They could do all the jobs that man's too weak to do or that are too dangerous or too much drudgery."

"Mining," Alice said, "and manufacturing."

"Exploring—the cold places and the hot places. The deeps of the sea and space. Rebuilding—making uninhabitable places livable." Jim's eyes were distant. "The important thing is that they can't compete. Man won't stand for it. He'll destroy them first. And they can never conquer Man, because he's too adaptable. Unless he lets them."

"That's wonderful," Alice said, her eyes glowing. "Tell Dad.

He can recognize a good idea when he hears it. He won't think you're so dumb then."

"I could probably like him," Jim said, "except he won't give me the chance. Not unless we find the constant. I guess I'll just have to play my heart out tomorrow."

"You can't do it, darling. You'd have to shoot in the fifties!"

"A golf ball takes some funny bounces," Jim said. He turned to the window and stuck his hands moodily in his pockets. He started. It was as simple as that.

"There *is* a constant," he said exultantly, swinging around. "Look, Al. Here's the key to my locker. Get my caddy and Saul's. I think you'll have more luck with the boy than I would. Give him—oh, five or ten dollars. And here's what I want you to do . . ."

In the middle of the explanation, Alice caught fire, too. As he finished, she gave Jim a quick, proud kiss and hurried out. Jim's eyes followed her admiringly for a moment, and then he reluctantly turned toward the dining room.

Jim dragged Dave Simpson, the tournament official, protestingly away from a hearty meal. "I've just had a wonderful idea," he said. "Why don't you put Saul and me together for tomorrow's round."

"*What!*" Dave exclaimed.

"Think of the crowds, Dave," Jim urged.

"But what about you? What chance will you have, playing with a man who has you down six strokes?"

"Oh, that's all right," Jim said bravely. "I don't mind. But if you're not interested . . ."

Jim moved to turn away. Dave caught him by an elbow.

"I didn't say I wasn't interested. If it's all right with you, I don't think anyone else will object."

Jim thought of Hatcher. "No," he said, "I don't think they will."

Jim walked away, whistling.

The reaction set in when he strode onto the tee next morning. The crowd was immense and noisy. It was all very well to plan something like this in the abstract. But, in the clutch, would his nerve fail him, as it had failed him before?

Alice was waiting for him, cool and lovely and infinitely desirable. She put her hand on his arm and warmed him with a smile.

On the other side of the broad tee, Hatcher's smile was mocking. Beside him, Saul, the robot, waited impassively. Jim knew then that it wasn't going to be as easy as he had thought.

It wouldn't be enough to hope that he had thrown a wrench into Saul's machinery. He would have to fight grimly, determinedly. He would have to play the greatest game of his life today, if he wanted to win.

The crowd was partisan. Like most Americans, they were pulling for the underdog. Jim knew they wanted him to play brilliantly, if only to narrow the gap and make the match thrilling and that, if he failed to come through for them, they would swing to Saul.

Even realizing all this, it warmed him as they cheered him up to the tee—knowing that what they really wanted was to see golfing history made. God willing, that was what they would see.

Jim's drive took a tail-end hook. It dived into the rough behind a clump of trees. He stepped back, grimacing. He would have appreciated a happier start.

As Jim watched closely, Saul took a ball from his caddy, teed it up, settled himself and swung. The ball sailed straight down the fairway, forty or fifty yards beyond the 300-yard marker. The crowd gasped. Jim smiled.

When he saw his lie, the smile was wiped away. Sensible golf would have been to play it safe, out onto the fairway, where he could hope to play his third shot straight enough for a par.

Sensible golf wouldn't win. Jim took out his two-iron, sighted through a small hole in the trees and swung at the almost-hidden ball. It whipped through the opening and rolled to a stop just in front of the green.

Saul's easy four-iron shot was dead on the pin all the way, but the crowd moaned sympathetically as the ball hit the back edge of the green and hopped into the rough.

Hatcher looked puzzled as he stood beside the green. Jim's close approach set up an easy putt for a birdie. Saul's recovery was long, and two putts gave him a par.

Jim smiled grimly. That was one of the six strokes he needed.

Jim's game sparkled—Saul kept finding trouble. While Jim was getting down in two on the next hole, Saul was over the green again and backed for a par three.

The third hole was shared in birdies, the fourth in pars, the fifth in birdies again. Then Jim eagled the par-5 sixth, and Saul played back and forth across the green for a 5.

Four strokes, Jim thought, and cast a glance at Hatcher whose face was worried and confused. Maybe now he was having doubts about his perfect machine.

But Saul matched pars with Jim on the next two, then got back a stroke on the ninth with a long putt while Jim was scrambling for a par.

Jim took a long breath as they walked to the tenth tee to begin the second nine, the crucial nine. He had come in with a scorching 30, while Saul had shot his worst nine of the tournament, a 33. If Jim hadn't been terrific, he wouldn't have picked up a stroke. It was going to be tough to keep up that pace.

When Alice lit his cigarette for him, her hand was shaking. He held the hand firmly and looked steadily into her eyes. In a moment the shaking stopped. "Thanks," she said.

"Nothing to it," Jim said, and hoped he sounded more confident than he felt.

Jim breathed a little easier when Saul's two-iron bounced far down the back edge of the tenth green. Jim played it carefully, landing on the front edge and sticking. Saul took a long recovery shot and two putts for his first bogey. Jim's two putts gave him a par. He was only two strokes behind.

They shared birdies on the eleventh and pars on twelfth. On the next, however, Jim got his second eagle, with a chip shot that dribbled to the lip, trembled and finally dropped. Unperturbed, Saul holed his putt for a birdie.

One stroke behind? Jim muttered hoarsely to himself. The strain was beginning to tell. He had to steel himself before each shot to keep from trembling.

They each took pars on 14, birdie threes on 15. On the short sixteenth, Jim's 7-iron dropped 10 feet in front of the pin, Saul's 11 feet behind. Saul's putt was straight in.

Jim's hand shook as he lined up the putt. If he missed this, he would be two strokes behind again with only two holes to go. He could never hope to catch up. He jabbed at the ball. It trickled off to the right, stopping a full foot from the hole. He steadied himself and dropped the next.

For a moment, he could feel the old, familiar sense of despair and rage creep through him. Then Alice put her arm confidently through his as they walked to the seventeenth tee. Fiercely, Jim drove his longest wood of the day. It still lacked 30 yards of Saul's.

Saul overshot the green by 40 yards and ended with a par-five. Jim calmed himself to make a 50-foot approach putt stop within 3 feet of the pin, but left himself a sharp downhill slope. He tapped the second one gingerly. The ball trickled to the lip and dropped with a cheerful thunk.

He was no Tod Winters, Jim told himself wryly, but he had his moments. Once more he was only one stroke behind. One stroke, and one hole to go. Pick up a stroke and tie, two strokes and win. Win Alice or lose her. It was like losing the world. A tie would be no good. There were excellent reasons why Saul's game wouldn't be off on the morrow. He had to get two strokes on this hole, somehow.

Jim's drive sliced behind a fringe of trees that divided the first and eighteenth fairways. Saul's drive, as usual, was long and straight. Jim wiped the sweat from his forehead. It was pain not to relax, not to quit, scream and curse.

The green was hidden, 130-yards away. He had to shoot over the trees blind. He swung easily, smoothly. The ball cleared the trees and dropped from sight. He barely heard the smattering of applause.

Jim watched Saul's approach land over the crowd at the back of the green. Jim walked up slowly. When he had forced his way through the spectators, he saw that his ball had landed on the green—but 25 feet from the cup.

The crowd formed a lane for Saul's third shot. It hit the green and scooted, coming to rest on the front edge. His putt was straight for the hole all the way. The hush broke into a moan. The ball had rimmed.

Jim figured it up. That would give Saul a five. He could win with a three. He studied the green carefully, noting the slopes, the lay of the grass. After a minute he decided on his line. He took his stance. Once more, an unnatural silence settled over the crowd.

Jim stroked the ball. It ran swiftly at first, then slowing, trickling over the last slope, nearing the cup, gently turning. Eternities passed, and the ball hesitated on the lip, toppled, disappeared.

The scene was bedlam. Alice grabbed his arm with one hand, thrust the score-card in front of his nose and jumped up and down screaming happily. Jim steadied the card long enough to read the score. Another 30—a 60 for the day. A 72-hole total of 255. A flock of broken records.

When the new U.S. Open champion walked to Saul's caddy and removed the ball from the boy's fingers, Hatcher was at his side. He was frowning.

"How did you do it?" he shouted.

Hatcher had ceased to awe Jim. Hatcher was not infallible. "Under certain, extremely restricted sets of circumstances," Jim said, "a machine is better than a man. But, over the long run, over the gamut of situations, a machine doesn't have a chance. It just can't compete."

Hatcher was still frowning. "I still don't understand."

"Here," Jim said, handing him the golf ball Saul had been using.

Hatcher stared at it. "This isn't Saul's regular ball."

"That's right." Jim laughed. "It's a new one, guaranteed to add twenty yards to the average drive."

Slow understanding crossed Hatcher's face. "But that's unfair," he said. "That's . . ." He began to smile, and the smile broke into a chuckle. "I'll be damned!" he said.

"There are no perfect golfers," Jim said. "There are only good ones and better ones. I'll be around in a few days to talk about men and machines—and competition. I have $50,000 to invest in our new business—making robots—*useful* robots."

WHO WANTS TO MARRY MONEY?

by Glynn Harvey

It was around ten o'clock on a Friday morning and I was hurrying around the corner of the clubhouse, head down, when I ran square into Roger Bartholdy. I mumbled an apology and was about to go on when I realized who it was.

"Tallyho!" I said. "I didn't recognize you without your horse."

This was a logical observation. The sight of Roger Bartholdy patrolling the terrace of the Pinehurst Country Club in golfing clothes was worth at least a notice in the Pinehurst newspaper. After all, Roger was master of the Moore County hounds and went around with the horsy set. You could put it down as a fairly accurate rule of thumb that the fox-chasing mob regarded golf as a footling pursuit, followed by idlers with overlapping arteries and interlocking brain cells.

In fairness, you might also put down that the Pinehurst golf crowd regarded the county cavalry—if at all—as a gang of eccentric stable swipes who dressed up in pink coats two mornings a week to go chasing foxes before breakfast. In short, never were two worlds farther apart.

When I barged into him, Roger reared back, nostrils flaring and eyes rolling wildly. For a moment I thought he might drop the putter he was holding and start pawing the air with his forelegs. Skittish was the word.

"Whoa," I said softly. Roger began to quiet down and even managed a cold smile.

"Oh," he said. "It's you."

I backed off and studied his haberdashery. Roger Bartholdy was certainly dressed to the nines, whatever that means. He was wearing a fancy red cap, and his golf shoes were so new they creaked even when he was standing still.

"You're beautiful this morning," I said, nodding approval. "But I think we ought to remove the price tag from the putter."

Roger flushed and peeled off the marker and muttered something I didn't quite get. I thought I detected a general air of petulance and, as he glanced toward the door of the ladies' locker, a faint suggestion of impatience.

"Well, I said, after a decent pause. I made a show of looking at my wrist watch. "I've got to get into town and back before our foursome tees off at noon, but I have time to listen to any kind of plausible explanation."

There's something about old Yale crewmen that annoys the hell out of me, and Roger Bartholdy was a real prototype. They have a generic tendency to be brusque and opinionated. That isn't just my own private observation; other Harvard men have remarked on it.

Roger was in one of his Napoleonic moods. He stared me up and down with a gaze that can only be described as steely. Then he pushed past me and strutted off. At the putting green he was joined by Mimi Elverson, and together they headed for the first tee.

I continued to watch, bemused by the scene, while Mimi teed off. As befits the perennial champion of the Pinehurst Women's Open, she whipped one well down the fairway. Then the master of the hounds, after nearly decapitating himself with his first effort, plopped one neatly onto the bowling green.

"View halloo!" I shouted and pointed to the bowling lawn. Mimi waved in reply, but Roger Bartholdy only glared and then trudged off behind his caddie. I noticed that the razor-sharp crease in his slacks was already losing its edge.

I sighed for Mimi. If Roger was going to trail the ball

through bush and bracken without his horse, it would be a long afternoon for her. Just watching that kind of game can be pretty tiring for a good golfer, and Mimi shot in the low eighties. There are those who argue that she ought to—she has nothing else to do since her father passed on and left her his millions.

As I turned back toward the clubhouse I saw Link Dreyer standing on the porch, watching Mimi and Bartholdy with a faint suggestion of a frown on his brow.

Dreyer was a big, easygoing guy who might have been a great golfer if his life hadn't been complicated by the fact that he had to earn a living. He might have been a good salesman too, if his craving for golf hadn't brought him in off the road like a homing pigeon every Thursday. As it was, he couldn't perfect his golf game; he had to waste too much time working. And he put in too many days playing golf to make any serious dent in the Carolina sales market.

Under the circumstances, of course, we all felt that the ends of justice and humanity would best be served if Mimi Elverson and Link Dreyer would quietly pair off and withdraw to some convenient rectory for the wedding. Then Link wouldn't have to waste Monday, Tuesday and Wednesday on the road. And Mimi could go about her golf with a high heart and a clear conscience, serene in the knowledge that she was serving society and not just reaping the fruits of compound-interest accounts.

Some astute observers of the social scene were inclined to believe that all this would one day come to pass. And certainly Link Dreyer was in there pitching to the pin; he was sensible enough to realize that he was missing a lot of fine golfing days. Mimi, on the other hand, was inclined to practice evasive tactics—but it was the consensus in the village that she just wanted to be chased a little bit. Women, I'm told, are like that.

Consequently, the sight of Link Dreyer watching his social security tack off down the fairway with Roger Bartholdy was most interesting. "It looks like somebody is playing your ball," I said gently.

Link turned to face me. A dark flush started up from his collar line. Perhaps that's why everyone was so genuinely fond of Link; he was such a total oaf; he even could blush.

"Isn't that Roger Bartholdy, the horse guy?" he said. Behind his horn-rimmed glasses, his eyes blinked in disbelief.

"Uh-huh."

Link turned this piece of intelligence over in his mind. "But he doesn't play golf," he said at length and rather suspiciously, as if testing the statement for a secret loophole.

I looked off down the fairway where Roger was emerging from the brush for the fourth time. "No," I said, "he sure doesn't."

Link frowned and pursed his lips. "Then," he went on stubbornly, "what's he doing out there with Mimi?"

"Well," I said airily, "he's not playing golf. We both agree on that point."

Link stared hard at me, and as he began to get the point his jaw dropped in astonishment. But I'll say this for Link Dreyer: Once he comes to grips with the subject he goes right to the mat. He looked quickly over his shoulder and then pulled me aside behind a pillar. "But Bartholdy's got lots of dough," he said hoarsely. Then, a bit anxiously, he added, "Hasn't he?"

I nodded. "They tell me his stable-boys make mops out of dirty old twenty-dollar bills and use 'em to clean the stalls," I said. "What's that got to do with it?"

"Well—" Link gestured weakly down the distant fairway.

I tapped him confidentially on the arm. "Don't let this get around town," I whispered, "but out there, in the world, people are still marrying for love."

Link stiffened and clenched his jaws. Poor guy. All his life he had either been in a bunker or under a shower when Dan Cupid posted the starting times. He recognized the word "romance" when he saw it, but he associated it vaguely with perfume advertisements.

"Love?" he said. And then he repeated it softly, over and

over. I backed him to a wicker chair and gave a slight push. Then I shrugged and started off for town. Empires might totter and dynasties fall, but if I wasn't back by tee time, I'd have to spend the afternoon at gin rummy.

As luck would have it, whom do I meet on Broad Street but Victoria Nelson, the editor of the Pinehurst Pilot. After exploring the customary conversational gambits, I casually passed along the bulletin about Bartholdy and his new diversion. Victoria took it standing up.

"I'm not surprised," she said. "I heard he was selling his horses."

"How come?" I asked. "Did he bow a tendon or something?"

Victoria looked at me queerly. "He's broke," she said flatly. "And the government's put a plaster on his paint business up North until he kicks through with two years' back taxes."

I tipped my hat to her, accomplished my errand and hurried back out to the country club.

I found Link Dreyer there hovering weakly on the fringe of a gin game, still convalescing from the effects of the block-buster. I dragged him out onto the porch and fed him the 11:00 A.M. newscast.

Righteous anger is beautiful to behold. Link gripped his hamlike hands into fists and the muscles of his forearms twitched convulsively. His normally cherubic face seemed to harden strangely. I was hoping that a small vein in his forehead would begin to throb, like it does in the movies, but nothing developed there except a few beads of perspiration. "Why, the lousy —" he began.

I cut him off. "Ah-ah," I chided him. "Temper never won the match. We've got to be cold and calculating, like Ben Hogan . . ."

Hogan's name worked magic. For a moment I thought the mention of Link's personal golfing deity would bring him to his knees. Instead he simply bowed his head momentarily. When he looked up again, the fury of the moment was gone. Gone, too, was the coiled-spring tenseness, though his eyes, behind the spectacles, were still glacier-cold.

He took my hand in a firm grip. "Thank you, Kelsey," he said humbly. "You're right. We must think." Then a look of panic came over his face. "But I'm not very good at that."

I poked his shoulder reassuringly. "Leave it to Kelsey," I said. . . .

Some people practice perfidy; others have conspiracy thrust upon them. I can't take full credit for what followed. The scheme was tossed into my lap, smoking hot, almost as soon as I got home: Jane, my wife, reported that her sister Margaret was en route for a visit.

Now, normally, a visit from Margaret fills me with the same sense of exhilaration as a ball out of bounds. Margaret is a schoolmarm of fairly formidable spirit who toils at her educational forge in distant Texas, hammering out sturdy little minds that someday will complete the winning of the West. That is, if Margaret doesn't get impatient and decide to finish up the job herself.

"Margaret?" I said blankly. "What happened? Did she flunk out?"

My spouse seared me with a look. "It's spring vacation," she said. "She's flying here for the week."

She waited for me to return to the attack, but a nasty little idea was seeping into a dark corner of my brain. I carried it gingerly out to the porch, where I sat quietly with it through the full incubation period. Ten minutes later, the plot fully hatched and scratching, I went to the telephone.

With my helpmeet eavesdropping, I unfolded my scheme to Link Dreyer. When I hung up she was standing in the doorway, staring at me as if I were something that had just wriggled out of the kitchen faucet.

"You're insane," she announced without any preamble. "Do you think Margaret is going to stand for such nonsense? Imagine! Masquerading as the widow of a wealthy Texas oilman, looking for a place to settle in the Sandhills . . ."

She snorted. "And a horsewoman, at that," she went on. "Why, the idea! Margaret probably thinks a snaffle is the past tense of sniffle."

Under Jane's withering barrage my bold project began to look shabbier and shabbier. "You don't think she'd go along with the gag, huh?" I asked glumly.

To my surprise Jane began to laugh. "Go along with it?" she exclaimed. "If I know Margaret, she'll dress it up so even you won't recognize it!"

It just goes to show you about women. Like I say, they're balky as jennies ordinarily, but rig up a scheme to ease some poor goof into matrimony and no piece of knavery is too foul, no plot too diabolical.

And Margaret, sure enough, went along with the idea. She sniffed suspiciously at first, but with Jane and me both working at her, she began to thaw. Then a formidable glitter crept into her eye and she began to embroider on her role with growing enthusiasm.

"And you want me to lead the hounds off on another scent," she said finally. "Is that it?"

"Just the one hound—Roger Bartholdy," I explained. "A pretty mangy cur, if you ask me. But if you can get him baying after you, just for a few days, Link will move in and win the championship by default."

A strange little smile softened the strong line of Margaret's mouth. "Sounds like it might be fun," she said dreamily.

I'll say this for Margaret: she isn't bad looking. I came to the conclusion that it was just those steel-rimmed spectacles that gave her the appearance of a drill sergeant.

In fact, when she arrived at the Moultons' cocktail party the next evening, squired by Link Dreyer, I began to think I had misjudged her—either that, or else Texas does something for women.

Jane had done a good job of planting her propaganda stories. When Margaret entered the room the clatter of tongues stopped as if somebody had snapped off a switch. There's something about a million dollars when it walks into a room that seems to focus attention. Everyone at the party looked Margaret over as though she were a six-foot sidehill putt.

Me, I was watching Roger Bartholdy—who was there, of course, with Mimi Elverson. When Margaret came in, he lifted his head like a hound catching the scent of a fox. I noticed he lingered over their introduction—getting quite a brisk run out of it, as we say around the tackroom.

Bartholdy would like to have carried on the conversation the rest of the evening, but Link broke it up by dragging Margaret off just as Mimi, a trifle grim, reminded Bartholdy that her glass was empty again. I caught Link's eye in passing and winked. He grinned happily. . . .

Sure enough, on Sunday afternoon there was a telephone call for Margaret—from Bartholdy. But Margaret wasn't there to receive the call. She had driven up to Chapel Hill with Link Dreyer to see the state university and they didn't get home until rather late. In fact, Jane and I had gone to bed when Link's old sedan turned into the drive.

"Say," I said to Jane, "don't you think you'd better tell your sister to concentrate a little more on Roger Bartholdy?"

She muttered something I couldn't make out. "What?" I said.

Jane's voice was muffled and fuzzy when she spoke again, but I'm pretty sure I understood her clearly. "Don't forget," she said, "that the backswing is just as important as the follow-through."

I didn't see Link during the next three days. He was rocketing around the Carolinas, selling just enough kitchen crockery to pay for his weekend golf losses. But on Thursday, when he showed up at the country club, I was able to announce important advances all along the front.

"Bartholdy had Margaret up to look at his farm Monday," I told him.

Link tugged reflectively at his ear.

"And he took her to the hunt breakfast Tuesday," I added, a little disappointed by his lukewarm reaction.

Link took off his glasses, held them up to the light, and then began polishing the lenses thoughtfully.

"And they went up to his farm again yesterday," I said peevishly. The guy's total lack of response irked me. We were standing in front of the pro shop and I turned away and strode over to the putting green, where I dropped a couple of balls and began batting them furiously around and about.

I suppose that's why I didn't notice when Roger Bartholdy came up. The first inkling I got was when I heard Link's voice, choking with anger: "Bartholdy, I want to see you."

I looked up as Link charged past me and I turned my head in time to see Roger advancing with a dark gleam in his eyes.

It was a pretty pallid battle and both principals would have been thrown out of the ring at the Garden. I don't know who opened fire first. Link threw a right over Roger's head and then Roger retaliated with a right hook that missed by two feet. Link jabbed twice with his left and didn't connect, and Bartholdy uncorked a haymaker that tore a gaping hole in thin air. After that they grappled and began to roll around on the lawn.

By the time we bystanders had got the warriors separated, unhurt but breathing hard, the affair had attracted quite a gathering from the club and the pro shop. It was the first time anything of the sort had ever happened in the staid purlieus of the Pinehurst Country Club, and oldsters who interpreted all disputes in the light of the rules of golf were shaking their heads and clucking their dismay.

It was Link Dreyer who first recovered his breath. "That'll teach you," he gasped, "to play around with other men's women."

Bartholdy glared venomously at him, but before he could reply Mimi Elverson pushed her way through the spectators and stepped up beside him. She stared coldly at Link. "For your information, Mr. Dreyer," she said, "I don't appreciate being made the subject of a common street brawl."

Dreyer blinked and readjusted his spectacles.

"And for your further information," Mimi went on, turning to wipe a tiny smudge of dirt off Roger's cheek, "Mr. Bartholdy and I have reached an understanding. Your brutal attack has only confirmed my judgment." She leaned forward and planted a light kiss on Roger's cheek.

Link gaped at her, and then he glanced at Roger and back to Mimi again. "You mean"—he pointed from one to the other, his forefinger swinging like a metronome—"you and him? You mean, you and he are—"

Suddenly Link lunged toward them. Roger Bartholdy, in alarm, started to assume the appropriate Marquis of Queensberry defense, but Link merely seized his hand and shook it excitedly. Then, before Mimi could fend him off, he swept her up and kissed her loudly on the cheek.

"Congratulations," he cried. "Congratulations to both of you. I didn't realize. I thought—" he stopped and turned abruptly to me.

"Where's Margaret?" he said.

"Home, I suppose," I said, puzzled by his giddy behavior.

Without another word, Link darted through the ring of spectators and ran toward the parking area. In a few moments his old sedan careened down the driveway like a hot rod. I turned to Doc Kerrins.

"What do you make of it, Watson?" I asked.

Doc shrugged. "A clear case of a mixed foresome," he said as he drew me off toward the cardroom. "Anyone for gin rummy?"

It was a quiet wedding, Margaret and Link's—nothing as elaborate as the one Mimi Elverson and Roger Bartholdy staged the following week. And Margaret made a handsome bride. She left her steel-rimmed spectacles at home.

She and Link are living now at the old Bartholdy place, which they bought from Roger. Margaret has opened a private school. Of course, we don't see much of Link these days. He's just a Saturday-afternoon golfer and his iron shots lack that old crispness; but they say he's a crackajack salesman—he's even taken on a couple of new lines.

We miss Link in the regular foursome. But Roger Bartholdy plays with us quite a lot, and he's not too bad if you give him a couple of strokes a side. He can't putt, though. Personally, I think those bowlegs of his have something to do with it.

But he's turning out to be a pretty fair gin player—for a Yale man.

THE MAKING OF A SPORTSMAN

by Thomas L. Stix

Golf plays an important part in our family life. That is just another way of saying that in our house the royal and ancient game receives the respect to which it is entitled. I suppose I should explain in detail. I'm forty-five, and I've been working at it since a bag of clubs was a driver, a brassie, a lofter and a putter. If you were very fancy you had a niblick. I had a niblick.

I've never been a Bobby Jones or a Chick Evans, but I'm pretty good as cub players go, and I still talk of giving up the game if I go over eighty-five. At Swallow Meadows, where I play, we take our golf pretty seriously too, and our six-man team has held the city championship for four of the last six years. Ned Banks is just my age, and he's been the club champion for so long it seems it's just a regular assignment for the chairman of the tournament committee to buy the club championship cup for him each year. I'm the sixth man on our team. Once I got up as high as third. But that was the summer my mashie was particularly accurate. I don't know what I do differently now, but—well, I'm the sixth man on the team.

Julia is our only child. She's eighteen. She knows golf is important, and some day she hopes to beat Glenna Collett. She doesn't hope so more than I do, I promise you. She has a nice even swing and I'm sure if she played her irons a little more crisply she'd be a real first rater. As it is she's the woman's champion of the Club. She's pretty too. If I looked at anyone as pretty as Julia who wasn't my daughter, my wife would have an awfully good reason to be angry. But I must be right about Julia, because the front of our house looks like a nice parking place. I guess if there is anything in the saying about safety in numbers, Julia must be the safest girl in town. Maybe I'm bragging; anyhow I happen to be awfully fond of her. But her game is good.

She was just up at Poughkeepsie for the crew races. There was going to be a big dance and a houseparty, and Julia asked me if she could get some clothes. I told her I'd give her a dress for every time she broke an eighty-six, and what does that child do. She goes out to Alec Cummings, the pro, and takes lessons for two days, and then she had four successive dress-winning rounds.

The day before she left, Julia got a seventy-nine, and I was just as excited as she was. That's the first time any girl ever broke eighty at Swallow Meadows.

"Dad, I haven't the heart to take it," she said.

So I said, "Come on, a score like that deserves the prettiest sport outfit in town. I'll shop with you myself."

I thought Julia would die laughing, and her mother too. But you ought to see her in that brown sport skirt and sweater, and her blonde hair. Maybe I'm an awful fool, but I was terribly proud of her, and as I said before, she's a grand girl.

Golf is pretty important to Mary, that's Mrs. Crane, because she has to listen to Julia and me at dinner on all the evenings that Julia is home. That's not as often as it used to be. Besides that her early American living room is spoiled, she tells me, because I insist on having those two cups on the mantelpiece, and one little golf ball—I did the seventh in one June, 1928. But that's nonsense. Any room looks better for a couple of cups. I only wish there were more.

Golf is important to the cook, because sometimes meals are late, and sometimes early. A few of the cooks have left, but this one doesn't seem to care. Maybe it's because I gave her the *American Golfer* to read. I don't know. What I'm trying to

show is that golf is important around our house. It's not over-
emphasized, but it has its place.

The last of this June I was playing in our regular Saturday
foursome. Right in front of us on the first tee were Jim Carney
and his son. I never recall having seen the boy before. He was
introduced around, and he seemed a nice personable youngster.
His father drove off, and then young Carney. He took a beautiful free swing at the ball. And it went. It had a second rise and
just enough hook so that it ran beautifully up the left side of
the fairway. Just about as nice a drive as I'd ever seen.

I turned to Ned. "Gee, he hit that ball."

"Oh," said Ned, "the boy is good. He was on the golf team at
Cornell. Got as far as the semi-finals in the inter-collegiates. He
ought to strengthen our team."

"Yes," said I, "I guess that means I lose my place."

No one said "No." And that was that. If I had any doubt in
my mind it was dispelled quickly enough. As we were going to
the sixth hole I saw young Carney play a shot from the pit in
front of the eighth green, right next to the flag, a beautiful
run-up shot out of soft sand.

I was telling Julia about those two shots at dinner. "Oh, Bob
Carney," she said. "He's a duck. Didn't you like him, Dad? He's
just home from college, graduated last week. I met him at the
Deke dance. He promised to come and see me."

As a matter of fact, he made good that evening. We were
sitting on the porch when up drives young Carney. Well, his
car was just one more added to the string. I guess porch sitting
is an older game than flagpole sitting, and even more popular.
Bob certainly is a mighty nice looking boy. He talked well too.
Not a lot of nonsense, like most of these college boys. Anxious
to get to work and do something. We talked for a while, and
then he and Julia and four or five others went off to the movies.
They surely were a good looking pair. And I said so to Mary,
but she just sniffed. She doesn't think any one is good enough
for Julia, and I guess she's just about right. Well, we saw a good

deal more of young Carney. He didn't miss many more evenings at the house than I miss two foot putts, and I'm a good putter. He seemed to have the inside track pretty soon, and sometimes his car was the only one in front of the house.

He and Julia played golf together some too, and he surely smoothed her iron play. I was liking him first rate when the club championship started. That was the first tournament he'd played in at Swallow Meadows.

We have sixteen qualifying in the first flight. I got in comfortably enough with an eighty-two, and Bob won the qualifying round with a seventy-three. Ned Banks had a seventy-four. We always qualify on Saturday, and the first round is Sunday morning. Bob came over after dinner and announced that the schedule had been posted, and he had drawn me as an opponent in the first round. "I hope we have a good game, sir." He was a nice respectful boy.

"What time would you care to play? I'll make my time suit yours."

We agreed to ten o'clock, and then he suggested that he call for me. Julia volunteered that she'd like to follow us around, and I said, "Fine, I'd like to have my own gallery." And she looked at me sort of funny and didn't say anything.

I knew I couldn't beat Bob, unless some miracle happened, and I guess he knew it too. Well, it wasn't a match, it was a runaway. I couldn't get my approaches up and he was hot, I halved the second hole, and at the end of the fifth I was four down. He played differently, it seemed to me, than I'd ever seen him play before. More intense, all concentration. He just reminded me of a machine. He was polite enough, but he didn't talk at all. He was grim. Tournament play, I guess, was a very serious business to Robert Carney. Well, he went out in thirty-six, and I had a forty-three, and I was six down.

It was all over but the shouting. Julia was following us, and he wasn't paying any more attention to her than nothing at all. On the eleventh he was well on with his second, and I was in the trap short of the green. My caddy wasn't very enthusiastic about my game at that stage, and he walked up to my ball, dragging my niblick through the sand.

Bob looked at him a minute, and then he said, "Mr. Crane, your caddy heeled your club in that sand trap. This is my hole. Sorry."

You could have knocked me over with a feather. It was the rankest kind of a technicality. I wouldn't have taken a hole that way for all Bobby Jones's titles, and here he had the hole and the match sewed up anyhow. I didn't say a word. I just picked up my ball and started for the next tee. I saw Julia look at him sort of quizzically and bite her lip. She didn't say a word. The match ended on the twelfth hole. He beat me seven up and six to play.

I shook hands in a perfunctory sort of way, and Julia didn't say anything. "Like to play the rest of the holes out, Mr. Crane?" he said affably as could be. I didn't. Then he asked Julia, and she said, "No, thank you," in no uncertain tone.

Well, I was sore. Good and sore. Between my rotten golf, my irritation, and three or four highballs I imagine I expressed myself pretty freely. There wasn't a dissenting vote in the locker room. Young Carney was a good golfer, but he was a rotten sport. I didn't say anything to Julia, and she didn't say anything to me. But I knew she didn't like it either. She's a sportswoman first and a golfer afterwards, thank heavens. That's Julia.

That evening we were sitting around after supper, and Mary asked Julia if Bob was coming over to take her out, and she said "No" and got up and went inside. And I didn't see Mr. Bob Carney for a week.

As every one expected, Bob Carney and Ned Banks won their way into the finals. We always play thirty-six holes in the finals at Swallow Meadows. The story of how Carney had claimed that technicality on me had gotten around, and I never saw such a unanimous gallery. They were almost to a man rooting for Ned Banks.

I didn't follow the morning round, but they came in for lunch all even. They each had seventy-three's, and the afternoon round promised to be a peach. Just as they started out I saw Julia reading a book on the clubhouse lawn, and I asked her if she wasn't going to follow the match, but she didn't seem interested.

So I went off with the rest of the gallery. They halved the first hole and Ned won the second, when he sank a putt all the way across the green for a birdie three. That put him one up. On the third hole Ned drove a beauty right down the center, and Bob hooked his drive into a clump of trees, and underbrush on the left. He went to where he thought his ball was and started to look for it, and then he pulled out his watch. Ned came over and everyone looked. Bob was looking pretty feverishly but he was keeping his eye on his watch as he looked.

Finally he turned to Ned, "Mr. Banks, my five minutes are up. I lose two strokes. I'll go back and drive another."

"Nonsense," said Ned, "let's see if we can't find it. What's the difference. Wouldn't be any fun to win on a technicality. Hey, wait a minute! Here's your ball. You're in luck. You have an open shot for the green, Carney."

Just then about two things happened. You could see Bob Carney's mind begin to work. Here was Ned Banks giving up a chance to get a lead of two up, because he didn't like technicalities. You could see it sinking in. The other thing happened inside my head. Here was a boy just as prompt to call a technicality against himself as he was against his opponent. Perhaps he wasn't such a bad sport. Just too intense.

Well, if Bob Carney was thinking a lot it didn't affect his game. And when they came up to the last hole they were still all square.

I don't think I've told you about the eighteenth at Swallow Meadows, but it's not a hard hole. It's not the best golf hole in the world either. A good second will always get you home. The drive is simple and there's a long pitch to the green. There are great big traps in front, and behind the green about thirty yards, is the swimming pool. I told the greens committee that was no place to put the pool, but it's there anyhow. Every once in so often someone dumps a ball into it.

Well, Bob has the honor and he hits a nice one down the center, about two hundred and fifty yards. Ned's is just as straight, but it isn't within twenty yards of Bob's ball, and of course he had to play. I never admired Ned's calm so much in my life. The whole Club's out there watching him. He studied his ball a minute, took out his old midiron and pitched it over the trap right on the edge of the green, about forty feet from the hole, a sure four. There was a lot of hand clapping, and Bob waited a minute. The crowd was just lining the green and no one was making a sound. Bob reached for a mashie and took his stance. Just what happened I don't know, but instead of hitting the ball cleanly, he cut it and it went on a line at a terrific speed. It was going over the green on the fly ticketed for the pool just as sure as shooting, when wham! The ball hit a bag that one of the caddies was holding and it bounded square back into the green, not a foot from the hole.

There it was, a sure three. One minute you knew Ned had the game sewed up and the next it was lost on a fluke. Every one started asking what the rule was. But I knew—it was a rub of the green. Tough luck for Ned. But the shot counted.

And then I looked over at Bob. His face was working, but his jaw was set. He walked up to the green, picked up his own ball, and then Ned's, and turned around to Ned. "Mr. Banks, that's your hole, of course, it wouldn't be any fun to win on a rank technicality like that. I couldn't possibly have gotten better than a five. Congratulations, it was a swell match."

I have seen lots of cheering and excitement on our home hole, but never anything like it before. Everyone was shaking hands with Ned, and with Bob, and congratulating them both.

And there I was pounding Bob on the back. "That's the boy," I kept on saying. "It's worth ten cups. You coming over to-night?"

He just grinned.

When I came home there was Julia sitting on the porch just smiling quietly, with her prettiest dress on, the brown one I had bought her the day she made a seventy-nine.

GOLFER AND CADDIE

by Edgar A. Guest

Mr. Golfer, I would warn you there's a youngster at your side,
And if you are fit to be with he will very soon decide.
He must watch the ball you play with. That is what he's paid
to do.
But as long as he's your caddie he'll be also watching you.
You're that growing boy's example. You will not have jour-
neyed far
Before you will have shown him just the sort of man you are.
If you break the rules he'll know it. He'll exactly keep the score
And he'll know the hole just finished was a "five" and not a
"four."
He'll go home and tell his mother: "I had So and So today
And I liked him, or I didn't." Mothers learn of men that way.
You may think it doesn't matter what you say or what you do,
But that youngster, Mr. Golfer, has both eyes and ears on you.

HE COLLECTS GOLF'S WACKY SHOTS
by Gene Gregston

BIG SPRING, TEX.

One day Gearge Wiehl, a golfer in St. Joseph, Mo., stepped up
to a tee and whacked a long drive down the fairway. He
watched with satisfaction as it sailed through the air—until it
came to an abrupt halt. A woodpecker, flying the other way,
had impaled the ball on its beak.

To John Morris Pipes, owner of a string of jukeboxes here,
the story of Wiehl and the woodpecker hazard was merely more
proof that the old saw about footballs taking crazy bounces
applies to golf balls, too. Since 1927, Pipes, an amateur golfer
and ex-caddy, has collected more than 3,000 stories of freak
shots, unusual holes-in-one and other golfing oddities. And a
checkup shows that Wiehl's story is by no means in a class by
itself. For instance:

In Beaumont, Tex., Kyle Wheelas drove a ball 90 miles. His
tee shot landed in the open cockpit of a plane as it was taking
off for Houston.

In Uganda, Africa, a local ground rule allows a golfer to put
a new ball in play without penalty if his shot lands too close to
a crocodile.

A California blacksmith once scored a hole-in-one with a
club he had fashioned out of an old automobile axle.

HOW HE STARTED

Pipes was a 14-year-old caddy at Dallas' Brook Hollow Country Club when he began browsing through the sports page in

search of little items about holes-in-one. He pasted them into a scrapbook. As he enlarged his collection to include freaks and oddities, he began copying the information on a typewriter. Now his home bulges with scrapbooks, typewritten sheets, magazines, old scorecards, papers and pictures attesting the authenticity of the freak shots. When he can, Pipes checks up on each item himself.

For example, after reading that George Cardwell of Winston-Salem, N.C., scored a 425-yard hole-in-one, Pipes wrote to Cardwell; now he has a picture of the golfer, plus a scorecard of the round. To Pipes this was important because Cardwell's blast was the longest hole-in-one ever recorded. Recently, Pipes heard of a 435-yard hole-in-one. But, on checking up, he found it didn't count: the ball had been hit, just as a test, by an automatic driving machine.

Not all of Pipes' items deal with Sunday golfers. The pros have a department, too. Recorded here are the time Sam Snead drove a ball 250 yards into a spectator's pocket; the time Walter Hagen broke a club trying to straighten it, borrowed a club and ball from Bobby Jones and then knocked in a hole-in-one; the time Tommy Armour took 21 strokes on a hole.

Armour's 21, incidentally, is not a record. He was outdistanced by a British lady with a determined streak. When she sliced her drive into a river, the ball floated, so she began swinging at it from a rowboat with her husband at the oars. After enough strokes to drench her oarsman, she finally hit the ball—into the woods. From there it was a long road to the green, and when she dropped her last putt the count for the hole stood at 166.

Another kind of marathon was recorded by Norman (Chief) Coy, a Peoria, Ill. boxer and wrestler. He once played 24 hours, covered 357 holes. And Ralph Kennedy of Mamaroneck, N.Y., has played at the most courses: 3,000. His roster includes every state in the U.S., every province in Canada, nine South American and Caribbean countries and the British Isles.

Although he has enlarged his field, Pipes remains most interested in the hole-in-one, and has made a special study of it. Aces, he finds, have no rhyme or reason. Some pros play all their lives and never score one; on the other hand, Jimmy Nichols, a pro with only one arm, has chalked up eight. Pipes has records of aces by 8-year-olds and 90-year-olds. His files show that the late actress Gertrude Lawrence scored an ace the very first time she hit a golf ball. In the second qualifying round for the U.S. Open in 1949, Ray Maguire, a Detroit pro, recorded two aces—and still failed to qualify.

Pipes delights in the ace with a twist—like the one Fred Jones scored at the Oklahoma City Country Club in 1949. A wealthy auto dealer, Jones was considering running for governor. As he stepped up to a tee, he commented to a companion, "I'd rather make a hole-in-one than be elected governor." He got his wish: he scored an ace, and he wasn't elected.

PIPES' FAVORITE SHOT

The historian's favorite freak shot belongs to Owen E. Cummings of Fortville, Ind. At the seventh hole, his second shot landed in four inches of water, behind a stone wall. Cummings took a vicious swing and topped the ball. It ricocheted off the wall and bounded into the cup for a 2-under-par 3.

The shot won him the hole, but lost the match. When he swung, the clubhead struck the wall, flew off and struck Cummings in the face. He was carried off the course unconscious.

There's just one thing missing from Pipes' collection of golfing lore. A long-time golfer himself, he once played in Texas amateur tournaments but gave that up when the competition began to include such up-and-coming youngsters as Byron Nelson and Ben Hogan. He still plays every week end, shooting in the 70s. But nowhere in his collection of golfiana does the name John Morris Pipes appear. He's never scored a hole-in-one, and, in all his years of golfing, can't recall a single unusual shot.

COUNTRY CLUBS
BUSINESS FOLLOWS THE GOLFER
from TIME Magazine

In fact and fiction, U.S. executives have always belonged to country clubs, and used them as much for business profit as weekend pleasure. But in today's expense-account economy, country clubs are assuming a new importance to established businessmen and young executives. With the spectacular post-war rise of golf, more and more companies are taking out country-club memberships for their men, both as a means of giving them a tax-free pay boost and as a sound business maneuver. There are few better ways for businessmen to develop new contacts, keep customers happy, sell their products and themselves.

In Los Angeles, one accountant deducted $20,000 in golf-club fees as business expenses over a period of years; when the Internal Revenue Service protested that the club was for pleasure, he won his case by proving that he could not even play golf. A lawyer won his case for a heavy deduction by proving that his country-club activities had a direct effect on his income. Furthermore, he hated playing golf.

Even the smallest companies like to have at least one country-clubber on their staff. One small Boston advertising firm has a low-70s golfer whose only job is to play with prospective customers, softening them up for the eventual sales pitch from another member of the firm. Bigger corporations may have a dozen memberships to hand out to their executives, chart their plan of attack as carefully as any sales campaign. They spread their men around in different clubs covering every customer market, make sure to put each man in the club where he can do the most good, upgrade the good producers. They look for his natural customers and avoid places where tight cliques make it impossible for a new man to make headway.

In a club, the young executive finds there are strict dos and don'ts. In some, second-, third-, and fourth-rank clubs, a member can get away with making a direct pitch for business, talk shop either on the greens or in the locker room. But at front-rank clubs, the hustler is shunned like the plague. The good clubs are hard to get into and expensive (up to $6,000 for the initiation fee alone), and most members resent an obvious mixing of business with pleasure.

The best approach is the indirect one in which the young executive never talks shop, never seems to be selling anything. Instead, he lets things take their natural course, picks up a game in the occasional twosome or threesome, makes polite conversation, may later offer to buy a drink, play a hand of cards, swap a story or two. Meanwhile, his wife is getting to know the other wives, his children are busy making friends in the club swimming pool. Gradually, if he plays a good game, he gets to be known, more people want to play with him, and he expands his circle of friends. Eventually, it pays off in dozens of direct and indirect ways. One young Milwaukee advertising man, for example, got himself on a club committee, worked so hard and so well for the committee chairman that he later landed a $300,-000 account from the chairman's company.

Contrary to accepted belief, the young executive-golfer seldom dubs his shots to butter up a prospective customer. The true golf addict, whether he is a company president or a minor purchasing agent, likes nothing better than watching—and getting beaten by—a crackerjack golfer. In Denver, Investment Banker Harry Buchenau Jr., who shoots a good game, estimates that fully 50% of his business comes from friends who enjoy

"The tournament players are about three holes farther on ahead."

playing golf with him. Says he: "Recently a friend called me to make up a foursome. I told him I couldn't play because I had a quota of stock to sell. He said, "Forget it; come on along. I'll take a third of it and we'll unload the rest on the other two.' "

At times, a businessman can sew up a client merely by fixing him up with a memorable game at his club. The one golfer everyone wants to play with is President Eisenhower, who tees off at Burning Tree. Every U.S. golfer dreams that some day he may be called upon to fill out a foursome with Ike. At Burning Tree, Firestone Lobbyist Thomas Belshe was once entertaining two Firestone executives when the call went out that the President needed two to make up his foursome. Before the Firestone men knew it, Belshe, who often plays with Ike, had arranged for his two astounded clients to whack the ball around with the President.

Some businessmen still feel that business and country clubs should not be mixed. But for most businessmen, the country club is as important a part of U.S. business as the adding machine. Says a Los Angeles lawyer: "The club is the meeting place, and any time you throw together men who have something to sell and men who have something to buy, deals will be opened and closed. This isn't the club system . . . It's human nature."

ANECDOTES,
ODD FACTS, OFF BEAT DATA

A SHORT HISTORY OF GOLF

There is no "Father of Golf." The best historical sleuths haven't been able to uncover the man "who dun it." It seems that the idea for golf surfaced in different parts of the world, at different periods of history.

In a basic sense, golf seems to be descended from the family of stick-ball games; centuries ago, people played forms of hockey, and polo. Golf seems to be a sophisticated and slightly urbanized form of these sports.

However, its evolution can be traced. Pictures, plaques, tapestry, ballads, poems, references even in Shakespeare's plays all give hints of a game similar to golf. In the slanguage of television, which seems to have become the major source of new phrases, here's a "run down" of the best golf scholarship on how the game started.

The Romans—Caesar played a game called "Paganica" which was played with a crooked stick and a leather ball packed with feathers.

The Dutch—Holland claims to have invented the game, and some of its evidence is in the form of an old Flemish manuscript that can be found at the famed British museum and which dates back to 1500 to 1520. The manuscript, a mixture of picture and text, portrays two men putting at a hole, while a third addresses his ball at a nearby tee. Dutch experts also bring forth the famous Delft tiles and plaques which pictures a game being played similar to golf. However, the game is unmistakably being played on ice.

The etymology of the word, "golf"—has been traced to the Teutonic term, from which the Germans have their noun "kalbe" meaning, "a club." From this springs the low Dutch "kolf" a sound that very clearly resembles that of "golf." But once again the meaning of the word is "club."

The Scotch—The strongest evidence points, repeatedly, to the Scottish origin of golf. There are Statutes going back as far as 1457, prohibiting the exercise of Golf, lest it should interfere with the far more important accomplishment of archery. But this was Golf they were playing. Equipment, crude; a leather bag stuffed with feathers for a ball, and a club cut from a bent tree branch—but Golf, nevertheless, a game of skill.

Then one fine day, King James IV of Scotland was discovered playing, as were many of the noblemen in the privacy of pastures by the sea, and the ban was henceforth ignored. Golf was free to grow again, eventually exercising its fascination so as to enthrall Mary, Queen of Scots, who became history's first woman golfer. An army cadet carried her clubs and to this do we credit the caddies of today.

The French—Even the French bring forth a Continental claim to the invention of Golf, with their game of "jeu de mail" —a game played cross-country, with a sort of croquet mallet, and to posts or raised marks.

We find the earliest mention of the sport in the New World, mostly in the police records near Nieuw Amsterdam circa 1780. Although, it must be confessed, we have no way of knowing for sure whether the "Gouff" referred to is hockey or golf. Savannah, Georgia, apparently had the first of all golf clubs, so-named legitimately and so-identified without question, as early as 1811. But the first club with a continuous existence was located "somewhere in Pennsylvania, but no records were kept." Therefore—finicky historians of the game brush off all previous candidates and anoint the St. Andrews Club near the City of New York with this honor.

In November, 1888, John Reid, Sr. of Yonkers, called together a group of five golfers interested in the game. These six comprised the charter membership of St. Andrews, for which they assessed themselves yearly dues of $5.00 toward the upkeep of their six-hole golf course. This was the official birth of the game on this continent. On its heels came the Country Club of Buffalo, New York in 1889 and then the Philadelphia Country Club in 1890.

In 1894 a momentous meeting took place, out of which came respectability and responsibility. Representatives of St. Andrews, Mount Hope, the Shinnecock Hills, Long Island Golf Club, the Country Club of Brookline, Massachusetts, the Chicago Golf Club of Wheaton, Illinois and the Newport Golf Club of Newport, Rhode Island got together. Out of their confab came the structure of the United States Golf Association.

Thereafter the game grew, slowly but steadily, through the next two decades until 1913, when a bombshell exploded the pastime right onto the front pages of all the newspapers from coast to coast and made the United States golf-conscious. For that year saw Francis Ouimet triumph, after a terrific struggle, over two top-notch British invaders in the play-off for the United States Open Championship, Harry Vardon and Edward Ray. The story was a reporter's dream come true. Ouimet provided us with our first really big success story in amateur sport —for in the finest Horatio Alger tradition, Francis was the poor but honest boy who achieved the dizzying heights of unalloyed success. He was a caddy; he was an American David to two British Goliaths; he slew the giants of English golfdom and hiked our national pride; he had overcome all obstacles to triumph in glorious American fashion.

After World War 1, all sports enjoyed an enormous upsurge, none more than golf, thanks to Francis Ouimet. Before long, a hard core of dedicated fanatics were busy spreading the word of what they made into a cult, very nearly a religion. For along came a young fellow out of Atlanta, Georgia named Jones, who was acclaimed as their high priest. What Ouimet started, Jones finalized. For in the person of this modest young man, who had captured, at the precocious age of 15, the Southern Amateur Championship—and who reached the finals of the National

Amateur at Oakmont, Pennsylvania two years later in 1919—
the cultists found golfing perfection.

By 1923, Robert Tyre Jones had become Open Champion—
and for the next seven years reigned in splendor over the game
both here and abroad. During this time he proselyted well—
and the ranks of the faithful swelled with converts. A veritable
horde of businessmen and executives who had started out showing a polite interest in the game, adopted it as their own and
worshipped Bobby Jones from Baltusrol to Merion, trooping
over fairways, across brooks and into ponds at a hundred different shrines around the land. Yet through it all, Bob Jones
never lost his head; he remained unspoiled.

Consider, if you look askance at such goings-on, not one
spectator in ten thousand ever played football; not one bleach-
erite in a thousand ever went beyond the sand-lot—so how can
they feel for the shortstop who boots one in the majors, or how
can they identify with the Babe, who slams one? But every
single man and woman on the fairways when the Open and
the Amateur were held each summer—these seekers of the
truth—they knew! Because they, themselves, had suffered the
agonies of the damned (anguished). They sought solace in the
play of their high priest and with him, they found consolation,
they found inspiration. For he was living proof that this
damned game *could* be played!

When Jones, with rare perception, retired in November of
1930, he bequeathed a legacy of purest gold. He had done more
than merely "everything" with the game of golf. He had, of
course, captured the Open and Amateur titles both in this
country and in England—a grand slam never accomplished before or since—but he had done more, much more. For Bobby
Jones had elevated the game of golf to the point where it
rivaled, indeed in some sections, supplanted baseball as our
national game.

The passing of Jones from the competitive scene saw the end
of an era as the great shadow of the depression settled over the

land. The stock market debacle threw a punch at the solar-plexus of pleasure and relaxation and with taxes up and memberships dwindling, all sports tightened their collective belts. Clubs fell like grain before the reaper; courses tumbled into bankruptcy and were sold to real estate promoters on a gamble; the numbers shrank from 1124 golf clubs attached to the USGA in 1930 to a puny 772 clubs by 1935; and traffic over eighteen holes was a dribble.

Then a new apoch arrived—the growth of the public course. Cutting expenses to the bone for potential golfers, the public course filled a crying need. Of course, during the depression, municipalities felt the pinch as well as individuals. Letting the facilities fall into a state of impoverished non-maintenance simply added to the already long list of defects of the public course. But it was better than no golf at all. And then came salvation in the form of the WPA. This government project, in July 1935, started using money for recreational purposes—and golf was a set-up! Between the years 1936 through 1940, the WPA built 207 new golf courses, to say nothing of the countless numbers of already-existing public courses it rehabilitated to the delight of millions of golfers. They picked up the slack and made golf available to all.

Today's trend is two-pronged—with the accent on municipal courses of all kinds, offering the sport right alongside the country club or golf club, many of which are in actuality little more than daily fee clubs, while retaining their USGA affiliation. Each makes available a little something "extra"—a dividend on your investment in time and money—but both the country club and the public course are in business for the same reason. They want to help you enjoy your golf.

THE SPORT OF PRESIDENTS

WILLIAM McKINLEY

Altho Taft is popularly credited with being the very first golfing President—actually top honors should go to President William McKinley (1896-1901). He played a few rounds in the summer of 1897 when he was on vacation at Lake Champlain. McKinley showed an immediate liking for the game, but as with most sports, his enthusiasm did not last long. He gave it up because of the walking it required; McKinley was not athletically inclined.

THEODORE ROOSEVELT

Teddy Roosevelt (1901-1908) tried golf, several times, but he found it wanting in action. It was far too slow for him. He loved tennis, boxing, riding, hunting—he loved strenuous action. Pussy-footing it around a golf course was too tame for the "Rough Rider."

WILLIAM HOWARD TAFT

President Taft (1908-1912) was really the first one to establish the game as a presidential pastime, and, incidentally, a good business for youngsters who wished to absorb the atmosphere and the technique by caddying; for Taft was also a good tipper. Al Houghton, a retired professional, recalls today that when he caddied for Taft, he'd sometimes find an additional quarter tip added to his regular caddy fee of 25 cents. Doubling the fee—a monumental tip for a caddy indeed! But Taft did things in a big way, always. Taft was a cheery, fat man, and his foursomes, swollen by secret service men and friends, were happy afternoons for everybody concerned.

Taft had a keen interest in golf, the first President to be so enthusiastic, for he truly loved the game. He invited the leading exponents of golf to the White House to play with him. His brother, Henry W. Taft, was one of the pioneers of golf and belonged to the St. Andrews Club. Therefore, it was no surprise to find President W. H. Taft present as Guest of Honor at the famous 25th anniversary dinner of the St. Andrews Golf Club held at Delmonico's in November, 1913.

William Howard Taft's remarks that night are worth repeating, for reasons which are pertinent and obvious: ". . . the game's virtues include, first of all, self-restraint and it calls for mental discipline and ethical training." Could anything be more appropriate today? Taft was a golfer at heart—he loved to play Chevy Chase, with summers at Murray Bay in Quebec. And he was good at the game, going around in the high 80's.

WOODROW WILSON

Wilson (1912-1920) altho not in Taft's class as a golfer—he seldom broke 100, often shooting 110 and higher—still rarely lost an opportunity to play while in Washington. During the summertime, he played at the Deal Golf Course along the Jersey coast. Wilson had played before he came to the White House, having taken up the game while he was at Princeton. Being a born pedagogue, he fancied himself somewhat of a teacher, but his miserable results soon made him quit trying to pass along instruction and concentrate on his own game, which ordinarily needed much attention.

Wilson addressed the ball as if he were about to reason with it—but it is a matter of record that the President rarely followed thru, invariably slicing in a manner as to bring tears to the eyes of his caddy. Wilson too would tip liberally, altho here as well he never quite reached Taft's generosity. Wilson would add an extra 15 cents to the quarter, regular caddy fee for the round.

Occurrences of historical significance quite often took place on Wilson's rounds. For example, those present comprising the rest of the foursome, report that Colonel House, who played often with Wilson, as did Grayson, the President's physician, quarreled frequently on the course. Regardless of who had won the honor by score on any hole, Grayson invariably gave the President precedence at the next tee—but Colonel House did no such thing! House, a tough-minded, independent cuss, insisted on going "by the book" (perhaps he was an incipient USGA official) and always wished to follow the proper rules of golf; hang Washington protocol! During their rounds, it is reported that the Colonel and the President had frequent and sharp controversies. No wonder those who played with them were not too surprised later on when they split over affairs of state.

Another event which took place during a Wilson round in 1915—a particularly enjoyable foursome at Chevy Chase, as it happens—was the breathless appearance of a special messenger, who blurted out the news that the *Lusitania* had been sunk.

Wilson played golf because of his doctor's urging, but despite his consistent high scores, he liked the game for the welcome relief it brought from his killing job.

WARREN G. HARDING

If Taft is credited with popularizing golf for the first time from the eminence of the White House, then Harding (1920-1923) deserves credit for being the most enthusiastic golfer, with the possible exception of Dwight D. Eisenhower. President Harding played two or three times every week, and he played very well, scoring in the 90's, and very often in the low 80's. An interesting sidelight is that he used secret service men as his scorekeepers—and sometimes, to their infinite yet smothered disgust, as caddies! Harding loved golf as exercise and as amusement, and he took an active interest in nation-wide affairs of golf.

In 1921—he was chosen as a member of the governing board of the USGA.

In 1923—he presented a trophy for inter-city team contests in public links championships.

San Francisco now has a municipal course named in memory of this most enthusiastic of all golfing Presidents.

CALVIN COOLIDGE

Coolidge (1924-1928) did not "choose to play the game." Coolidge was not much of a golfer anyway, and he remarked when asked about this, that the game was rather expensive for the average pocketbook. He played in desultory fashion on the Columbia Country Club links in 1921, and he had his own ideas on how to dress for the sport, which you may find interesting if not inspiring. The President would show up wearing old, frayed pants which had long since seen their best days; a white canvas hat; no coat at all; and instead of golf shoes, a pair of sneakers. Actually, Coolidge made few attempts at golf—he much preferred his mechanical hobby horse which he had had installed in the White House.

FDR

Franklin Delano Roosevelt (1932-1945) played some golf when he was Assistant Secretary of the Navy (a spoon from the Roosevelt bag now rests in the Burning Tree clubhouse at Washington). But, after polio incapacitated him, his previously good game had to be abandoned. FDR thereupon concentrated on swimming and sailing above all other sports, with a good bit of deep sea fishing for action.

DWIGHT D. EISENHOWER

It has been many a year since the occupant of the White House has been a man who so loved golf (1952-   ). And there is this to be said of Ike's zeal and interest. If he hadn't taken to the game so well, it is entirely possible that his doctors might have prescribed it as a wonderful means of relaxation from his taxing responsibilities. It was Eisenhower who had a putting green installed on the White House lawn—and just recently, he is having one built at his home, in Gettysburg.

If there is a more popular golfer in these United States than the winner of the U.S. Open Championship, he is in an enviable position indeed—yet Ed Furgol, the winner of the U.S. Open in 1954 came in second to Ike in a poll conducted by the Golf Writer's Association of America as having made 1954's most outstanding contribution to the game of golf! The President received 394 votes, 73 more than the 321 polled by Furgol of St. Louis. This great honor carries with it one year's possession of the William D. Richardson Trophy and a plaque for permanent possession, a treasured token of a rare golfing honor.

INDEX OF GOLF INFORMATION

INDEX OF GOLF INFORMATION

MAGAZINES

"GOLF WORLD," Pinehurst, No. Carolina, 1 yr., $5.00, (foreign) $6.00.

"GOLF DIGEST," 611 Davis Street, Evanston, Illinois, copy, 25¢, 1 yr., $2.00 (US & Canada).

"GOLFING," Golfing Publications, Inc., 407 S. Dearborn St., Chicago, 5, Illinois, copy, 25¢, 1 yr. (5 issues), $1.00 (Canada) $1.25, 3 yrs. (15 issues), $2.00 (Canada) $2.50.

"THE GOLF COURSE REPORTER," Box 106, St. Charles, Illinois, per yr., $3.00.

"GOLF LIFE," 10380 Wilshire Blvd. (Rm 207) Los Angeles, California, 1 yr., $3.00, 2 yrs., $5.00, copy, 25¢.

"THE GOLFER" (a voluntary non-profit magazine), 3rd & El Camino, San Mateo, California, 1 yr., $3.00, 2 yrs., $5.00, (foreign), $3.50, 2 yrs., $6.00.

"PROFESSIONAL GOLFER," 134 La Salle Street North, Chicago, Illinois, 1 yr., $3.00, copy, 25¢, (foreign) $4.00 per year.

"GOLFDOM" ("The Business Journal of Golf"), 407 S. Dearborn St., Chicago 5, Illinois, 1 yr., $2.00, Canada, $2.50, copy, 25¢.

"CLUB MANAGEMENT," 408 Olive Street, St. Louis 2, Missouri, 1 yr., $2.00, 3 yrs., $5.00, copy, 35¢.

"USGA JOURNAL & TURF MANAGEMENT," U.S. Golf Association, c/o "Golf House," 40 East 38th Street, New York 16, N.Y., copy, 30¢, 1 yr., $2.00.

BOOKS ABOUT GOLF

GOLF BOOK SERVICE, 42-05 Layton Street, Elmhurst, New York. Will send bibliography on golf books, history, golf songs, humor, etc.

FILMS ABOUT GOLF

How to Film About Golf. "Tommy Armour Golf Series." Castle Films. Catalogue available at your photography store or at: Castle Films, 1445 Park Avenue, New York City. Films available for rent or purchase.

THESE FILMS, WHICH INCLUDE INSTRUCTION, COMPETITIVE AND SCENIC MATERIAL, MAY BE PURCHASED OR RENTED BY GROUPS

The following films are available to groups on a rental or sale basis from the firms indicated. Addresses of the film sources are given at the end of the listings.

Play Better Golf (1948)

Reel 1: Lloyd Mangrum, Sam Snead, Patty Berg and Jim Ferrier demonstrate fundamental grip, aim, swing.

Reel 2: Same 4 pros show techniques in overcoming special hazards, i.e., high grass, sand traps, etc. Putting, chipping covered.

Both 10 minutes, 16 mm sound, black and white. Rent $2.00; sale, $19.75 each. Bailey Films, Inc.

Famous Fairways (1949)

Includes play on six famous American courses: Pine Valley, N.J.; Pinehurst, N.C.; National, Southampton, N.Y.; Oakmont, Pa., Pebble Beach and Cypress Point, Calif. Includes some instruction.

30 minutes, 16 mm color, sound. Rent free; sale, about $140.00 (inquire). A. G. Spalding & Bros., Inc.

How To Play Your Best Golf (1955)

Tommy Armour demonstrates his techniques on three reels: Reel 1, Grip and Stance; Reel 2, Swing Away; Reel 3, Short Game.

Each reel 10 minutes, 16 mm sound, black and white. Sale, each reel, $29.75; all 3 reels, $79.95. Castle Films.

Beginning Golf

Bob MacDonald and Les Bolstad make fundamental points in film designed to teach groups of beginners. Includes "Golf Instructor's Guide" and introductory student's handbook.

35 mm color slidefilm, sound or silent. Sale only, $33.00 (sound), $25.75 (silent). National Golf Foundation.

The Rules of Golf, Etiquette (1954)

Golf's etiquette is explained. Bobby Jones gives introduction, Ben Hogan appears in several scenes.

17½ minutes, 16 mm color, sound. Rental only, $15.00. National Education Films, Inc.

Legend of the Masters (1948)

The story of the 1948 Masters in film. Claude Harmon was the winner. Film features many others.

20 minutes, 16 mm, color, sound. Rent, free. PGA of America.

Keep 'Em in the Fairway (1954)

Five PGA swing fundamentals are demonstrated by Hogan, Snead, Mangrum, Barber, Middlecoff, Burkemo, Oliver, Demaret, Little, Nelson and Suggs. Compares stars with average golfer.

38 minutes, 16 mm sound, black and white. Rent, free (renter pays transportation costs). PGA of American and Life Magazine (any office).

44th Canadian Open (1953)

Play-by-play account of this Open, played at Scarborough Club in Toronto. Dave Douglas won by a shot over Wally Ulrich.

33 minutes, 16 mm color, sound. Rent, free (renter pays transportation costs). Canadian Travel Film Library.

Honor Caddie (1949)

Stars Bing Crosby and Bob Hope and features shot-making of 15 top pros and amateurs. Also describes Western's caddie-scholarship program.

22 minutes, 16 mm color, sound. Rent, $7.50. Western Golf Association.

Community Planning Gets a Golf Course (1955)

Shows step-by-step process of getting a golf course—from initial "talking" stage to the construction and successful operation of course.

22 minutes, 35 mm color, sound slidefilm. Rent $5.00 (renter sends check for $30.00, $25.00 is refunded upon return of film); sale, $30.00. National Golf Foundation.

Addresses of Sources

Bailey Films, Inc., 6509 De Longpre Ave., Hollywood 28, Calif.

Canadian Travel Film Library, 630 Fifth Ave., Suite 658, New York 20, N.Y.

Castle Films, 1445 Park Ave., New York 29, N.Y.

National Educational Films, Inc., 165 W. 46th St., New York 36, N.Y.

National Golf Foundation, 407 S. Dearborn St., Chicago 5, Ill.

Professional Golfers Association of America, 134 N. LaSalle, Chicago, Ill.

A. G. Spalding & Bros., Inc., 161 Sixth Ave., New York 13, N.Y.

Western Golf Association, Golf, Ill.

FAMOUS "FIRSTS"

The first USGA Championships, held in 1895, attracted a grand total of 32 entries for the Amateur—and only 11 for the Open. The next two years, 1896 and 1897, saw 16 qualifiers at 36 holes. 36 holes was prescribed tournament course from 1894 thru 1897—then 72 holes thereafter.

Two tournaments were held prior to 1895; both in 1894; one at match play; competition at the St. Andrews Golf Club, with L. B. Stoddard defeating C. B. Macdonald 1 up; the other, at medal play, at the Newport, Rhode Island Golf Club, wherein W. G. Lawrence took top honors with a 188 for 36 holes.

The first public links play started in 1922, under the auspices of the USGA. At first tournament (1922) there were 18 team entries representing various cities competing for the Harding Cup; and there were 140 individual entries for top honor. Chicago won first Harding Cup; Eddie Held of St. Louis came out on top among the individual contestants.

The first international term used in golf was BOGEY, commonly called "Colonel Bogey"; which means a score, higher than par, fixed as a standard for the ordinary or average golfer to shoot at. If, in example, par actually was 74, then BOGEY might have been established at 77, or 78. Par, what you should make, is fixed by the architects of the course.

The First golf course (First in the hearts of golfers the world over, that is) is without doubt the most famous of them all—the Royal and Ancient of St. Andrew's, in Fife, Scotland. Pioneer in the United States among links is St. Andrew's in the Yonkers, New York area.

The first golf Hall of Fame created in 1941 with a committee under sponsorship of PGA; situated in Evans Scholar's House at Northwestern University, Evanston, Illinois. (Additional players were nominated by Golf Writers Association, which, along with Western Golf Association, took over responsibility in 1949.)

The Hall of Famers: Walter Hagen—Robert T. Jones, Jr.—Francis D. Ouimet—Gene Sarazen—Willie Anderson—Thomas Armour—James Barnes—Charles Evans, Jr.—Jock Hutchison —John J. McDermott—Alex Smith—Jerome D. Travers. (The first four named were original selections of first PGA committee; others were added afterward.)

WHAT THE USGA IS

The United States Golf Association is an organization created by golfers, for the benefit of golfers, and controlled by golfers.

No one can play the game without being affected by USGA work, whether it be the rules for play, or the rules governing markings on iron clubs, or the best methods of greenkeeping. USGA work has an impact upon every player.

The USGA is a voluntary association of golf clubs and courses.

It operates solely for service to golf, not for profit. Any excess revenue eventually goes back into the game.

That is the only place to which it can go, because USGA officers and committee members donate their services and pay their own expenses, even to the championships and meetings held all over the country.

The Association is managed by an Executive Committee of fifteen members, elected annually by the Regular Member Clubs. There are fifteen standing sub-committees, comprising some 400 persons throughout the United States.

The USGA maintains several offices with paid staffs:

EXECUTIVE OFFICE, 40 East 38th St., New York 16, N.Y. All matters except greenkeeping are handled here.

USGA GREEN SECTION REGIONAL OFFICES: MID-ATLANTIC—South Building, Plant Industry Station, Beltsville, Md.; NORTHEASTERN—College of Agriculture, Rutgers University, New Brunswick, N.J.; SOUTHEASTERN—Georgia Coastal Plain Experiment Station, Tifton, Ga.; SOUTHWESTERN—Texas A.

and M. College, College Station, Texas; WESTERN—Davis, Cal.

HOW THE USGA BEGAN

The origin of the USGA is interesting historically and as a clue to the continuing nature and purposes of the Association. The USGA was created because in 1894 two "Amateur Golf Championships of the United States" were sponsored by two different clubs. There were two different "Champions."

In other phases of golf there were no uniform standards.

That was why five clubs formed the Association, on December 22, 1894.

They needed a central governing body to establish uniform rules, to conduct championships and to develop the fine elements of sportsmanship in golf.

THE GAME TODAY

The Spirit of Golf

Just as every club needs its own governing board, so must golf have a national authority.

The need of a guiding spirit has grown as golf has grown. Golf clubs and courses acting alone cannot do certain things. They must have unity in a national organization impartially devoted to the good of the game—else they will have disorder. Golf is their lifeblood: the good of golf is their good.

Without the spirit of the game, what would the game be? Every day we see striking examples of the deep need of good fellowship and fair play among men everywhere. Sports help us learn them. Consideration of the other fellow is a great thing in golf.

Having an ideal of sportmanship, golf thus makes a rich contribution to man's welfare. It helps produce health and balance. The USGA "exists for the purpose of promoting and conserving . . . the best interests and the true spirit" of golf.

As Grantland Rice put it so clearly:

For when the One Great Scorer comes
To mark against your name,
He writes—not that you won or lost—
But how you played the Game.

How the game is played is a main concern of the USGA.

The Size of Golf

Golf in the United States today is of great size. Following are estimates compiled by the magazine *Golfdom* for 1954:

3,500,000 golfers—men, women, children, including caddies —who play ten rounds or more annually

5,147 golf courses as of March 1, 1955.

583,700 acres devoted to golf

$1,089,000,000 in land, courses, clubhouses, equipment, furnishings

64,100,000 rounds of golf played,

$48,707,666 factory selling price (excise tax included) of golf clubs, balls, bag and miscellaneous golf equipment sold by companies in Athletic Goods Manufacturers Association in 1953. This represents 38% of total athletic and sporting goods sales (fishing and hunting equipment not included). Manufacturers sold 4,071,245 golf clubs for $26,000,505; 32,598,624 golf balls for $17,318,042; and 495,-422 golf bags for $5,217,791.

$75,000,000 annually spent to maintain courses and grounds (USGA estimate)

Golf's need for a national authority is greater than ever.

USGA MEMBERSHIP

USGA membership is of two classes—Regular Member Clubs and Associate Member Courses.

Regular Membership

Regular Membership is open to any regularly organized club in the United States. A regularly organized club is a permanent club composed of individual dues-paying members who manage their own affairs through officers and committees whom they select. Such club must operate permanently at one golf course, but it need not control the course where it plays. (Regular Membership is thus open to not only a private club but also a club of golfers using a public course.)

Regular Membership entitles a club to all USGA privileges. Annual dues are:

(1) Club operating at a course of 18 holes or more—$35.
(2) Club operating at a course of less than 18 holes—$20.

Associate Membership

Associate Membership is open to any golf course in the United States which is not controlled by a regularly organized club. (This applies mainly to public and daily fee courses and their managements, but not to regularly organized clubs operating there.)

Associate Membership entitles a course to all USGA privileges except voting rights and eligibility of the course's patrons for the USGA Amateur and Women's Amateur Championships. Annual dues are:

(1) Course of 18 holes or more—$25.
(2) Course of less than 18 holes—$15.

WHAT THE USGA DOES

The names of the fifteen standing sub-committees give an idea of what the USGA does:

RULES OF GOLF	WOMEN'S
CHAMPIONSHIP	PUBLIC LINKS
IMPLEMENTS AND BALL	SECTIONAL AFFAIRS
AMATEUR STATUS AND	JUNIOR CHAMPIONSHIP
CONDUCT	GIRLS' JUNIOR
HANDICAP	MUSEUM
MEMBERSHIP	SENIOR CHAMPIONSHIP
GREEN SECTION	BOB JONES AWARD

Below are brief examples of USGA services:

General

1. Making uniform standards and giving decisions and information on:

Rules of Golf
Amateur status
Handicapping
Tournament procedure
Golf balls and implements

Such standards keep golf enjoyable. Without them, chaotic and costly conditions might result: there probably would be widely different rules in different sections and freak golf balls and implements might be introduced, to change the very nature of the game. The USGA guards against such deterioration of golf.

2. Cooperation with district associations and their clubs.

3. Public relations for golf nationally, and dissemination of authoritative golf information. This includes publication of the official organ "USGA JOURNAL AND TURF MANAGEMENT" seven times a year. The JOURNAL is a meeting place for golfers to exchange ideas and a medium for USGA decisions, comments and information on such subjects as Rules of Golf, handicapping, tournaments, amateur status, greenkeeping methods, golf balls and clubs, USGA championships, playing hints, new trends in the game, golf history and background, including information on the USGA Golf Museum and Library. Every member club and course receives one free subscription to the JOURNAL. Individuals may subscribe at $2 annually.

4. Sundry information on records, certain statistics, types of competitions, etc.

5. Representation of American golf in friendly relations with golf governments of other countries.

Competitions

1. Conduct of eight Championships annually, with more than 6,000 entrants:

OPEN	AMATEUR PUBLIC LINKS
AMATEUR	SENIOR AMATEUR
WOMEN'S AMATEUR	JUNIOR AMATEUR
WOMEN'S OPEN	GIRLS' JUNIOR

2. Sponsorship of three international amateur team matches:

With the British Isles:
WALKER CUP, for men
CURTIS CUP, for women
With Canada and Mexico:
AMERICAS CUP, for men

These competitions promote understanding, good fellowship and love of the game among players from all sections. The international matches have been a factor in improving international relations. The events are wholesome outlets for man's competitive urge. They develop self-reliance, self-control and consideration for others. They are a part of a healthy social pattern.

Green Section Service

The USGA Green Section is a scientific agency which assists the USGA member clubs in upkeep of their golf courses. Among its services are:

1. Visits and written reports by Green Section agronomists to USGA member clubs and courses which subscribe for the Regional Turf Service. This service is provided through the Green Section's several Regional Offices to bring the best available information within comfortable reach of all USGA members, at reasonable fees.

2. Cooperation with the United States Department of Agri-

culture, and coordinated financing of turfgrass research by State and regional agricultural experiment stations.

3. Advice by correspondence to any USGA member club or course on such matters as:

Soil testing   Turf culture   Seed
       Watering   Fertilizer
       Control of pests, diseases, weeds

4. Tips for economical and efficient course maintenance.

5. Distribution of research information through the USGA JOURNAL AND TURF MANAGEMENT, sent gratis to all members, and Regional Turfletters, sent to clubs subscribing for the Regional Turf Service.

6. Development of trained workers in turf management.

The Green Section is free from commercial connection. Its opinions are based on scientific experiment and wide observations, and are unprejudiced. It has produced many of the excellent and economical greenkeeping practices now standard on most courses.

The USGA expends on its Green Section a large part of all receipts from membership dues, besides all Regional Turf Service fees.

An outside source estimates that the Green Section has saved America's golf courses at least 20 times all the money paid for USGA membership dues in the Association's history.

No club or course can afford to be without the Green Section's help. It is important to all golfers. It helps them have the best possible playing conditions for minimum cost.

"Golf House": Golf Museum and Library

The USGA has a Golf Museum and Library in "Golf House," its New York quarters. Here are permanent exhibits of many items of historical value—clubs used in winning Championships, such as Robert T. Jones, Jr.'s famous putter "Calamity Jane II"; a fine collection of other clubs, balls, medals, pictures, documents.

Here is a splendid golf library, available for easy reference by golfers.

The Museum and Library have been built up by contributions from golf-lovers over the world.

Thus, the USGA is preserving a visible record of the evolution of elements in the game.

"Golf House" is a real golf center. It is a monument to the devotion of several thousand golfers, clubs, associations and other organizations who gave funds to buy and equip the building. All golf-lovers are cordially invited to visit "Golf House."

WHY GOLF CLUBS AND COURSES SHOULD BE MEMBERS OF THE USGA

Every golf club and course should be a member of the USGA, not only to receive the tangible services described herein but also to insure maintenance of an impartial, non-commercial governing body.

The USGA's work affects and benefits all clubs, all courses, all golfers. They have needs which can be served only by such an organization.

If there were no USGA, where could golf turn for the things outlined here? Suppose this work stopped: would not golf, and every club, be injured?

A club which believes in these things has a moral duty to support them. USGA membership is within easy reach of all. But non-membership is a silent vote against USGA work.

Non-members all benefit from the USGA. As a small example: although they pay no membership dues, they print on their score card "USGA Rules Govern" and do not hesitate to write when a ruling or other information is needed. Further, they all use greenkeeping practices which have been developed by the USGA Green Section. If all clubs were parasitic, taking without giving, there could not be a national authority.

Fortunately, all clubs and courses are not like that. The spirit which motivated the USGA founders in 1894 is alive and growing.

By as much as a club takes part in USGA activities, by just so much does it increase the Association's effectiveness, and by just so much does the club benefit itself.

The primary purpose of the USGA is, then, to carry on the fine things of golf: fair play, good fellowship and the general good of the game—things which are essential in the greater game of life.

A PHYSICIAN LOOKS AT GOLF

By Alvin A. Schaye, M.D.

Golf is a splendid form of physiotherapy and psychotherapy. In shorter words, it improves the body and the mind. However, the dosage should be regulated to the tolerance of the patient. Addiction may well bring on a clinical syndrome (or pathological malady) that has not yet found its way into the medical books.

The classic sign and symptoms of this obsessive disease may be characterized as follows:

1. A complete withdrawal from all other interests in life.
2. Momentary convulsion seizures which may occur on or off the golf course. These are nothing more nor less than practice golf-swings which the patient is unable to surpress.
3. Incoherent mutterings or periods of talking to one's self. These are recollections of badly executed shots.
4. Extreme agitation in stormy weather. This is due to the fact that the addict is suffering from withdrawal symptoms.

The treatment of this condition is exceedingly difficult. Even if it were possible to contrive that the patient spend all his waking hours on the course playing a perfect game of golf, he might well die of monotony. I try to explain to these patients that hitting a golf ball perfectly is somewhat like an eclipse. Everything must be in exactly the right place at the right time. And then I ask them, after all, how often does an eclipse happen? Those patients who still possess a slight degree of rationalization may respond to this type of reasoning but the percentage of cures is very small.

Actually many of us lose sight of the fact that golf should be sport, exercise, and I might even say, fun. It is not given to many of us to be a concert pianist, major-league ball player or chess expert. Why then should we harbor the delusion that we can attain the quintessence of perfection with every golf shot? Why should we develop a feeling of self-abnegation before a golf expert? Why should we flagellate ourselves over an inglorious miss? Finally, why, on a nice sunny day in the country, should we fret, fume, become tense, lose poise and become unhappy? My first bit of advice is to LEARN TO LAUGH while on the golf-course even if it be at yourself.

There are many benefits to be derived from playing golf. In the realm of physiotherapy, the type of exercise especially for middle-aged golfers is excellent. Walking is one kind of exercise. The amount of bending involved improves the back muscles and the posture. Swinging develops the arms and shoulders; endurance improves; the general circulation and body tone improve and I believe with this, the glands of internal secretion function more smartly.

In the realm of psychotherapy golf can delight the mind and senses. There is the detachment from the vicissitudes of one's daily routine; the release of one's sadistic impulses in striking at the ball (sublimation); the sensory delight at hearing a good, clean crack after impact, the smell of the air, the springiness of the soil and even the shade of the woods.

No effusion such as this could possibly be complete without some do's and don't's. One should become conditioned, if possible, in the early spring when the weather is cooler. Don't do too much too soon. Don't push on when you are over-tired. Don't rush around the course. If you haven't enough time, play fewer holes or don't start. Try to avoid accidents by standing in relatively safe places, watching where you are going, taking care about swinging clubs and warning golfers within possible reach. Don't get mad or hostile. Don't get superior or intolerant. Play the course and not your opponent.

Exertion in hot weather is entirely a matter of acclimatization. Extensive studies on this subject have demonstrated the following facts. Heat, especially when one is expending physical energy, will cause an increase in the pulse rate and a demand for greater cardiac output. The skin will demand a more adequate blood supply so that the sweat glands can function better. Acclimatization to the heat depends entirely on the ability of the organism to sweat better. This will help keep the body temperature from rising. Acclimatization to heat improves with exposure to heat and is entirely dependent on better blood supply to the skin. In short, the heart and vascular system bear the brunt of exposure to heat. It is, therefore, particularly important that people who have not become acclimatized to heat, avoid excessive exertion in hot weather. Taking salt tablets will not avoid any strain on the vascular system. Salt tablets will replace the salt lost in sweating which seldom, under ordinary conditions, attains serious proportions. Drinking liquids (of any kind) will replace the fluids lost in sweating but here natural thirst is a reliable guide to the amount of fluid replacement required.

There are two medical conditions, heat exhaustion and heat prostration, which can be brought about by excessive and prolonged exposure to the heat. Heat exhaustion is due to loss of salt from the body. Heat prostration is due to an effect on the heat regulating center in the brain which goes berserk and allows severe rise in body temperature. Under ordinary circumstances these two conditions do not occur. The danger to be guarded against is neither of the two conditions mentioned above but the excessive demands made on the heart. Do not overexert yourself in hot weather unless you are properly conditioned to it.

Exercise requires the utilization of sugar stored in the body. Because of this the blood sugar content becomes lowered. A study of the blood sugar done on golfers, hole by hole, showed that as the blood sugar diminished, the distance they drove the ball decreased. Raising the blood sugar by eating a chocolate bar improved their performance.

This is particularly important to people who take insulin, as exercise is the equivalent of an extra dose of insulin. The symptoms accompanying excessively low blood sugar are a feeling of faintness, weakness, palpitation (racing of the heart), unsteadiness and inability to concentrate. A sweet drink or a piece of candy will correct the condition promptly. Incidently, smoking a cigarette will cause a temporary rise in the blood sugar.

A final word upon a matter which is a little out of my field, ethics. I doubt whether golf has any beneficial effect upon one's integrity. I do not mean that an honest man becomes unethical but neither does a tricky character become more honest. The point is best made by relating the following story. An old gent, while walking through a grave yard, came upon a tombstone bearing the inscription "NOT DEAD—JUST SLEEPING." He looked at it, pondered for a while and said, "Man, you ain't fooling nobody but yourself."